Images of an
Australian Enlightenment

Images of an
Australian Enlightenment

The Story of Lachlan and
Elizabeth Macquarie's Treatment
of the Convicts as a History
Tale for Today

AUSTIN LOVEGROVE

Published in 2019 by Unicorn,
an imprint of Unicorn Publishing Group LLP
5 Newburgh Street, London
WIF 7RG

www.unicornpublishing.org

A catalogue record for this book is available from the British Library

Printed in Turkey for Jellyfish Ltd

ISBN 978-1-912690-04-6

Contents

To the memory of

Charles Manning Hope Clark AC
Australian historian (1915–1991)

'History, to be great as history, must have a point of view on the direction of society. It must also have something to say, some great theme to lighten our darkness …' [1]

Sir John Erskine Starke
Victorian Supreme Court judge (1913–1994)

'Reformation should be the primary objective of the criminal law. The greater the success that can be achieved in this direction, the greater the benefit to the community.' [2]

Acknowledgements

One of the many pleasures attending the writing of a book comes at the end of the process when one sits down to write the acknowledgements. All those wonderful memories! The anticipation of each overseas or mere interstate research trip; multiple visits to places to be enjoyed, almost all trips in search of just the right print, one trip to put 'pen to paper' for the first time. These places, from the majestic harbour city of Sydney to historic London; from Crieff in the Scottish Highlands to Skipton in the Australian Felix. In the latter two – the towns – scenic beauty was largely the source of the pleasure. In the former – the two cities – it was much more. Those varying emotional cocktails of awe, admiration, horror, sadness, anger, as one contemplated when walking around these two places the people and events they unwittingly hosted. In Sydney, it was the Macquaries, who knew what they were doing, yet suffered for it. In London, it was the British politicians, who did not know what they were doing, but who triumphed. In all the places visited in the search for prints, sometimes elation, more often disappointment. Nonetheless, it was far from all serious stuff. For there were the characters along the way, men and women, the memory of whom still generates a warming chuckle and entertaining anecdote. Thank you for contributing to this medley of emotions – all part of the joy of historical research and writing.

In these places too are the institutions and small businesses critical to my putting together the ninety-five images so pivotal in the telling of the Macquarie story as an enlightenment and history tale for today. The institutions are especially the State Library of New South Wales (incorporating the Mitchell Library) in Sydney, and the National

Archives at Kew in London; but also and outside these major centres, the Tasmanian Museum and Art Gallery in Hobart along with the Devon Heritage Centre, Exeter, England. In these institutions one is handling documents and objects which both inform history and made history. They are to be regarded as a wonder to behold. At these times, one must not forget that this is this made possible by the conscientious and hard-working staff behind the scenes, the men and women responsible for putting them before the researcher and producing high quality copies of them on request.

As far as the purveyors of antique and fine prints who contributed at least one print or illustrated book to my collection are concerned, there are too many to mention. Though four stand out. Principal among them must surely be Grosvenor Prints in the London neighbourhood of Seven Dials. This is not simply because that is where I sourced many of my rare and old prints. Enriching this was the nineteenth-century romance of the shop; those large, overflowing, dusty old folders which you are left to trawl through with a tingling expectancy of that next print perhaps being sought-after treasure. Ah, the joy of collecting! A second important source of fine antique prints was Sebra Prints of Melbourne. Then there are those many shops where I acquired one, perhaps a couple of prints. Again, two in this category stand out for me, though the items themselves were not the most collectable. In England, it is Petersfield Bookshop in Hampshire. After being told of my interest in Lachlan Macquarie and Elizabeth Campbell, they came up with a copy of 'Historical Record of the Seventy-Third Regiment', illustrated, published in 1851, and bearing Lord Archibald Campbell's coat of arms opposite the title page, the book itself concluding with a memoir of Lachlan Macquarie. The other is an original rough caricature sketch of a maniacal John Macarthur by the Australian poet Hugh McCrae, dug up by Douglas Stewart Fine Books of Melbourne. At this point, it would be remiss of me not to mention the Rebecca Hossack Art Gallery in Fitzrovia, London. It was on a visit there I was introduced to the work of the Aboriginal artist Rosella Namok and her 'Kaapay and Kuyan' motif, which was to prove fundamental to the telling of this story. Alastair Nicholson facilitated my making contact with Rosella in Cairns.

An author requires a foundation from which to embark on a substantial project. Over the four or five years during which I first thought about this topic, then set about undertaking it, finally bringing it to completion, I had the pleasure which comes with the honour of working at one of the world's elite law schools, The Melbourne Law School, at the University of Melbourne. In particular, I must record my gratitude to the Law Librarian, Carole Hinchcliff, whose friendly staff offered much support, while she herself has been a ready source of needed encouragement.

As I write this, fond memories flood back of my time at Goodenough College, a London residential college, where in the Spring of 2018, armed with a stack of hand-written notes, and with London University's Senate House Library nearby, I sat down to write the first chapters of this book. What a spot to commence a creative exercise! The solitude and beauty of Mecklenburg Square; the College's fine facilities, its most helpful staff, and … and its broader location – the intellectual and cultural district of Bloomsbury. How one would like it to be that Charles Dickens, who at one time had a home around the corner, here first conceived of Magwitch, the convict character he would later introduce to the world as a man.

Images play, as intimated above, a key role in this work. It is one thing to collect them, another to reproduce them fit for fine publication. This strung-out task fell to Jim Morris of Classic Colour Copying, Melbourne. The nature of the job posed a challenge; for two images it was particularly demanding, such was the poverty of their quality. Yet, this offered me the advantage of seeing a master printer at work. Incidentally, it was the Australian historian, Geoffrey Blainey, from whom I came to understand the potential of the image – word imagery in his case – in the telling of history, in making it memorable.

There were many others who made themselves available or did something to assist me, and who are appreciatively, in some cases fondly, remembered, though their part was lesser rather than greater in the overall scheme of things.

Finally, it delights me to acknowledge two very different groups, far apart, though unknown to each other yet working together. In London, Ian Strathcarron and his team at Unicorn Press, who were most solicitous of making the book what I wanted it to be, and most wise in offering advice on how to bring this about. In Hawthorn, Victoria, the staff of my local coffee shop, 'Who's Harry?'; every morning they enlivened my flagging spirits with their warm greetings and kick-started my weary mind with their fine coffee.

Part 1
Lachlan and Elizabeth Macquarie's treatment of the convicts

Chapter 1

Introducing the Macquaries and this Story

TWO BIRTHS; TWO deaths: without the latter, the former would be today of no significance. Indeed, there would not be a story to tell, one of lives re-made at the time, and a philosophy of enlightenment for the treatment of criminals today. The births are those of this tale's heroes, the Scots, Lachlan Macquarie on 31st January, 1761, and Elizabeth Campbell on 13th June, 1778. The deaths are those of Jane Jarvis (15th July, 1796) and Murdoch Maclaine (5th July, 1804). In the context of this story, we rejoice at the births, but how should we regard the deaths, and what should be our accompanying emotions?

Maclaine was Lachlan's uncle and Elizabeth's brother-in-law. His dying is what brought them together. Lachlan had come to bid his uncle farewell, while Elizabeth was there to help her sister run the household at this difficult time. Thus, at Lochbuie House, on the Isle of Mull, they met for the first time. Yet this death should not trouble us too much, since Maclaine was in his seventies – a good age for the day – and Macquarie had taken his time to come up from London in response to his ailing uncle's plea. In any case, for our story to have the significance it does, Murdoch Maclaine did not have to die – a grave illness would have sufficed. Rather what mattered was the timing; the fact that Macquarie, a soldier, was not abroad on duty at the time.

Not so for Jane Jarvis; she had to die. And it was an event most tragic. She was cruelly young – just 23 years old. Moreover, this left Lachlan a grief-stricken widower. Now for several years he lived without his previous zest for life, as a man bereft of his love of society with its gaiety and attendant status, and as a soldier no longer with the drive to rise to the heights of the military establishment. Nonetheless, her death had two most profound consequences for the rest of his life. The first was spiritual, the second prosaic but as important. When Jane was in his life, the ground of Lachlan's being was his love for and devotion to her. Her death created an emotional void, one which had to be filled. It was. In its stead, there sprang up within him a powerful, consuming, and enduring desire to do good; in particular, to befriend and advance the lives and interests of those upon whom fate had cast a shadow. And so, he dedicated himself to those who struggled to survive, whom society treated harshly, and looked down upon not with the eye of pity but in contempt. Though he himself could no longer enjoy happiness, he would bring it to others. As to the second consequence, Macquarie was now in need of a wife. For this role, he chose Elizabeth Campbell. Well-bred yet practical, she would make a good officer's wife, such was his reckoning. In time he was to discover she was much more. She was sustained by a religious faith, one inclining her strongly to the service of others. Moreover, she was possessed of a most formidable character – this lady was not for turning. In what was to define Macquarie's life's work – the governorship of the British convict colony of New South Wales, from 1810 to 1821 – she was to become one-half of the very essence of a modern power couple.

So do we face a very confronting fact, namely, without Jane's death, Lachlan Macquarie's life, while being that of a good man, in all probability would have been marked by the pursuit of pleasure and professional advancement, but little else. Without Jane's death, the story of Macquarie's life is likely to have amounted to no more than material for an entertaining light novel. While with Jane's death came Macquarie's epiphany, and a man very different than he would otherwise have been went out to the convict colony. Moreover, with Jane's death, enter Elizabeth Campbell. Such are the vicissitudes of life. Thus, it came to be, in regard to the treatment of crime and criminals, we have two lives worth knowing about, worth understanding, worth emulating. This is what this book is about.

What exactly is it about these matters making this story worth telling? The fact is, Lachlan and Elizabeth Macquarie's attitudes towards the convicts, and their policies for dealing with them, were radically different from the thinking of the government and people of Britain whom they represented. The Macquaries thought of the convicts as having goodness within their souls: accordingly, they intuited, there was no need for more than moderate punishment; rather, the emphasis should be on measures designed to help these wayward men and women turn their lives around, lead good lives and, once free, participate in society according to their individual capacities. How different from the official policy, under which convicts were regarded as people for whom goodness was foreign to their natures: accordingly, it followed, let there be harsh, even brutal punishment as a deterrent, with no thought for the convicts' reclamation; then, once free, to be treated as a moral canker, ever to be kept on the margins of society; better, to be excised from society. Moreover, the Macquaries' approach to the treatment of the convict and, more generally, to the prevention of crime, was an indivisible part of social justice. Again, how different from today, where we think of social justice as aiding the worthy, and criminal justice as punishment for the bad.

Both the British and Australians think of themselves as enlightened and point to their pursuit of medical and scientific advancement, along with an ever-greater sensitivity to human rights and justice. Nonetheless, as the people of these two countries bathe themselves in self-satisfaction in regard to these things, they remain strangely oblivious to their punitive criminal justice cultures, though the sentiments and attitudes underpinning them remain unchanged – the excesses of brutality aside – since the days of convict Australia. What makes this remarkable is that in the Age of the Macquaries is to be found the idea of the treatment of the criminal as part of what it means to be enlightened. This needs to enter the national consciousness in both Britain and Australia as a step towards their social advancement.

Moreover, punitive criminal justice cultures are to be found in other so-regarded enlightened countries across the globe, there being no better instance of this than the United States. Thus, the Macquaries have a story for much of the world. Without knowing our history, we are not challenged to consider learning from our history.

This overview places the source of this particular contribution to enlightenment as the Macquaries themselves. Indeed, it was. But it should be seen as part of a greater enlightenment, a national consciousness of enlightenment, namely, what we now call the Scottish Enlightenment. This was a period spanning a hundred or so years from around the mid-eighteenth century. It was manifested by pioneering advances in science, great insights in the humanities, and by thinkers who championed reason and humanity. It provided for the nation's citizens a climate of intellectual ferment, an expectation of a greater understanding of the world, a better way of doing things, and the inspiration to be part of the action. It is impossible to think this did not capture the imagination of the Macquaries, each with a native intelligence and an instinctive humanity.

Both were proud Highlanders and patriotic Scots. Elizabeth, certainly, celebrated Scotland for the unique perspective and values with which this land had imbued her. This story, then, is not only a story about two Scots, it is a Scottish story.

TELLING THIS STORY

In this work, images (portraits, landscapes, buildings, objects) are dominant. Text, although substantial, is somewhat background. The story is told in large measure by way of the images – they are no mere illustrations, acting as leavening to lighten the text. These images are not few and scattered, but numerous and ever-present. Moreover, not just any reasonable image of a person, building, etc. is used, as in the case of illustrations; nor just any significant and relevant work of art, as in an exhibition. Rather, an image here must convey something about a person or what a building, scene or object represents. It must say something, something which could not be said, or said as well or succinctly or memorably, with narrative alone. And ideally the images will be found attractive, sometimes amusing, certainly substantive and, it is hoped, thought-provoking, even confronting. Moreover, each image should act to animate a past life, recreate a reality. Most importantly, these images are intended to stimulate the reader's imagination and stir their emotions, all with impact and beyond the potential of words. In contrast, the role of text is, for each image, to outline its background and context, to offer an interpretation of it, and to link it with preceding and following images, and more generally to fill in the details of the story. This, however, is only one side of the role of the working image in this work. For as text called for images, so there were images upon being serendipitously sighted which demanded text.

Why images? In the preceding material lies only part of the answer. This book seeks to inform and then – unashamedly – persuade you, the reader, to a point of view about how the community ought properly to deal with the problem of crime. This is a matter of great importance to the public at large; one about which you personally probably opine regularly, and may well do with conviction and not a little animation. Two things follow for the telling of this story. First, it must have the potential to appeal to you, the thoughtful man and woman in the street – the proverbial Everyman. The book's language must be lay; it cannot take the form of a heavy-duty or arcane academic piece of work. Moreover, with images its presentation can be made more engaging, and will be less demanding of words. Second, because the problem of crime arouses strong emotions, ones often with a graphic element, this book attempts to engage both the reader's affective and aesthetic faculties. Images, often more than words, have the capacity to do this.

In view of the role of images here, this work may be cast as one of the Law's 'picture books'[3].

STRUCTURE OF THE STORY

The acknowledgement of the Macquaries' work taking place on the land of the Australian Aboriginal people – the continent's First Peoples – and the consequent appalling price paid by them is fundamental to the telling of the story. As part of this, the book's organisation is influenced by the Indigenous moiety stories[4] 'Kaapay and Kuyan'. The eminent Aboriginal artist, Rosella Namok of the Lockhart River, has represented in painting this traditional understanding of social organisation among her people. She describes the underlying idea thus: 'Everything is divided two ways … people, lands, story places … they belong one way or other way … it's important you know which way'.[5] In fact, the two elements of the Kaapay and Kuyan motif do not represent so much anything specific as, together, their proper difference.[6] Following from this, there will be a 'right way' and a 'wrong way' of doing things. This concept offers a structure for the ideas underpinning this story. The Macquaries' attitude towards the convicts and their approach to their treatment had its ardent supporters but, alas, also its vehement critics who did their best to discredit the Macquaries' ideas and to destroy their work. The former resided largely in the Colony, but the latter were to be found not only in the Colony, but critically in the British parliament and government. Underlying this, as intimated above, the Macquaries' attitudes towards the convicts and their policies for dealing with them were radically different from the thinking and understanding of the government and people of Britain whom they represented. It was along this fault line the Macquaries' policies were implemented, and they as a team rose; it was along this fault line they as individuals came closer together when their polices were overridden, and they as team fell.

As a symbol of Aboriginal historical pre-eminence in this Land and as the source of this book's organisation, I commissioned Rosella Namok to paint 'Kaapay and Kuyan' applied to the treatment of crime and criminals and to the two ways identified in this story, namely, the Macquaries' way and the way of their opponents and detractors. This painting (see p.18)

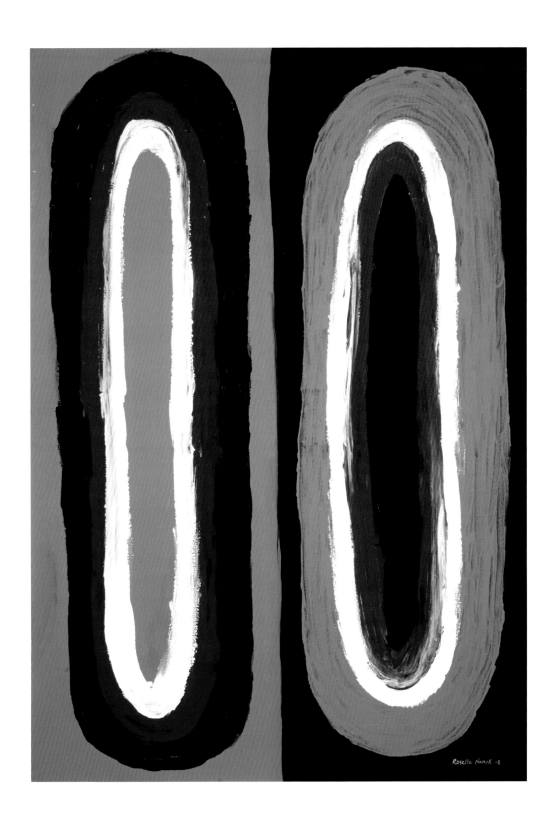

(opposite)
'Kaapay and Kuyan'.
Rosella Namok. 2018.
(acrylic on canvas;
w: 61cm, h: 90cm)
(Viki Petherbridge,
photographer.) (Personal
collection.)

is primary within the text, providing an embedded framework for the arrangement, selection and interpretation of material between and within the chapters.

The ovals are Namok's 'Kaapay and Kuyan' motif. The colours – Lockhart River ceremonial pigments – represent the story and its message. Yellow ochre is the way of reform, inclusion and hope; black, the way of punishment, marginalization and further degradation. White proclaims this a story of enlightenment; red ochre warns against the wrong way. As this image is pre-eminent in this text, so let it remain pre-eminent in your mind as this story unfolds.

This chapter concludes by introducing the Macquaries: their backgrounds and aspects of their characters, together with their meeting and their marriage; then follows his appointment as the governor of New South Wales. Subsequent chapters deal with his governorship, her part in it, the opposition they faced, what apparent failure meant for them personally, and the significance of their lives and work for the treatment of crime and criminals today.

THE MACQUARIES

Lachlan Macquarie: his background and character

Five-foot ten in height, sandy haired, ramrod straight when parading, a face portraying calm and presenting a genial smile to the world; such was the physical manifestation of the man, Lachlan Macquarie. But what about his personality, his inner man? What did he bring to the command of Britain's remote, southern convict colony? About this we must turn to his early life and circumstances.

Lachlan Macquarie was born on Ulva, just off the Isle of Mull, Scotland. His father was a carpenter, who shared a tenant farm belonging to the Duke of Argyll, he himself being too poor to work it alone. There is nothing here, at first blush, offering a child a material base from which to rise. But, perhaps with thought, we can discern something for his psyche? In fact, there was straw from which bricks could be made. His mother was the sister of the current chieftain of Clan Maclaine – Murdoch Maclaine – and his father was a cousin of the last chieftain of the Macquaries. On his mother's side a comfortable family of modest status, certainly; alas, on his father's, money and position were very remote. There is nothing much apparent here. There was, however, the fine residence – Lochbuie House – Uncle Murdoch was planning to build on his estate. No doubt Maclaine, who had taken young Lachlan under his wing since his father's early death, talked excitedly about this project to his young nephew. Perhaps, just perhaps, there was in this enough to inspire an ambitious and imaginative young mind. Nevertheless, Lachlan would need to find the right ground to build upon. This he soon did.

Lachlan left this harsh, primitive, confining enclave as a young teenager. It was to Edinburgh he went. Scotland's capital was to be his introduction to sophistication and his gateway to advancement in the world. In Edinburgh he boarded with a school master, where he learned basic reading, writing and arithmetic, along with some geography and history. Macquarie in the course of his life was to see much of the world's geography at first hand. What this rustic lad, though now wider-eyed, could not have imagined then, was his becoming part of the history of a continent yet to be settled by Europeans; more particularly his being, along with a girl not yet born, one of its great improvers, whose work would offer an object lesson in social justice to the world.

Edinburgh did not hold him long. At fifteen he was off to North America as a volunteer with Uncle Murdoch, where the American War of Independence was approaching its last stages. Maclaine had enlisted in the British army for no higher reason than a pressing need for money. Lachlan went with the ambition of joining the British army as a career soldier. We can no more than speculate about the young man's thoughts and emotions at this time. Almost certainly dominant would have been high expectations, and an attendant thrilled anticipation. The army alone offered him a road out of poverty, isolation and lowliness. If he could participate in winning battles around the globe, become an officer, rise through the ranks, he would acquire wealth and live in style, mix with the highest in the land, attend glittering parties, be consulted on world affairs – he would be a man of consequence, a man who mattered in London. Hmm! And he would return to where it had all started, now as a Hebridean hero. Most probably his adventurous young mind, along with a desperation to rid himself of his present circumstances, would have engendered a reckless disregard for the horrors of war: he would have to maim and kill, see his comrades and friends scream in agony or die slowly from deadly diseases; and of course, he would risk the same fates himself.

The next year Lachlan Macquarie obtained an ensigncy – his career was under way. And when in 1781 he was commissioned as a lieutenant, he was no longer a soldier, but an officer. O joy! Now on the first step of a ladder he would climb to military seniority, one culminating in acceptance into the Establishment. Well, this was his dream, one constituting an enticing hope, a driving ambition. Then followed deployment in Jamaica,

'Seventy Third Regiment. Storming of Seringapatam 4th May, 1799'. Copied from R. Cannon, *Historical Record of the Seventy-Third Regiment*. Parker, Furnivall and Parker, London, 1851.

after which he returned to Scotland on the Army's half-pay list, managing his Uncle's estate on Mull. During this period at war, he had seen fighting on the sea, but not on land.

Macquarie's next period of overseas service, 1788-1802, took him to India, Ceylon, and Egypt. On this tour of duty, he did take part in live fighting. One action was the assault on Seringapatam in 1799 at which – perhaps significantly for Macquarie's future – Arthur Wellesley, the future Duke of Wellington, was present. One year earlier, also in India, Macquarie had recklessly exposed himself to danger in a two-week campaign. The image depicting the battle of Seringapatam reminds us that the boy Macquarie became a man and made his way in the world as a soldier.

Successful military campaigning underpinned future promotion. In the short term, it meant prize money – often big money. By 1803 Macquarie had amassed 10,000 pounds, a fortune at the time. As a consequence, when he returned to London, this man of humble birth had the means of acquiring the trappings needed to participate comfortably in the elegant and extravagant lifestyle of the highest in the land. As importantly, in the military this rustic had the opportunity of acquiring much needed social skills.

These skills first came in the officers' mess, then by way of special appointments. One of the most significant of these was in 1800 as confidential military secretary to the Governor of Bombay, a relationship which grew to be one of confidant, friend and mentor. In this role Macquarie resided at Government House, which offered him experience in the intimate company of good society. In fact, he spent time there periodically for the next six years. Over this time Macquarie grew in stature. He learned high-level administrative skills. He mixed with increasing ease and enjoyment. Along with this, the breadth of his understanding of life and the depth of his conversation rose to a higher plane. This company included such elevated people as Sir James Mackintosh, a patrician figure, whose future lay in parliament as an eminent Whig politician. He was a man reputed for his brilliance and learning, and a conversationalist par excellence; he too was a man possessed of humanitarian and reforming instincts. We meet him again later. It was company such as Mackintosh's which taught Macquarie much and reinforced his own compassionate world view. Macquarie's appetite for more was whetted.

Greater satisfaction soon followed. In 1803 the Duke of York – Commander-in-Chief of the British Army – appointed Macquarie Assistant Adjutant-General in the London district. So, we find Macquarie in London: now with the conversation of an educated man, apparently socially sure-footed and confident; dining with the likes of the Duke of Clarence, delighting himself at glittering parties; being driven through the streets of London in a fine carriage, drawn by his two handsome black chargers, on his way to an audience with their Majesties, or returning from a function or engagement to his accommodation in chic St. James's. The joy of it all for this man of humble birth!

As though in celebration of his life to date, Macquarie commissioned the notable artist John Opie to paint his portrait. Opie did Macquarie well, giving him the very image which he wanted to project to the world. Here he appears as handsome and suave, a dignified officer and gentleman, at home in the best society; a man pleased with himself and optimistic about his future. A man proclaiming to the world that he is ready for bigger things. This was the real Macquarie – well, at least on

(opposite)
Lachlan Macquarie (c1804). J. Opie. Copied from S. Ure Smith and B. Stevens, *The Macquarie Book: The Life and Times of Governor Lachlan Macquarie*. (Tenth number of 'Art in Australia'.) Art in Australia, Sydney, 1921.

one of his very many good days. Yet, in this image, Opie did us – the viewer – well too. For look into Macquarie's eyes. In light of his dress and deportment, we might have expected them to be radiant, they revealing a man most pleased with himself, they perhaps looking down upon us, in this projecting a certain hauteur. But no, there is both something more and something quite different going on inside the man. There is about his eyes a softness; there is about his eyes a certain sadness, disappointment, insecurity, and uncertainty.

The softness emanated from the deep and sure humanity of Macquarie the man, who felt and practised compassion when he came across life's sufferers and battlers. Around this time, he had purchased an estate on Mull and was contemplating how he might improve the lives of the peasants on it. As part of this, to any man who built a comfortable cottage for his family, he determined to contribute fifty per cent of the cost. The turn of events later in this tale will demonstrate this act of humanity to represent not an isolated aspect of his character but something fundamental in the core of his being.

Macquarie was 'pleased with himself' to be sure, but far from contented. He desperately wanted more; it was an ambition accompanied as much by an enlivening anticipation as by a disturbing fear of failure, and with good reason. By 1800 Macquarie was increasingly re-engaging with his future. Nonetheless, the loneliness and the profound sense of an irreplaceable loss widowerhood had brought to his life were still very much part of his existence. Moreover, these were not the only things afflicting Macquarie's mind. Though the elite mixed with him, though he flattered them and showered them with valuable gifts, Lachlan the person never really mattered to them, and they would soon forget about him. Now, such slights caused psychological scarring to men like Macquarie: his self-regard suffered; and his desire for advancement in his professional life first cooled, then fired the more, in a discombobulating cycle. In the end, Macquarie's strength of character won the day, steeling his ambitious drive. One real problem remained. The Powerful hazarded his promotion, because men like Macquarie relied on the patronage of the great and the good to reach the heights of the military. This was in light of the painful, disillusioning fact before him: he had some way to go, and big were the steps, before he would be an officer – and hence a man (yes, 'man' not merely 'soldier') – of real consequence. Macquarie learnt at first hand the flaws in society's clay.

Society too learned about the flaws in Macquarie's own clay, with almost ruinous consequences to himself. The fact is, Macquarie had a predisposition – latent for the most part – to deceive in order to advance his purpose. On one occasion, he misrepresented the circumstances of two young relatives for whom he was trying to secure commissions. On another occasion – it was upon returning from India – he consciously made a claim for an already-paid sum of money. The Duke of York, jolly fellow that he could be, was not amused. Fortunately, for humanity's sake, he ensured the likable Macquarie survived. Survived too with an intimate understanding of human weakness, and – perhaps tellingly – the beneficiary of a compassionate response to wrongdoing.

Elizabeth Campbell: her background and character

There is little to be said about the early phase of Elizabeth Campbell's life. As a late eighteenth-century girl, personal hopes could be but few. Rather, she would be the subject of her parents' expectations. And of limited scope they would be: a marriage of contentment to a man of at least her father's status and means. Despite this, as a young woman of the time, she had much to be satisfied with, much to offer. She was the daughter of John Campbell of Airds, and with her family lived in a fine gentleman's residence looking out over Loch Linnhe and its majestic surrounding landscape at Port Appin, Scotland. This background, along with a rounded secondary education in London, prepared her for good society. She presented as a lively, straight-talking, cultivated young

Aird's House (c1975). Copy from and made by Canmore, Historic Environment Scotland, Edinburgh (SC 569502).

Elizabeth Macquarie (c1810). Digital image from the State Library of New South Wales, Sydney (MIN 237). This portrait of Mrs. Macquarie bears a striking likeness to MIN 70, a portrait of Mrs. Macquarie dated to around 1810.

woman, having a wide range of interests and skills, including architecture and music. Guests would admire the improvements to the landscape at the front of Airds House, which she planned and had implemented, and then once inside would delight in her accomplished playing of the violoncello. To appreciate the standing of her background, we need no more than view this modern photograph of Airds House (see p.25), largely as she would have known it, the small asymmetrical addition to the right aside.

Nevertheless, despite this familial style, Elizabeth can experience no more than half a life; she must wait until picked out by a man as a wife, and then live and find fulfilment largely through him and within the boundaries of his world. Until then, she is to remain at home, amusing herself, helping her mother entertain and her older married sisters with chores when they need her. Her father would have had reasonable hopes of Elizabeth being found by the right man; but not even in his flights of fancy would he have foreseen her leaving a legacy to the world, one worth remembering and understanding two hundred years later. Rather contentment for him as a father would have been Elizabeth living happily and fulfilled as a wife and mother in a house comparable to Airds.

Let us imagine Elizabeth's mental world at this time. Surely she would have experienced increasing concern about her future, since marriage came late for her. Not all women married, after all. There was always the chance of spinsterhood, with its loneliness, unspoken shame, absence of maternal fulfilment and domestic self-expression. To the extent these matters exercised her mind, how great her apprehension. Yet, there was almost certainly more going on within her. We know from her later life that she was a spirited woman, capable of wielding power with the intention of leaving the world a better place for others. But of this aspect of her character, as a young woman, was she aware? Certainly, she would not have been encouraged to think this way. But her perceptiveness would have allowed her to discern it in men; why then could it not be for women? We can only surmise. Nonetheless, known to her or not, troubling to her consciousness or not, Elizabeth was a simmering cauldron of reforming drive. This is far from the person we discern in Elizabeth's 1810 portrait.

This portrait of Elizabeth Campbell presents her as an attractive young woman though certainly no beauty. She is simply dressed, demure, looking out innocently though not directly at us, with her head sweetly leaning to the right – every bit, a middling gentleman's daughter, his 'Little Girl'. This is probably how she would have appeared in person to those not well acquainted with her; how she might have appeared to Macquarie on introduction. This is a personal image which might have been extracted from a family portrait. The passivity of her pose is striking. She appears no more than part of something more; set back in the frame, as though waiting for us to come to her; not showing herself off. Is not this a woman born by nature to serve, not to give orders, let alone to frighten? How different we will find her 1819 portrait! Though what concerns us here is that there is much about Elizabeth to have pleased Macquarie – certainly – but nothing to shake him, to challenge his striking, charming, beautiful, wealthy first wife, Jane Jarvis.

The marriage of Lachlan and Elizabeth

In 1804 when Lachlan met Elizabeth at Lochbuie House their emotional needs were so different as to render an encapsulating, all-fulfilling emotional union between them impossible. The facts are most unfortunate. He was a man looking for a wife to replace Jane qua wife. His grief had subsided sufficiently for him to once more be realistic about his personal life. Yet he was not a man looking for love; indeed, this was not open to him, because he was a still in love with his most beloved Jane. By way of comparison – tragically – the virginal Elizabeth was looking for love; but at twenty-six years of age there was a whiff of anxiety in the air. Perhaps she would have to find happiness with a man who no more than admired her and would treat her well.

Macquarie – the handsome, brave, socially accomplished officer – soon paid her attention. Elizabeth sparkled! This watercolour of Lochbuie House, though delicate, radiates vibrancy. Through it we can enter Elizabeth's mind and capture how she now perceived the House and all about it. Macquarie's attention was not surprising in the circumstances. She was amiable, an accomplished gentleman's daughter, and the practical side of her nature – her preparedness to muck in, to get her hands dirty, to organise – struck him favourably. This notwithstanding, his behaviour towards her was little more than the minimum called for in the circumstances. She did impress him, though apparently no more than for the utilitarian reason that she would make a good officer's wife, at home and in the field. Within months he proposed; she accepted promptly. This was all new to Elizabeth. How she hoped the mutual emotional sparkle she had expected all along would soon follow. Yet nothing – poor Elizabeth.

Worse was to come. Quickly her muted delight turned to disappointment, her hope gave way to doubt. She soon learned that Macquarie had named his new estate on Mull, the very place where they would settle down and call home, 'Jarvisfield', in memory of his beloved

Lochbuie House. Based on a digital image kindly provided by Lorne Maclaine of Lochbuie, who dates the painting to around 1822; it was painted by a French army officer, a guest at the time. This image, of very poor quality, was masterfully transformed by Jim Morris of Classic Colour Copying, Melbourne.

first wife. Along with this, she was asked to postpone their wedding, as Macquarie had determined to serve with the army in India for the next three to four years and, yes, she was asked to keep their engagement a secret. Why did he not want to take her with him? And why did she have to summon him back, on threat of a broken engagement? About this, we can only speculate. Perhaps he decided to allow himself a fling before settling down to a marriage without romance. Whatever was going on, one fact is inescapable, he had coldly left Elizabeth behind to wonder and

The YEAR 17   Page

No.

William Horn ~~of th~~ resident in this parish (Bachelor) and Elizabeth Bale resident in ~~of~~ this parish (Spinster) were married in this Church — by Banns — this thirtieth Day of August in the Year One Thousand eight Hundred and seven — by me O. L. Meyrick (Rector)

This Marriage was { William Horn ⌐ his mark
solemnized between Us, { Elizabeth Bale ✝ her mark
In the { Richd Hoskin
Presence of { William Jewel

No.

William Sleeman of this parish (Bachelor) and Ann Allin of this parish Spinster were married in this Church — by Banns — this twentieth Day of October in the Year One Thousand eight Hundred and seven — by me J. Pearce offg Minister

This Marriage was { William Sleeman
solemnized between Us, { Ann Allen ✝ her mark
In the { Richd Hoskin
Presence of { John Allin

No.

John Allin — of this parish (Bachelor) and Martha Cole of this parish (Spinster) were married in this Church — by Banns — this twenty eighth Day of October in the Year One Thousand eight Hundred and seven — by me O. L. Meyrick (Rector)

This Marriage was { John Allin
solemnized between Us, { Martha Cole
In the { Richd Hoskin
Presence of { John Cole

No.

Lachlan Macquarie Esqre of the Parish of St James Westminster Widower — and Elizabeth Henrietta Campbell of this parish (Spinster) were married in this Church — by Licence from the Archbishop this third — Day of November in the Year One Thousand eight Hundred and seven — by me O. L. Meyrick (Rector)

This Marriage was { L. Macquarie
solemnized between Us, { Elizabeth Henrietta Campbell
In the { ... Meyrick
Presence of { Elizabeth Meyrick

fret. In any case, he did respond to her ultimatum, and returned, though at pace indicative of a man in no hurry.

On this unromantic footing did their nuptials proceed, and they were married at Holsworthy Parish Church, Devon, on 3rd November, 1807. Macquarie, now with a wife, comforted himself – well, at least up to a point. Elizabeth, having forced herself to accept pragmatism, now – strong woman that she was – would set herself the task of transforming Macquarie's admiration for her into a deep attachment, real affection, perhaps even love – O bliss!

THE APPOINTMENT OF LACHLAN MACQUARIE AS GOVERNOR OF NEW SOUTH WALES

Despite all Macquarie's entreaties to the great and the good to advance his prospects – sometimes almost to the point of demeaning himself – by 1808 he faced some most unpalatable facts: the now 46 year-old Lieutenant-Colonel's rise through the ranks had been slow by the standards of the day; moreover, there was every possibility of him having hit his professional ceiling. Then came New South Wales. Although the circumstances of Lachlan Macquarie's appointment to the governorship of New South Wales would have done nothing to buttress his uncertain ego, nonetheless, he certainly would have quickly come to see it as an opportunity for his frustrated ambition. He would do well in the Colony, and then come back to greater things – well, this is what he intended. Importantly for this story, Macquarie's drive to do something for himself, to achieve, was left intact, unmoderated. The problem is, frustrated ambition in a man's career will leave its scars. So it was for Macquarie; he became a man in too much of a hurry. His promotion happened this way.

At the time, Macquarie had command of the 73rd Regiment of Foot. Then the British government decided to send this regiment to accompany Brigadier-General Nightingall, who was to replace the mutinied Bligh as Governor, with Macquarie as the Lieutenant Governor. However, Nightingall demurred, and the Government quickly looked elsewhere. Macquarie grabbed his chance, submitting his application. The decision fell to Viscount Castlereagh as Secretary of State for the Colonies (Colonial Secretary), who had reports on Macquarie from Arthur Wellesley – the future Duke of Wellington – and the Duke of York. Who were these men on whom Macquarie's fate fell? And what reasons did they proffer? We know from their titles alone they were society grandees. This, however, tells us nothing about their characters as real people like us, and how

'The Duke of Wellington'.
Published by T. Kelly,
London, 1815.

this might have determined their thinking about Macquarie. As is the way in the telling of this story, we turn to images. Actually, in this case caricatures (or images with a touch of caricature) serve well, since they may reveal more, not being bound by the dictates of status.

In the Duke of Wellington, we see pomposity and condescension; in the Duke of York, we see the fast-living bon vivant, who in his love-life and gambling scandalized the monarchy; and in Castlereagh as a young man, we see a sensitive and gentle, ethereal aristocrat.

Wellington was anything but flattering: the man Macquarie, while a business-like, indeed likable sort of fellow, was to be found wanting of judgement in difficult situations so critical for high office. This notwithstanding, perhaps Castlereagh reasoned, Macquarie was not being considered for high office – really. No, he was simply being asked to run a small, far-flung convict colony. All this required was a steady,

(above left)
'"Here's a health to the Duke of York" "wherever he goes" .... Coldstream Guards'. 371. Published by Bowles & Carver, London, [c1793].

(above right)
'Robert Stewart, Viscount Castlereagh'. From the portrait by Sir Thomas Lawrence. [early C20th, photogravure]

firm, predictable, reliable, unimaginative hand; a senior army officer, but not one of the first order. After all, what big judgements were required? As for initiative, this was something definitely not wanted, so far from the centre of power. This was Macquarie – surely. Here was the man for the job! And perhaps the Duke of York, who had very good grounds for expressing serious reservations about Macquarie's character, knew himself, understood human weakness, and spoke kindly of him. Of course, no one thought to make any serious enquiries about the woman who was poised to become the new colonial governor's wife. Blissful ignorance! So, Macquarie it was: the new big-wig in a land of social outcasts and working-class would-bes.

Thus, it came to pass, on 22nd May, 1809, our heroes set out set out on board the 'Dromedary', with a cargo of the deemed unworthy, intended-to-be-forgotten convicts in tow, on a perilous, seven-month journey to a land few had seen and which no one who mattered wanted to see. As to the Macquaries' emotions: for both of them, excitement and anticipation, to be sure. For him, also joy and apprehension: an immediate reward, and a hurdle to be jumped for a future greater prize. Of more consequence though, both the Macquaries, each in their own way, harboured a transcending need to prove something to someone else.

This is what proved crucial to this story. Not by way of determining what the Macquaries did. Rather, it transformed their work into a mission, it imbued this with a sense of urgency, and them with combativeness in the face of opposition.

The Colony of New South Wales had a new governor and – most significant on this occasion – a new governor's wife. Lachlan and Elizabeth, two Scottish warriors, rooted in their Scottishness, qualities together symbolized in these two images: a clansman, as a warrior, and wearing the Macquarie tartan, taken from McIan's iconic Scottish tartans series; and a piece of early nineteenth-century Campbell tartan, as Elizabeth would have known it.

(above left)
'Macquarrie'. R.R. McIan, artist. L. Dickinson, lithographer. Published by Ackermann & Co, London, [1845].

(above right)
The Campbell/Black Watch Tartan. A piece of this tartan was kindly provided by Peter Eslea MacDonald, Tartan Historian, Scotland. It is matched to the shades of this tartan around 1820. (Eric Sierins, photographer, 2018.)

Chapter 2

The Macquaries' Colony

LACHLAN MACQUARIE AND his wife Elizabeth, she proudly at his side, were welcomed with all due ceremony at Sydney Cove, and he sworn in as Governor on 1st January, 1810. This chapter is the first of two dealing with the Colony as the Macquaries found it upon their arrival – its general appearance, the daily lives of the people, and the people themselves. The present chapter considers what about the Colony would have struck the Macquaries, having regard to what they themselves brought to the Colony – their ideals and the forces animating their minds. These would determine what they saw needed to be done, and how they would go about it. Along with this, there is an introduction to the leading social groups and some of the major figures with whom the Macquaries would have to deal as they sought to implement their plans. First, though, we consider the Indigenous peoples, and life as it had been, and now had become, for them.

THE INDIGENOUS PEOPLES

History and humanity demand this ordering: first the Aboriginal people, then the Europeans. For this puts before us – assertively – a most sobering reality. This great tale of criminal justice, with its potential to enlighten the world today, took place on the lands of a dispossessed people and at an incalculable and lasting cost to them. In respect of this – sadly – Macquarie's governorship at one point was to be part of this shadow of shame.

What rendered the British occupation of New South Wales horrific was not their settling on the continent – the sweep of history tells us if

not them at that time then someone else later. Rather, this action in effect represented an invasion, because the land was settled on British terms and enforced militarily with fatal fire. There was not even any pretence at sharing the land, allowing for the Indigenous peoples' interests, negotiating British settlement around their earthly needs, spirituality, traditions. No sense was shown of the Aboriginal people being fellow human beings, equal in their shared divinity.

What the British chose not to respect was the traditional owners' different way of life, their different understanding and use of land. For the Aboriginal men and women, unlike the British, there was not individual ownership of land but a communal right to the land. For food, they did not farm the land, but hunted, gathered, and fished upon it. They did not confine themselves each to their own plot. Rather, they camped and wandered at large, though keeping within the territory of their own

'View of Sidney in New South Wales (Taken from Bell-mount)'. 140. [After a work by J. Eyre.] Published by J. Whittle & R. Laurie, London, [1814].

people, one which would cover an expansive area. Moreover, and just as important, the Indigenous and British expressions of spirituality were diametrically different. For the British, the worship of their God took place within a consecrated building; the land upon which it stood held no spiritual significance. It could be moved at convenience. In contrast, the Aboriginal people had their sacred sites, whose spiritual significance lay in and was integral to a particular site or tract of land – no other; they could not be moved. Indeed, almost every feature of a tribal landscape had mythological significance with deep ancestral origins for its occupants; it was the locus of the peoples' dreaming.

Thus, the British action of displacement devastated the First Peoples: it starved their bodies; it deprived them of their spirits; it destroyed their culture; it degraded and ruined them. Ultimately, it took their lives, physical and spiritual. How well the image of Port Jackson captures the reality of dispossession by the displacement of one people at the hands of another with a different and incompatible way of life. It is a view across Port Jackson (Sydney Harbour) from just inside the Heads to a distant, developing Sydney town, with a group of Aborigines, now outcasts, camped well beyond the ever-expanding city limits.[7] This town now occupied land upon which Aboriginal people had once lived traditional lives, but no longer could, indeed were not allowed.

This picture of dispossession around Sydney, was repeated again and again on the lands beyond. As the Colony grew and became in need of more land for villages and farming, the displacement of its Indigenous inhabitants took place over an ever-growing area and at an ever-increasing pace. Along with this, the local Aboriginal warriors resisted with ever-greater force and less effect, the British in turn with ever-greater violence and greater effect. The extermination of a way of life, and of a people, was well underway.

In respect of the Aboriginal people, what did the Macquaries see as they first walked around Sydney upon their arrival? Well, there were those of the Indigenous population who chose to assimilate into the white man's ways as best they could. They imitated their dress, learnt their ways, acquired work skills; indeed, they fitted in and contributed to the basic running of the Colony, apparently contentedly. Many actually lived within both worlds. They adapted as best they could to their new circumstances in ways consistent with their traditions, and as part of this they would move between the town and the countryside. Then there were those who to varying degrees could not cope. They comically mis-wore items of European clothing and often disported themselves half-

naked; they lay drunk in the street; they begged to survive; new diseases emaciated them and rendered fit bodies corpses. A tragic parade of human caricatures, a picture of degradation and misery. What to the Macquaries would not have been readily apparent, but was very real, indeed was the cause of much of this suffering, was abuse in all its variations and amounting to the worst kind. Then, when the Macquaries travelled into the countryside, what awaited them? As in the town, so it was in the villages, save on a lesser scale. And if they had ventured onto

'Nouvelle-Hollande: Nelle. Galles Du Sud. Norou-Gal-Derrie s'avançant pour combattre'. XX. N. Petit, artist. B. Roger, engraver. Printed by Langlois, [1807].

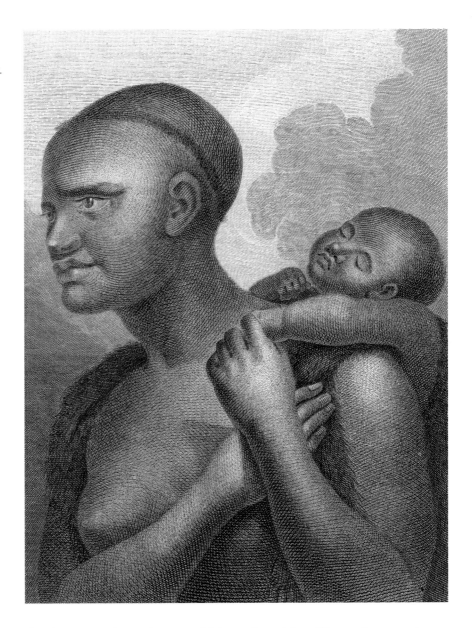

'**Une Femme De La Terre De Van-Diemen**'. Pl. 7. 9. Bernard. [J. Webber, artist. J. Caldwall, engraver. Published by Hotel de Thou, Paris, 1785.]

the frontiers, there they would have found hostility and terror: brave warriors resisting, killing, as their traditional land was being cleared by newly arrived settlers; native families cowering, both most uncertain about their safety and futures. So too others: some who had stolen farm animals and produce from land they believed was rightfully theirs; some who lay dying, victims of reprisals by the settlers.

At this point we must pause and understand the nature of our thinking about these dispossessed peoples. The fact is, we are dealing with them not individually but en masse, and meeting them not in life but as words on the page of a book. The inevitable effect of this will be to incline us to think of real people in the abstract, not as living flesh-and-blood individuals, not as fellow human beings; it will be to shield us from understanding their hurt, feeling their pain. This risks matter-of-factness when there should be animated emotion. Let us reflect, then, upon the portraits of two Indigenous people of the time (see previous spread), one a warrior in New South Wales, the other a Bruny Island (Tasmanian) woman.

Look at, study, each of these images, each in its own way arresting, troubling; indeed, the latter, hauntingly evocative. The warrior: imposing, bold, proud and fearsome; perhaps entertaining a false hope of overcoming this new, most menacing foe. How might he have died? A musket blast to the guts, his life ebbing away in agony? Quite likely. As to the woman, her face betokens deep fear. How at that moment might she have been seeing her future and that of her baby? She abused, raped and taken as a white man's moll; her baby snatched from her and cast out as detritus? Most probable. In light of this, we face a most uncomfortable reality: as the British – free settler and convict, alike – fought to prosper and took pride in their success, Aboriginal men fought to survive and faced death; while European women looked to their children's futures with great optimism, Aboriginal women feared the horrors which might befall theirs.

This all-too brief account of this aspect of Australian history should not be thought of as strangely out of place in this story about the Macquaries' treatment of the convicts. Rather, it is integral to the second part of this book, where we consider this story as a history tale for today. To the Macquaries, as they passed through the Heads for the first time, the scene before them (see p.36) would not have represented the displacement of the Aboriginal people. No. They, in their excitement, would have perceived something quite different: a blank canvas upon which to paint for the British government a picture of a different society; a world which for the convicts was reforming and accepting, and which for their children was socially fairer. Remember this, remember too, this warrior, and this mother and baby, and there let their images resonate, be unsettling, be motivating.

THE MACQUARIE GOVERNORSHIP BEGINS

Imagine the ebullience of the Macquaries on their arrival. Any tiredness from their arduous voyage would have been soon been swept aside the moment their ship entered Sydney Harbour and they were confronted with its majestic splendour. As they drew ever closer to the city, at last entering the Cove, and then prepared to disembark, their air of expectancy would reach its climax. Thus, with feet unsteady and minds overwhelmed, they stepped on to land and processed to Government House, their new home.

After a few days settling in and with the swearing-in now over, it was down to business, to see what they had taken on. For Macquarie himself, the occasion for the ramrod straight, senior officer, and the consequential projected sternness, had passed; now to be moderated – no more than somewhat, though – with a genial smile and general ease of manner. In contrast, Mrs. Macquarie, in her first vice-regal days, was surely uncertain about how to conduct herself before the curious throng. Great pride in her position, anxious not to over-compensate for her slight nervousness – both understandable in light of her youth and absence of any experience in the limelight. The need for the dignity her husband's office demanded – one perhaps bolstered by her inherent tendency to superiority. But did not her Christian precepts demand humility? Yet, might this not cheapen her, and the people be emboldened to take liberties? We can only speculate how she resolved these dilemmas.

In any case, as the Macquaries inspected their new home, how might the locals, both the high and the low, have beheld their new first-family? What manner of man and woman might they be? The men of the colonial upper class would be hoping for a governor who would keep the peace and look after their interests so they might prosper; their wives more interested in whether Mrs. Macquarie would be a lavish entertainer, even include some of them informally in her society. The convicts' interests would have been far more basic. They would have looked at his and her eyes: did they betray a certain steeliness, or was there a softness to be discerned? Did their expressions project a concern or more a disregard for the little people? In respect of this, the men would have been thinking of their backs, the women of their families. What both groups were actually getting in the persons of the Governor and Mrs. Macquarie never crossed the people's minds.

As the people were looking over the Macquaries, the Macquaries were assessing what lay before them as governor and governor's wife in their new, isolated little world. What might their backgrounds and experiences in life have predisposed them to look for as they acquainted themselves with the Colony? And how might these influences have predisposed the Macquaries to react to what lay before them?

THE MACQUARIES' MINDSETS

Lachlan Macquarie

Macquarie's mind was the product of a number of influences. The first came when as a Highland lad the potential part played by the laird impressed itself on him. The laird – the owner of a large estate – exercised great power over his tenant farmers and their families. He could help them, and give them and their children the chance of a better life; or he could exploit them, and drive them down. He could attempt to ameliorate their necessarily harsh conditions, or he could leave them to wallow in misery. Lachlan admired the former lairds and dreamed of becoming one of them. As a lad too, he saw widespread drunkenness and deprivation among these farmers and other Highland people; and crime too, much of it involving property, but including violence. Moreover, he observed that crime continued despite punishment. Most importantly – so it was to prove – as Lachlan matured, his practical but perceptive mind saw more, thought deeper. It made a connection between deprivation and drunkenness and degradation, and between deprivation and crime; and related to this, a link between deprivation and crime and the ineffectiveness of punishment. He discerned goodness, decency and much talent in many of the wayward peasants, and moral wretchedness and stupidity among many of those whom society deemed 'the great and the good'. Also, significantly, Macquarie realized that goodness and decency alone did not protect a man or woman from falling into crime. In the face of deprivation and temptation, one also needed a strong, resilient spirit – something the Creator did not bequeath to all.

Then, for the young Macquarie's impressionable mind, now tuning itself to the world's realities, came the army. As an officer he would come to admire the common soldier's bravery and persistence under fire, his cheerfulness and doggedness in adversity. He saw trouble-makers in the camp be heroic on the battlefield. Of especial significance for his future life, he would have reached similar conclusions about many of the criminals who had chosen the army as an alternative punishment to gaol. Macquarie despised – though too wise, too ambitious, to let it show – those officers who neglected their soldiers' welfare, more especially those who punished otherwise good men mercilessly, and who cared naught for their lives. Moreover, to Macquarie's chagrin, prize money and promotions were going to the affluent, the well-born and the well-connected, less so to the deserving, the worthy, and the most talented. Some of the ablest men were foot-sloggers being ordered around by fools.

'Seventy Third Regiment'.
Copied from R. Cannon, *Historical Record of the Seventy-Third Regiment.* Parker, Furnivall and Parker, London, 1851.

He appreciated how all this might frustrate, crush or stir up resentment in a man, indeed alienate a man. So, we find Macquarie's generous nature often turning a blind eye to his brave soldiers' wild behaviour and forgiving their misdemeanours. For these reasons did he look out for and promote their interests to the limited extent open to him.

Nonetheless, Macquarie's military training had inculcated in his very core the importance of obeying one's superiors and being obeyed by one's inferiors, and the necessity of officers administering discipline to maintain order. These tenets governed his thinking and behaviour as an officer though, in respect of discipline, his benevolent, feeling nature was disposed to moderation and mercy, and baulked at wanton harshness.

'William Wilberforce Esq.'.
J. Russell, artist. J. Heath, engraver. [Published by W. Finden, 1807.]

Macquarie's army service both reinforced and deepened his nascent understanding of human nature and the antecedents of criminal behaviour. It also left him with a strong autocratic streak. The young would-be laird and the maturing officer became the Governor man. The army was most significant in Macquarie's life in another respect. If he had not been an army man, he would not have been appointed governor of New South Wales, since the British government had determined in light of the recent contretemps in the Colony that the next governor required a military background. The image (see p.43) of three soldiers of Macquarie's old regiment, the 73rd Regiment of Foot, the regiment which accompanied him to the Colony, reminds us of the important influence of

Macquarie's army life on Australia's early social history; in particular, its role in his enlightened thinking.

More generally, experience had brought Macquarie a profound preparedness to forgive human weakness. We may suppose this was not simply because he was self-aware of his own faults – this is common enough among people. Perhaps for him this came with the rare gift of understanding what it should mean for his treatment of others: as he overlooked his own shortcomings, so he must forgive others theirs. How could he forget the Duke of York in this respect? Along with this, experience had taught him to appreciate the wisdom of looking for goodness and talent among those in whom the many saw only badness and assumed inadequacy. In respect of this, Macquarie faced what was for him a most unsettling reality. Many of the so-called 'great and good', whom one side of his nature so admired, and whose company he sought and enjoyed, cared not a fig for those of worth but born lowly or struck down by fate. These things rankled, though there was nothing he could do about this – individual acts of kindness, generosity and forgiveness aside – since at this stage of his career he needed the patronage of these men. Macquarie's time would come.

Of themselves, these qualities represent an aspect of goodness, one prompting no more than benevolent actions in everyday life. So, something else linked with this had to be going on in Macquarie's life, something transforming him into the great the man he would become. It was. In the decade or more before his governorship, and before he would have entertained holding such a position, his mind was being prepared to incorporate these qualities in something greater. In this way Macquarie himself was being prepared to be not just a good man, or just a great man, but one of the truly great and good men of history. This we may suppose came about by way of a major figure present at the time, someone at work both in Britain and in Macquarie's mind. It was none other than that great social reformer, William Wilberforce. His preoccupation was not acts of individual kindness. Rather, it was to bring justice to a whole class of people by way of the abolition of slavery, and by this means render men and women of Britain more civilized beings.

This portrait of Wilberforce (opposite) presents him as the earnest, intelligent, neat man he was, and the books and papers around him reveal respectively his subject – the abolition of slavery – and his means – parliamentary. There is about him here an air of peacefulness and gentleness, despite the intensity of his feelings for his cause. After a tireless and protracted period of campaigning, Wilberforce won his first

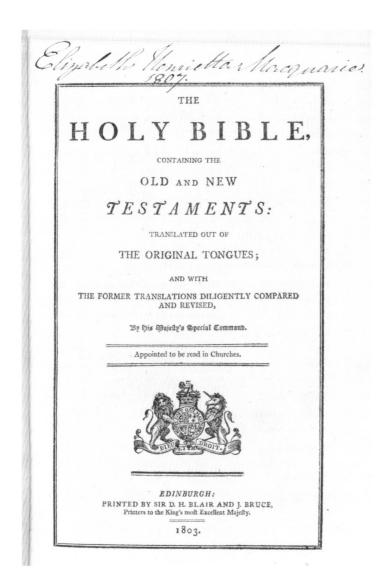

Title Page of Mrs. Macquarie's Bible. Digital image from the State Library of New South Wales, Sydney (B 1685/6).

parliamentary success in 1807. Macquarie was to bequeath him the epithet 'Real Friend of Mankind' and celebrated his life and work during his governorship. Why? Perhaps from Wilberforce came Macquarie's understanding that an individual could use his influence to better the lives of a whole layer of society. Thus, as Macquarie had seen Wilberforce, the parliamentarian in England, legislate on behalf of slaves, so Macquarie, now colonial governor, would rule in the interests of the convicts. The man Wilberforce, though of body hunched and diminutive, and of manner gentle and persuading, was in Macquarie's mind and life a towering figure and a potent transforming force.

but as the end of punifhment is not revenge of crimes, but propagation of virtue, it was more becoming the Divine clemency to find another manner of proceeding, lefs deftructive to man, and at leaft equally powerful to promote goodnefs. The end of punifhment is to reclaim and warn.

Elizabeth Macquarie

In order to appreciate what Macquarie might see as important as he first looked over his little kingdom – this term captures how he regarded the Colony – we have looked generally into his background, and then elaborated on specific aspects of it, namely, his clan heritage, military career, worldly experiences, and the man he admired most. For Mrs. Macquarie, also of significance was her Highland tradition – as it was for Macquarie – but separately, her education and cultivation, religious faith, and a man of learning.

The clan for Mrs. Macquarie meant something different. As a woman she sought not a noble laird as a model. Rather, her inspiration was necessarily the caring and loyal clan member – the woman who looked out for those who were suffering or in need and, on finding them, assisted and ministered unto them; her particular focus being the children of the poor.

As to cultivation, well laid-out floral displays, verdant landscapes and fine buildings, each in their own way, delighted Mrs. Macquarie's senses and elevated her mind, all speaking to her of a civilized world. Then, when Mrs. Macquarie went inside her home, works of art and music served the same purpose. In respect of education, she would have understood the importance of formal learning, realizing how it had enriched her own life. In the wide sophisticated world of London, she would have seen how it could raise individual lives, particularly for men – perhaps a lawyer not a clerk, a tradesman not a labourer, more generally, one of life's drivers not life's driven.

Along with these things, there was Mrs. Macquarie, the devout Christian. Every Sunday she humbly worshiped her God: she praised him, sought his forgiveness, and listened to what he had to say to her. At home, she read her Bible (see p.46) – both the New and the Old

Testaments. Christian belief was not enough; God required Christian actions of her. Passages of Scripture which spoke to her, she noted. One of the messages upper in her mind was the prophet's exhortation to 'Learn to do well ... relieve the oppressed ... plead for the widow' (*The Book of Isaiah, Chapter 1, verse 17*). Important also to her understanding of Christianity as matter of practice were the writings of learned fellow disciples, such as that noble moralist and pre-eminent man of letters, Dr. Samuel 'Dictionary' Johnson. In her copy of James Boswell's biography of Johnson, we find by way of a marked passage Johnson impressing upon her (see p.47):

> ... but as the end of punishment is not revenge of crimes, but propagation of virtue, it was more becoming the Divine clemency to find another manner of proceeding, less destructive to man, and at least equally powerful to promote goodness. The end of punishment is to reclaim and warn.

O how these words must have rung in Mrs. Macquarie's ears to telling effect, when she came to the far-flung penal colony. Once there, one of her duties soon became clear: to bring comfort to others. What did not occur to her was that, in time, she herself was to need comforting from the slings of those whose image of the same God was very different. Religion too differed for Macquarie, though in no way leading to conflict between them. It was simply the case that while for Mrs. Macquarie her faith was determining – indeed, driving, governing – for her husband it was not. Macquarie was a believer – surely – and he was certain religion had moral value for Mankind and was therefore important. But belief for him was of the mind not, as it was for his wife, part of one's soul and spirit.

These just-canvassed influences on the Macquaries are not sufficient of themselves to explain why they did what they did as governor and governor's wife. The fact is, not all who are confronted with poverty feel pity, are moved to alleviate it; rather, they see personal fault and feel contempt. And, when they are confronted with criminals, they do not look for goodness within and seek to bring it out, but see wickedness and demand condign punishment. Similarly, not all who come across blighted and frustrated lives see injustice and seek reform; instead they invoke weakness and assert the need for maintaining life's natural order. As it was for Macquarie, so for Mrs. Macquarie. While she thought of education and opportunity as the right of all, others regarded it as properly the privilege of a few. Though her God was loving and desired this love be bestowed

'New South Wales 1810. View of Sydney, from the West Side of the Cove. No. 1'. [J. Eyre, artist. J. Clark, engraver. Published by J. Booth, London, 1810.] Published by W. Dymock, Sydney, 1884.

on all, others worshiped a God who commanded the harsh judgement of sinners. Something more is needed to explain their shared perspective. Perhaps within their psyches an inherent generosity of spirit, a sensitive capacity for empathy, a … Who knows what? We are now in the deepest recesses of the human mind, inaccessible to the self, let alone others.

In the light of this background, we may accompany Lachlan and Elizabeth as they first acquaint themselves with their new home, now in a better position to see the Colony as they saw it, and to appreciate their take upon the place and the people.

THE MACQUARIES INSPECT THEIR COLONY

Macquarie's first concern is civil unrest. The previous governor – Bligh – had been overthrown in a rebellion led by a cabal of turbulent citizens, one involving the military. Yet, it is not that Macquarie fears something similar, after all he is – unlike his predecessor – a military man, and the regiment of which he has just relinquished command – the 73rd – has

'St. Phillips Church'.
J. Fowles, artist. W. Harris,
engraver. [Published by
J. Fowles, Sydney, 1848;
republished, c1880.]

accompanied him to the Colony. No, Macquarie's concern arises because he wants to be an improver, not a suppressor, and for this he requires a quiescent population. Thus, the soldier in him first looks for signs of unrest: tension in the air, malign or furtive expressions on people's faces, whisperings by some against others, signs of secret cabals. In fact, there is nothing to worry him; indeed, much to delight him. For both Macquarie himself and Mrs. Macquarie soon discern a people far from obviously forlorn or downtrodden; indeed, among some – perhaps no more than a small number – an audible buzz and unmistakable purposefulness as they go about their daily lives. Commerce in general – shop keeping, manufacturing, fishing and trading – is quietly bubbling along in its own parochial, unambitious way. Nonetheless, over the people's spirits there hangs a shadow, lighter for the free settler than for the convict: somehow the place and they belong to someone else; additionally, for the convict, somehow their future lies in someone else's hands.

Mrs. Macquarie's attention, though, is primarily elsewhere. The majesty of the greater setting of her new home – the harbour – is the equal of the situation of her family home – Loch Linnhe. O joy! But what about the town itself? Well, it is settled on a small cove. A surrounding ridge falls to the head of the cove, creating a valley through which a stream flows. From the harbour approach to the cove, the scene appears picturesque, and the town might be described as pretty. This image (see p.49), portraying Sydney from the west ridge, shows how the buildings might have appeared to the naked eye, somewhat removed, and in the right light.

This representation of Sydney deceives, however, as Mrs. Macquarie is to discover. The people's houses – often also serving as their place of business – are for the most part mean and small, little more than ad hoc structures. As she moves around the town, she finds herself asking: where are the open squares, and the parks and gardens, to rest one's body, to calm one's mind, to delight and inspire one's spirit? As to the customary public buildings, they are typically make-do accommodation, run-down, shack-like, not fit for purpose. Nothing here to indicate even a nascent cultivation. The Church – St. Phillip's – is better; but to this first-lady's eyes, falls well short of the beauty, the stateliness, required for Sydney's House of God (opposite). We hear from Mrs. Macquarie a very displeased, 'Huh'. Then an almost imperceptible conspiratorial smile plays on her face. How fortunate she brought that architectural pattern book with her! Macquarie feels similarly, but his thinking includes a degree of self-centredness. Great leaders require grand buildings as accoutrements, edifices serving as monuments. What a setting the topography of the place offers for this purpose – an outdoor panoramic gallery, he exclaims!

As Macquarie thinks about himself and his legacy, Mrs. Macquarie's mind turns to other things, in particular the needy. Nearby, just up from the docks and across from the Rocks, is a place housing orphan girls. The wretchedness of the building, the girls' want of education, indeed their general state of neglect, saddens her, maddens her. But what really cuts her up is the appalling abuse experienced at night by these poor abandoned girls. The problem is self-explanatory. The Rocks are home to lecherous, single convict men, and the ships disgorge idle, randy sailors. Neither group has far to go for fun and satisfaction. As the official party is hurried away – such an unsavoury place for a lady, you understand – this woman of the Bible would have recalled her Lord's words, 'Suffer the little children to come unto me and forbid them not: for of such is the kingdom of God' (*The Gospel of Mark, Chapter 10, verse 14*).

In regard to welfare more generally, there is much to be done. Where are the schools for the ever-increasing numbers of children of the free and convict alike – the next generation? The comparatively small numbers of the wealthy and the well-off rely on tutors to educate their young ones. But this is not an option for most free settlers, let alone the convicts who comprise the great majority of the population. This is just one of the

'Le Serpent noir. (Nouvelle-Galles-du-Sud)'. N. Maurin, artist, after a sketch by J. Arago. Kaeppelin & Co, lithographer. [Published Paris, c1839.]

aspects of colonial life in which, for the Macquaries, there was to be no distinction between free settler and convict.

Suddenly we are distracted, as are the Macquaries, particularly Mrs. Macquarie. Screams pierce the air; they come from a site on the outskirts of the town. Mrs. Macquarie manifests an uneasiness; but had she witnessed the unedifying sight she would have been sickened. A convict writhes in agony, his back bloodied, several ribs now exposed, this part of his body torn asunder by 200 brutally administered lashes. Around the triangle a group of rough diamonds, most of whom have been punished similarly, are taunting the man because he has shown weakness. Lachlan spares Elizabeth the worst details. He, a soldier, has seen it all before, and is not as troubled as she. Nonetheless, he can readily agree it should not be a public spectacle, and actually shares her distaste, if not her horror – Sydney is a penal colony and punishment must remain part of daily life. 'With moderation', Mrs. Macquarie appears to utter sotto voce and with some disgust. Almost certainly unfinished business for her. We know Macquarie was thinking similarly, though he says no more on the subject at the time.

The gubernatorial couple continue on their way, exchanging observations about this, pointing to that. Soon apparent is the Colony's desperately inadequate hospital facilities. The people have to put up with medical care – in-patient and out-patient services, alike – delivered in what amounts to little more than makeshift and almost derelict structures. It must not be allowed to remain that way.

In all this, Mrs. Macquarie does not forget about herself. Though she acted with humility towards the lowly, she was not a humble woman. She was a woman of self-regard, always aware of her status as the daughter of a gentleman, now the wife of a governor, her mind comfortably justifying these conflicting expectations and demands. Government House and the landscape about it would not do. About this she would brook no argument. For a start, the building itself was too small to make the right statement about the significance of its occupants, both to visiting dignitaries and to the local population. Along with this, their private quarters were cramped, making living there uncomfortable; as well, there was no grand room for entertaining. And Lachlan would surely want his Beloved to have an extensive parkland garden for her pleasure! She was right; indeed, his pride applauded the consequent works, and he delighted in the pleasure that was hers. Macquarie, himself, had practical concerns about the place. He was viceroy, thus being not only the Monarch's representative but – unlike today – the Colony's chief administrator. For this he required considerable office space, not only for himself, but also for his staff.

There were other people for Macquarie to consider. Of greatest priority were the Deputy Judge-Advocate[8] and the Governor's Secretary, whose positions properly required a gentleman's town house. Other items of infrastructure found themselves on the Macquaries' 'to do' list. Surely most striking as they made their way around the town and its outskirts would have been roads and streets – they needed levelling, straitening, widening, extending – and the dearth of well-constructed bridges.

Outside Sydney the principal settlement was Parramatta, about fifteen miles west. There the governor had a modest country house. Soon it became Mrs. Macquarie's habit to go there and relax, away from the noise, grime, odours, hustle and bustle, and the pervasive coarseness of the people and the buildings. In Parramatta life was quieter, and the rural undulating landscape brought her peace. There the people, as in Sydney, went about their daily lives looking out, rarely down, a few even up. To Macquarie's delight, commerce was thriving too, here being mostly agricultural – crops, sheep and cattle. Yet not everything pleased Mrs. Macquarie: the governor's country residence did not meet her domestic standards, and the parish church – St. John's – was too modest as a place for the worship of Almighty God and as a sign to all of His presence in this world.

The countryside around Parramatta and what the Macquaries saw there would have both confirmed a city insight – namely, for the Indigenous people, dispossession begat misery – and compounded the profound unease it caused them. While in Sydney, they could not escape the sight of a people whose lives had been rendered wretched and their culture eviscerated by white man. This is what lesser people than the Macquaries took as evidence of the Aboriginal people being lesser than they. Most troubling to Macquarie, occasionally such thoughts got into his own head. Once in the country, the absurdity, the wilfulness of these thoughts became overpoweringly apparent. Away from the settlements he did not have to look too hard to see a proud people in command of their environment, in control in circumstances where settlers as interlopers floundered and felt fear (picturesquely depicted on p.52).

So much for the Colony as a place; what about its people?

THE PEOPLE OF THE COLONY

What would the Macquaries have looked for in the people, what might they have found telling about them? In fact, the Colony represented an intricate social web. Like all webs, it looked weak, but was strong, and could trap the unsuspecting to their surprise and social chagrin, even their downfall. In this case, the social web comprised four major groups. These were the regimental officers, the free settlers, the convicts and the emancipists (convicts who had served their sentences and were now free). Both between and within these groups there were significant differences in legal and social status. The critical legal difference was between the convict and the three other groups; however, not all convicts had equal legal status, these differences materially affecting their daily lives. Moreover, within the three free groups, the emancipists' legal rights as a matter of practice were not the equal of the two other groups. Along with this, they were treated as social and moral inferiors. These were differences the Macquaries, being the Macquaries, did not always observe, or observe as had been customary, and for which he as governor would later pay a price.

The Regimental Officers
The regimental officers had well-founded claims to social exclusivity in the Colony, to be considered part of the Establishment as of right.

Indeed, the attendance of the senior officers at Government House parties and functions was de rigueur. And for a man to be invited to dine with the officers in their mess was a mark of his personal social status in the Colony. The military's duties were various, including the supervision of convict work parties, and chasing down bushrangers. Their principal role though was to protect the governor and his colony. In practice, they might take upon themselves the role of powerbroker and, if the governor did not please them, challenge him, cause him trouble, even try to overthrow him. As a soldier Macquarie understood these things well, and he was most conscious of the previous governor's fate. Nonetheless, his autocratic nature and sense of self-importance did not let this affect his thinking. He the Governor, he a military man himself, he Macquarie, would not allow their feelings – they mere subordinates – to prevent him from doing what he thought was right. Well, this is how he thought when he looked at them. When they eyed him off, some of them would have been thinking differently.

The Free Settlers

The vast majority of free settlers had risked the perilous voyage to New South Wales to improve their lot in life. They largely came from the lower ranks of society, often having lived menial lives without the prospect of advancement. Thus did they have pluck. Thus were they ambitious, some with the intention of going far. Thus did they have initiative, some to the extent of becoming ruthless thrusters. Not a few were actually men and women of great capacity. Some did go far materially, even socially; more than one founded a dynasty. These were the exclusives, at the top of the Colony's social pyramid. With this came a felt need to fashion a high-society for themselves. With this went exaggerated displays of wealth, together with insufferable aloofness, both belying a social uncertainty and personal insecurity born of their lowly birth. Touch them and they were brittle; disturb them and they prickled; challenge them and they hit back hard. In respect of the last, note well, these men and women comprised a group who had fought life and won. These were not people who were going to cower to a governor who sought to challenge their social position and, especially, their material interests. A problem for Macquarie was that he had not dealt with their likes before. He was not alive to their potential to be disruptive. Moreover, the military and its means, which he had used in the past to quell those who had rebelled against his orders and wishes, were not open to him in the case of this lot. Indeed, the military were to become part of the problem. Compounding this, as an autocrat he struggled with diplomacy once an initial gracious overture on his part had been rebuffed. And Mrs. Macquarie's thoughts about the affected airs and graces of the exclusives? To this self-assured daughter of Airds House and governor's wife – bemusement. And should the thrusters take her Beloved on, even displease her, the question would be what actions she would take, not what thoughts she might entertain.

One of the leading thrusters was John Macarthur, who had come to the Colony as a military officer, but now was most energetically seeking his fortune as a pastoralist. To his colonial contemporaries, he was 'Jack Bodice', a scornful reference to his now social pretensions in light of his father's occupation as a mercer. Historians have given him the epithet 'The Perturbator'. For nature had primed him to move through life on a constant war footing. Every challenge to his material interests, every perceived slight, however minor or unintended, brought volleys of fire as part of a campaign of personal hostility designed to destroy. Not the sort of fellow a governor would want among a small colonial population. In any case, the Macquaries were not to meet him for some years, since he had been forcibly returned to Britain for the leading part he had played in the overthrow of Governor Bligh two years earlier. But meet him they eventually would,

'John Macarthur'. Hugh McCrae, artist. [1920s.] [Unpublished.]

and it did not end well. Macquarie on arrival soon learnt a lot about this larger-than-life character by repute – he was still the talk of the town. Macquarie would have, well he should have, readily appreciated that this was not a man to be persuaded to a view contrary to his perceived interests, and his inevitable return would spell trouble. This image of Macarthur the citizen represents a forbidding caricature of Macarthur the man. Here is someone who could look down on you, even though he be on a level below you. It is of a man, at once haunting, ghostly, menacing, dangerous and destructive, certainly stormy, perhaps even mad. His portrait (opposite), in pencil, light of touch, only in outline, has the character of a shadowy mental image. Surely, one to disturb a man's equanimity, to lurk irremovable in the far reaches of his mind though most unwelcome.

Another of the thrusters amongst the free settlers was one Samuel Marsden. He was actually a man of God, who had felt the call to minister unto His far-flung flock. Jesus of Nazareth, whom he most devoutly praised and worshipped, might have expected him to forgive sinners and to comfort the weak. The Macquaries – themselves both believers – would have thought similarly. They accordingly would have prepared on meeting him to express their admiration for him as a cleric and their strong support for his ministry. Greet Marsden they duly did, in fact warmly though without much thought. Yet when the Governor and Mrs. Macquarie returned to Government House, the day's formalities over, and sat down together to mull over the day's events – a practice of this devoted couple – did any first doubts about the Reverend surface in their minds? Did she – perhaps more than he – on reflection wonder whether in Marsden's face she saw not a so much a pure man as a puritan? Perhaps a man predisposed by nature to look for sin, rather than goodness, in his fellow man; perhaps a man whose predilection was condemnation, not love. Time might tell. It did! In any case, what is certain, they would not have detected the danger he too represented for them. For about Marsden, when in the presence of an authority figure, there was a hint of submissiveness about his demeanour. Yet he, like Macarthur, was potentially dangerous and menacing to a governor who crossed his interests. Though in Marsden's case these interests were spiritual – what he sincerely believed to be God's interests. Moreover, when Marsden attacked an adversary it was always at night and behind their back. He was not mad, but he was one of the Colony's madmen. In this respect, the Macarthur caricature evokes Marsden.

As for most of the rest of the free settlers, they got on with their various lives, in the main unremarkably. Some had come as professionals – doctors, architects, teachers, and the like. Their numbers were few. Far from a few had arrived with the intention of continuing in or of turning their hands to the land or business and trying their luck. Often these businesses would have amounted to little more than a store or service run from a shack that was their home. Significant numbers of others had come as 'mechanics',[9] applying all sorts of trades, at the dockyard and lumberyard, more generally around the town, and in the countryside. Alongside them laboured the semi-skilled and the unskilled. Of this mass of voluntarily displaced humanity, a few made fortunes on the land or in business, and built matching mansions. Many had to content themselves with moderate success and comfortable lives, ones often better than would have been theirs at home. Some little more than made ends meet, even existed in varying degrees of poverty. Their rough-hewn accommodation would have reflected this, thereby casting a somewhat shabby appearance over the town.

Macquarie would not have disapproved of the very successful, because he would have regarded them as providing a necessary boast to the Colony's prosperity, something required in order to realize his own bold ambitions as Governor. And he would have applauded their mansions for the beauty and opulence with which they endowed the town and its surrounding landscape. Yet the people he and Mrs. Macquarie would have despised and deplored – from whom they would not have hidden these feelings when they came across them – were those who without qualms were advancing their own interests at the expense of the honourable battler, whether convict or not.

The third and fourth social groups – the convicts and the emancipists – are integral to this story and warrant their own chapter. Apposite to this is the Colony as a place of punishment, and the punishment of the convicts in the Colony. To these matters we now turn.

Chapter 3

The Convicts

THIS CHAPTER EXPLORES the Colony's convicts as people, the Colony as a place of punishment, and the punishment of convicts in the Colony. The convicts were the Colony's principal group. At the time of the Macquaries, the convicts and their children made up around 85 percent of the population. In fact, the convicts comprised two social groups, namely, the convicts and the emancipists. The former were those serving the sentence which had brought them to the Colony; and the latter were those who had served this sentence and were now free citizens. Well, as intimated above, free but not the equal of those who came free, in terms of the British Government's treatment of them and the free settlers' attitudes towards them. Branded thus as one, their fate as a legal convict was to remain a social convict. The legal distinction between convict and emancipist thus conveniently ignored, especially by the higher free settlers; insignificant in one way, most significant in another.

THE CONVICTS AS PEOPLE

The convicts as convicts

So, who were the convicts? The convicts were criminal offenders who had been sentenced to transportation across the seas, or whose death sentence had been commuted to transportation. The vast majority were men, although the numbers of women were not insignificant, especially in the early days. Most of the men were aged around the mid-twenties; for the women, the common age range was a little lower. Nevertheless, some were no more than teenagers, while others were well into middle-age.

Consistent with this, on arrival they were primarily single. Those who were married often brought their spouses with them. These people, though primarily of the cities and large towns, actually in many cases had found themselves there, being no longer able to survive on the land, often the victims of crop failures, and increasingly land enclosures. Nonetheless, not a few were those whose mentality inclined them to think that only suckers worked. As to their crimes, these predominantly were ones of dishonesty, typically theft of some sort, often house breaking and entering, sometimes robbery. Other offences in the criminal calendar of the day, such as rape and other serious crimes of violence, were represented in the Colony, but these were very much the exception.

It is an entrenched part of Australian folklore that the convicts as a group were not serious offenders; rather, they were individuals who had committed one or two offences of a minor kind, and found themselves caught up in a harsh, unforgiving system. Some did fit this description, but it wildly distorts the true picture. The fact is, the convicts were primarily of the criminal classes, and to be found among the under-class and the working-class. A convict may have committed only one offence, but it would better be thought of as the man or woman's first detected offence or the first of potentially many. For the most part, the convicts' disposition to criminality was to a greater or lesser extent entrenched. While there were among the convict population those whose offence did represent no more than an uncharacteristic lapse, this type did not constitute this population's general character. This is not to suggest the convicts as a body were deeply and irredeemably anti-social. They were not. Rather, the truer picture is of the vast majority of them falling between these extremes.

It would be all too easy in light of this brief demographic overview to think of the convicts as a largely undifferentiated mass. Again, this they were not. They were individuals varying in character and circumstances. These three images representing different types of convict well illustrate this diversity, along with their humanity and individuality. They might be labelled thus: 'Degraded and heavy-hearted', 'Spirited and wild', and 'Charming and devious'.

In 'Degraded and heavy-hearted' we see the common convict (opposite), one who lived in straitened circumstances at best, perhaps poverty, not infrequently degradation. Sometimes these were the circumstances of their birth; other times these men and women had fallen into them through a misfortune – unemployment arising from industrialization was a major cause in the cities – with which they could not cope. Then there were those whose plight could be traced to neglect along with emotional

(opposite) **'Morning'.** W. Hogarth, artist. T. Cook, engraver. Published by Robinson & Robinson, London, 1797.

PEG and BOBBY.

A Burlesque Parody, on that Tender Song call'd Love & Glory. ____ Written & Sung by Gaby Grim.

1
Young Bobby was as blythe a youth,
  As ever grac'd an attic story,
And Peg, so fair, had ne'er a tooth;
  She mended chairs, He sought for Glory.

2
Fair Peg, disguis'd, and void of fear,
  Join'd Bobby's hand, so fam'd in story,
And nightly robb'd each trav'ler dear;
  She for pure Love, and He for Glory.

3
At length, attack'd by runners three,
  Peg fell, besmear'd with wounds so gory,
And Bob was hung on Tyburn-tree;
  She died for Love, and He for Glory.

and physical abuse as a child and young person. For others the cause was personal: human weakness, laziness, or the bottle had ensnared them. The crimes of these people were most commonly simple acts of dishonesty to meet a desperate need for food or to enjoy a modest pleasure, both of which were otherwise out of their reach. Folk such as these appeared as life's little ones, whose criminal ambitions were similarly modest, for they took little thought for tomorrow. In the compassionate, they would evoke pity. These men and women were the ones whose circumstances – often along with their temperaments – rendered them most vulnerable to the vicissitudes of life. Among them were both the skilled and semi-skilled workers, and the dogsbodies. Often de-humanized by those above them, their usefulness was seen as life's heavy-lifters. Yet many were

'Peg and Bobby: A Burlesque Parody, on that Tender Song call'd Love & Glory'. 449. Published by Laurie and Whittle, London, 1806.

people of hidden abilities and unrealized ambitions. While they may have appeared broken by their cruel misfortunes, there were those among them those who had the potential to shine when given a chance in life. We shall meet one of them – a woman – in due course. Of these truths, the Macquaries were most conscious. From deep within them sprang a moral directive to give these creatures a 'fair go', a helping hand, in life. More difficult to understand and for whom to have compassion were those whose offending went beyond the mere meeting of earthly needs, whose offending was far more serious. Yet, here were to be found those whose moral compasses had been destroyed by the wretchedness of their lives. This anomic state Macquarie well understood, having seen it among the poor of Mull. A state well captured in Hogarth's 'Morning' (p.61).

'Spirited and wild' (see p.62) represents a different type of wrong-doer. These individuals were more than just an everyday nuisance, a part of the shabbiness of city and town life, as were many of the former. These were the men, and occasionally women, whom every traveller dearly feared, and who stuck terror into their hearts as victims. They were life's dashers, appearing as bolts from the blue; and they could disappear as does lightening, often relieving their quivering targets of valuable possessions. They were often a cut above the common criminal. Among them were those capable of taking life by the throat; here was derring-do. Indeed, in the late 1700s one of their number was to father a man whom Australian historians have dubbed 'The Native Son'. Both became firm favourites of the Macquaries, and appear later in this story.

While there was some overlap between the preceding two types, the 'Charming and devious' represents a very different type of convict. As the image (see p.63) suggests, they were often of a higher class, and often well-educated: indeed, solicitors, doctors, architects, and the like. Yet some would come as simpler folk with a hidden a talent for business and harbouring overweening ambition. The crimes of these people were generally ones of dishonesty, but not of the garden variety and not so much in the face of pressing need. Rather, they would commit a financial fraud or forge a document purely for selfish gain. People such as these comprised a small segment of the Colony's convicts. Nevertheless, in light of their talents and drive, they had the potential to play a leading part in progressing the Colony's material wealth and cultural life. This many did, a few becoming significant figures of Australian history. Their potential – indeed the potential of most of the convicts – was something the Macquaries understood very well.

These are some of the convict types from the range among the convict population. They represent no more than instances of broad, loosely defined types, at that. Thus, many convicts were heavy-hearted, but were not degraded. Others were spirited, but not wild. Yet others were devious, only when cornered, and were certainly not charming. Moreover, there were the variations across the types: the wild who could be charming, and so on. These pictures serve to reveal something about the convicts beyond their aggregate demographic characteristics. They also, though fictional, attest to the convicts as individuals; people who had their own names and personalities. Convicts as fellow human beings, with their hopes, more often their disappointments. They had their reasons, ones often not well understood to themselves, certainly not well thought out, for doing what they did. With their crimes might come sometimes gloating, sometimes

"He seized me by the chin."

'He Seized Me by the Chin'. A. Dixon, artist. Copied from C. Dickens, *Great Expectations*. (Eight original illustrations by A.A. Dixon.) Collins' Clear-Type Press, London [early C20th].

shame and regret, often nothing more than impotent resignation. Sooner or later, they might attempt to live better lives, to make good of themselves, or they might not. At their core, most of them were in many ways just like us. We meet some of them later.

These demographic data and character sketches considered alone leave us well short of a proper understanding of the sort of people the governors greeted as the transport ships disgorged their human cargo onto Sydney Cove. They were no longer the men and women we met above. Very different, indeed! For by then they had endured the brutalization and degradation of having been a transport. This experience involved several stages. After their court appearance and conviction – often before as well – there was imprisonment in a local gaol. After this, followed the journey to the docks. Many men would spend time in the hulks on the banks of the Thames as they awaited transportation. Finally, there was the ocean voyage across the seas. These could be the circumstances of a convict's life for several years, even more. Physical suffering and pain, and humiliation, were its hallmarks. Of the convicts subject to this treatment, many died, even more fell gravely ill, all but a few suffered appalling physical hardship, and not a few were left with psychological scars which might never fully heal. It would not have been worse if their bodies had been vigorously rubbed every day with a coarse brush. As for the body, so for the mind.

No more than a few features of each stage of the process are needed to sear into our mind's eye the horror of it all. The local prison: filthy; rat-infested; rags for clothing; freezing in winter; scraps for food; abusive, cruel gaolers. Then the trip to the docks: in a carriage exposed to the elements; the women, often half-naked; open and subject to the to the leering, jeering mob. The hulks: the physical conditions similar to the gaols; the wearing of leg-irons; and ironed, heartlessly supervised, often back-breaking labour. These are the circumstances under which Charles Dickens introduces us to the convict, Magwitch (above). Recall his physical state and ruthlessness, and his desperation, as he threateningly accosts a terrified young Pip.

'Hold your noise!' cried a terrible voice, as a man started up from among the graves at the side of the church porch. 'Keep still, you little devil or I'll cut your throat!'

A fearful man, all in coarse gray [sic], with a great iron on his leg. A man with no hat, and with broken shoes, and with an old rag tied round his head. A man who had been soaked in water, and smothered in mud, and lamed by stones, and cut by flints, and stung by nettles, and torn by briars; who limped and shivered, and glared and growled; and whose teeth chattered in his head as he seized me by the chin …

The man, after looking at me for a moment, turned me upside-down, and emptied my pockets. There was nothing in them but a piece of bread … he ate the bread ravenously …

'Now lookee here', he said, 'the question being whether you're to be to let live. You know what a file is?'

'Yes, sir.'

'And you know what wittles is?'

'Yes, sir'.

After each question he tilted me over a little more, so as to give me a greater sense of helplessness and danger.[10]

Then the convicts, after all this suffering and torment, and in this state of physical and mental wretchedness, faced an apparently interminable voyage across the seas to the Colony on floating, bobbing, heaving and rolling hell-holes, sometimes becalmed in stifling heat, sometimes nearly frozen in an Antarctic southerly. There, stuck in the bowels of the ship, hungry, perhaps covered in sores, with little opportunity to move, rats and lice their constant companions, amid the stink of unwashed bodies, and vomit. All this, and overwhelmed by the terror of the unknown.

How a convict handled this torment varied with each man and woman's psychological make-up. Thus, the weak remained crushed. The resilient realized their potential to bounce back to their former selves. The spirited resolved to do something better in their now new lives. The already resentful and the more criminally inclined were candidates to join the recalcitrant and the deeply embittered, those harbouring a generalized hostility and viciousness to all around them.

Such were the criminal and social detritus the British cast adrift; such were the human souls Lachlan and Elizabeth sought to save. No wonder the Macquaries in their less sanguine moments despaired of the base natures, even apparent irredeemability, of some of these men and women. Nonetheless, what prevented these self-appointed missioners from faltering was their understanding of the problem and profound commitment to the cause.

The convicts as emancipists

The emancipists were the convicts who had served the sentences for the crimes bringing them to the Colony. Thus, they were legally free men and women, and in practice enjoyed most of the rights and privileges of the free settlers. In regard to how they lived, what they did, and where they went, for the most part their lives were the same as those of the free settlers. Many established farms on small acreages; many set up stores or other little businesses – pub ownership was much favoured by emancipists. Some chose a working life on the sea as a fisherman or a trader. In particular demand were the mechanics – the blacksmiths, the carpenters, the ship builders, and so on. Often their small businesses were run as cottage industries. Very many, though, supported themselves as semi-skilled workers and labouring factotums. Perhaps the greatest number worked for wages, for both the government as well as the free settlers and other emancipists. In regard to the former, they might hold positions of no little responsibility, such as the senior constable of a district or a works supervisor. Not a few little better than subsisted; many – perhaps most – could be regarded as living in at least moderate comfort, especially in light of their backgrounds. In a minority of cases, these men, and occasionally women, did very well for themselves, even achieving the status of wealthy; several created little empires. As for the professionals among the emancipists, they typically would pursue their chosen profession.

Nonetheless, the emancipists, considered as a group, did differ in one significant respect from the free settlers. More emancipists came from the lower, and particularly lowest strata of society, and very few knew the high society with which the officer class would have been familiar back home. This is a difference which would manifest itself in their everyday behaviour, and importantly in the attitudes of the officers and free settlers towards them. While these people would do business with them and profit from their skills, they for the most part practised a policy of social exclusion towards them. It was an affectation more pronounced at the higher levels of colonial society, yet present at all levels. The emancipists were as a class socially coarser, but not nearly to the extent the setters with their pretensions would acknowledge. To outsiders who visited the

Colony at this time, this self-delusion was a source of amusement. To the Macquaries, it was more an irritant, and with good reason.

As far as the Macquaries were concerned, the convicts and emancipists were far more than people of one or another legal status. No, they represented lives characterized to a greater or lesser extent by goodness and worth, lives with the potential to be re-made, to be worth living, even to flourish. More fundamentally, they were to become living proof of the moral bankruptcy and social disability of Britain's policy of transportation as a response to crime.

THE COLONY AS A PLACE OF PUNISHMENT

No account of the convicts can be complete without a description of the Colony as a place of punishment. New South Wales was not just any colony; rather, it was one especially established as a penal colony. Meaning is important here. What must be clearly understood is that the convicts were transported as punishment, not for punishment. In the Government's eyes, the convicts' punishment was their being cast asunder from Britain, their loved ones, their friends, their work, their green and pleasant land, and for this exclusion to seem an eternity – this and this alone was their punishment. What is being described here, then, is not the convicts' punishment but their way of life as they served this sentence.

Around the time of the Macquaries' arrival, the Colony was a much more normal place than an outsider would have been predisposed to imagine. It stemmed from three facts. First, the fact of the convicts not being there for punishment. Second, in the early days, escape was not thought a significant practical option in view of the Colony's remoteness and the harshness of the surrounding countryside. Third, the Colony needed workers not only to run place as it was, but also to develop it as more and more convicts and free settlers arrived, and as children were born to them. So too did the free settlers and the increasing numbers of emancipists need the labour and skills of ever more men and women. These were the three parameters together framing all four aspects of convict life: the nature of their work; their places of work; their conditions of work; and their accommodation. Each of these is briefly considered in turn, before moving to the matter of the punishment of convicts who re-offended while still serving their term of transportation.

We need to have in our minds this picture of the Colony as the Macquaries found it should we wish to understand properly their treatment of the convicts.

Nature of convict work

While the free settlers and emancipists contributed to meeting the Colony's labour needs, their numbers were too few – far, far, too few – to satisfy its demands. It fell to the convicts to be the ones who met this need. This meant it was the convicts who did most of the work, filling jobs from the highest to lowest in status. Thus would a doctor, arriving in the Colony, work as a doctor, a school teacher as a tutor, a mechanic as a mechanic, a seamstress as seamstress, a labourer or a domestic as a slogging dogsbody or servant. Appreciate what is going on here. Many of these later convicts would have been acquiring a skill for the first time or learning a new skill. As important, not a few of the convicts would have been experiencing, often under a light coercive touch, a disciplined life for the first time, or at least a very long time. And there would have been life's lowly developing a sense of importance, perhaps having been promoted to a position involving some responsibility. The Macquaries would have seen this, and known that it was good, being to the benefit of both the Colony and the convict.

Places of convict work

Convicts on arrival were either directed to work for the government or were assigned to work for a free settler or emancipist. With respect to the former, a lawyer or clerk might find himself in an office. Many mechanics would be employed at the dockyard or lumberyard, or on government building sites and roadworks in and outside the town. Meanwhile, the labourers would be playing the part of the heavy and the light machinery of the day. In regard to assignment: the factories and farms were largely run on convict labour, the women playing their part along with the men. This involved in the main blue-collar work, but businesses were in need of clerks and other assistants. The convicts, the women in particular, played a key role in running the homes of the wealthy; together they were the maids, the nannies, the valets and the tutors. It was no different for the governor and his wife. The less affluent profited from their services too, particularly those on the land. What was important about this to the Macquaries is that the convicts commonly worked in the very same places as the free settlers, alongside and together with them.

In regard to the allocation of convicts in the workforce, an important penal principle is to be found. It will be obvious on second thoughts: what work a man or woman did was primarily determined by what they had to offer, not the seriousness of the crime which had brought them to the Colony. The former included the nature of their skills, of course;

but it also covered other characteristics as well, such as their strength, apparent willingness to work, native intelligence, and so on. This principle describes a practice which emerged not from any theory of justice but from a common-sense view of what might, and in fact what did, work to the Colony's best advantage. This principle will emerge again, this time in regard to the release of convicts from their term of penal servitude. Here, understand, it became integral to the Macquaries' treatment of the convicts; accordingly, they were to expand its application and apply it most enthusiastically for the purpose of the convicts' rehabilitation.

Conditions of convict work

The convicts generally worked from early morning until the middle of the afternoon, with a break for lunch, except on Saturday when work ended around midday.[11] The rest of the day was theirs, until the mid-evening curfew. Sunday was their own. For some this free time meant innocent recreation; for others it meant carousing in the pubs and dens of iniquity. Many treated it as an opportunity to earn money, either at their place of work, or at another. In fact, the skilled among them could demand good – even very good – money. In regard to the treatment of those on assignment, many masters treated them firmly but fairly, even helping them to get on in the world; while others exploited them and dealt with them ruthlessly to the point of abuse. Good workers could expect, and in some cases demanded, indulgences; these most often were quite simple, such as coffee and milk, but might be more generous, and take the form of extra rations. As an aside it should be noted, there were those among the ambitious who were offered a very good deal; their masters might allow them to start their own business on the side in return for some benefit, or might invite them into what was in effect a partnership. Some took advantage of such an arrangement to great personal benefit. We meet one of them later. In any case, a convict assigned to the right master, and with a measure of ability and initiative, was well placed to make a new start in life. This same observation could be made for the convicts in government service and under the control of a supervisor. The working conditions of the well-behaved convict, whether it be clerking or labouring, were comparable to those in Britain for a similar occupation. Build in the time they had to themselves, and we have conditions often easier than would have been theirs as workers in Britain. Convicts were anything but slaves, an important truth captured in this image of convicts constructing a road in the countryside.

In respect of clothing, assigned convicts were indistinguishable from the free, as were most in government service (something apparent in the

'Groupe de Convicts
dans un Défrichments'.
de Sainson, artist.

image, above). They were just as shabby and tawdry, or in some cases just as neat and finely attired, as the free. Those working in certain jobs for the upper classes might well be dressed in livery. For most, whether in government or private service, dress accorded with the nature of the work being performed and the convicts' position in life. So too for their designation. The polite terminology for a convict was government man, assigned servant – even just servant – labourer, and the like.

What would strike visitors to the Colony is the freedom enjoyed by many of the convicts as part of their work; indeed, for all during their generous hours of recreation. The convicts were always on the move, out and about – going to or from work, moving between jobs, or as part of their job. In respect of the last of these, they might range widely, say bringing farm produce from some outlying district to the docks in

Sydney, a round trip of several days. And, outside of work, might be seen riding or walking jauntily to a pub or other place of relaxation and entertainment; or appear darkly, stalking the town late at night – albeit against the regulations – with malice on their mind.

The Macquaries, as they acquainted themselves with the Colony, observed a town being laid down and virgin bush being opened up. All – rough-and-ready though much of it was – the product of the convicts' toil. As Macquarie himself pondered over this, we need little imagination to suppose he was perhaps reminded of the lowly convict soldiers who won battles for their generals.

Convict accommodation

The convicts working for the government had to find their own accommodation. For many it was in the slums at The Rocks. Others lodged in the homes – more often shacks – of the poorer free settlers about the town. For this, the government provided them with an allowance. Each morning it was left to them to find their way to work. As to those on assignment, it was their masters who were responsible for their accommodation and keep. These convicts typically would live in separate quarters, the amenity of which would be commensurate with the master's status and means. For most, this was somewhat primitive.

Two very important points about colonial punishment will have become increasingly apparent. The first is this. Transportation as a punishment for crimes committed in Britain meant a life outside of Britain and some restrictions on personal freedom. But, and what a 'but' it is, life in Britain for many, perhaps most, of these people was to a greater or lesser extent miserable and without prospects – for them Britain was not a green and pleasant land. Moreover, in many cases, the circumstances of their lives in Britain did not afford them much opportunity to enjoy their freedom. The second point – equally significant – is related but follows a parallel track. When one has regard to the nature and conditions of the convicts' work and of their accommodation, this life as punishment might well be thought of as something very different from punishment's traditional punitive character. Rather, it had the potential to be a process of re-socialization and opportunity for renewal. For the typical convict, is not this punishment as rehabilitation? Think about it! To the Macquaries' prepared minds this would have been self-evident. In contrast, the instinctively harsh and those to whom social processes were opaque would have lamented over what to them was punitive leniency and weakness. The former idea was to underpin the Macquaries' plans for the Colony; the latter was to underpin the overthrow of his governorship.

THE PUNISHMENT OF CONVICTS IN THE COLONY

There are two relevant matters here: first, the punitive aspects of the convicts' sentences for their crimes committed in Britain; second, the punishment imposed for offences committed by the convicts in the Colony.

Transportation as a punishment

Sentences of transportation were most commonly imposed for terms of seven or fourteen years. For many convicts the period was, as a matter of practice, less. There were three mechanisms at work here, namely, ticket-of-leave, conditional pardon, and full pardon. Most common was the ticket-of-leave. A convict, on receiving this, was free to work and live as he or she pleased, and to move about the Colony without restriction. While those with skills to offer could do well, the lesser ones were open to exploitation by unscrupulous employers, in regard to how much they were paid, and to the extent their wages were paid in-kind. For most convicts, these 'tickets' were granted later rather than earlier in their sentence. The grounds for a 'ticket' was sustained good behaviour. Nonetheless, a convict of substantial means might be granted a 'ticket' on their arrival in the Colony. A conditional pardon, followed by a full pardon, would follow later, if at all. Only upon completing their sentence, or being pardoned, could a convict leave the Colony. Many convicts were the beneficiary of a 'ticket'. The 'ticket' system was instituted to relieve the burden convicts placed on the Government; a second consideration was their perceived potential to encourage good behaviour. Once emancipated, a man, as a means of helping him on his way might be granted a parcel of land to farm, along with stock and grain, perhaps one or two assigned convicts, and with government support for twelve months.

There was severe punishment for convicts who breached work or other regulations under which they lived in the Colony. Regulatory offences covered matters such as a convict's refusing to work or obey orders, acts of insolence, absconding, and so forth. A supervisor or master was not permitted to administer punishment. They had to take the delinquent before a magistrate. The most common penalty was a flogging. By their very nature floggings were always brutal; indeed, they could be draconian. A typical flogging might involve 100-150 lashes, but some magistrates thought up to 300 were needed to do the job in certain circumstances.

For particularly serious or repeated breaches, a convict might find himself in a hard-driven gaol-gang. The former was the experience of many of the convicts. Some because they were work-shy, others because they had acted out in response to particularly poor treatment. The latter was the fate reserved for the most recalcitrant among them.

Punishment for criminal offending

For criminal offending, the convicts were punished along with the free according to British law. The difference was that here, transportation was to the remote penal settlements of Coal River (Newcastle) on the mainland and Norfolk Island in the Pacific Ocean. Moreover, as practised in the Colony, transportation was in effect not as punishment but for punishment, and it was for the particularly recidivist and the very serious offenders, and those considered to be dangerous. Life in these places was intentionally hellish. As an alternative to transportation, there were the brutish goal-gangs, involving unremitting, back-breaking labour on the frontiers. By way of contrast, for the petty offenders, the British brought their stocks to the Colony.

As Macquarie thought about the system of punishment in the Colony, perhaps his mind turned to the Highlands, and he recalled the views he had formed about punishment there. As for Mrs. Macquarie, did not the wise moralist Dr. Johnson advise that severity was pointless and the purpose of punishment ought to be to turn people towards goodness? Thus, in this as in other aspects of colonial life they had witnessed, it is easy to discern how the Macquaries' instincts and early experiences prepared them to see the Colony as they did.

* * *

The Macquaries undertook the preparatory work of inspecting the Colony so as to appreciate what they faced as Governor and Governor's wife. They were soon acquainted with the facts, and with this came a sense of equanimity. The state of the Colony was much better than might have been expected, especially in light of the ructions it had undergone in the immediate past. Once back in Government House Lachlan and Elizabeth relaxed, each slipping into their own reverie, yet thinking along similar lines, and with the same contented and gentle smile. In just twenty-two years a town had grown from bushland-nothingness, notwithstanding its life-threatening remoteness. Now, after ups and downs, it was settled, bubbling along in all its rawness and simplicity. One observation did

'Arthur Phillip Esq. Vice Admiral of the Red Squadron'. [F. Wheatley, artist.] Page, engraver. Published by J. Gold, London, 1812.

particularly pique Macquarie's imagination. It was that some of the convicts – in particular, those who had that right mix of talent, push, and thick skin – were doing rather well for themselves. So, why not this for many of the others, if they were given the right assistance and encouragement? Hmm. How he did tingle with excitement! This was his opportunity. Remember, Macquarie was a man who sought to do good and to leave his mark, before moving on to then an even greater calling. At the same time Mrs. Macquarie's mind was dancing merrily to its own tune, though in harmony and in equal emotional measure. She too sought to leave her world a better place; moreover, this would require activity, plans and arrangements – O how she loved doing and organising!

At this moment Macquarie's mind turned to Arthur Phillip, the inaugural governor, who in just five years had laid a solid foundation against the odds. Macquarie greatly admired him and had corresponded with him about the Colony. The town as it stood was surely a monument to his elemental greatness – he must never be forgotten. Now fortune had bequeathed its future to him – well, in practice, he knew it would be them. Lachlan turned to Elizabeth, looked up at Phillip's portrait (see p.75), and said simply, 'Now us'. They must take it to the next stage, rebuilding, transforming, elevating its physical and social fabric. In regard to this, they were lucky, so they mused. The time was ripe, because nothing about the place was set in stone, and there were no established mores, nor was there a national identity. (About the first and the third of these, they were right; as to the second, alas.) Lachlan and Elizabeth each raised their glass to Phillip's portrait, and drank a toast to his memory. The 'Age of Arthur Phillip' was over.

Then they turned as one to each other and toasted their future together in the Colony. The next great era, 'The Age of the Macquaries' was about to begin. That night they both slept soundly – facts are better than dreams.

Yet when Lachlan and Elizabeth arose in the morning, the soporific effect of fine wine having worn off, there was about them an anxious urgency. As we know, for each of them there were multiple passions at work. For Macquarie one is worldly recognition. Here is a man whose ambition is overweening; a man who is convinced his true talent has not been recognized and has not been given the opportunity of manifesting itself. Hence, we find a man with a blinding drive to achieve, so society's highest prizes might be his. By way of contrast, Mrs. Macquarie is a woman whose desire is to please her God. For her, the world has not seen enough of His presence. Thus, she seeks to bring Heaven to Earth for the greater good of others. That will be her reward.

Then there is the hidden, all-powerful presence of Jane Jarvis. Her importance to Lachlan is to be found in the letter he wrote to his Uncle Murdoch in January 1797, less than a year after Jane's death.[12] (On the same day he expressed the same sentiment in a letter to his brother Charles.) The critical lines in the former are:

Since I cannot now be happy myself in this cruel world, I wish to see others at least so. – I shall therefore endeavour to do all the good I can

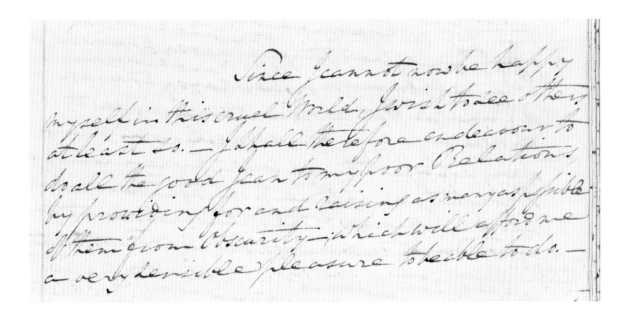

**Lachlan Macquarie
to Murdoch Maclaine.**
31st January, 1797. Digital
image from the State
Library of New South
Wales (A789).

to my poor Relations by providing for and raising as many as possible of them from obscurity – which will afford me a very sensible pleasure to be able to do.

Henceforth, Lachlan will dedicate his life to giving succour to the needy, to providing the deprived with the means of advancing their position and status in the world; not only 'advancing' them, but in this way protecting them from a life of poverty and wretchedness with its attendant risk of crime. (In this letter, Macquarie also mentions his intention to assist financially boys on Mull who are not relatives.) This letter should be treated as one of the most important documents in the annals of criminal justice and, indeed, in Australian history. Thirteen years later, and in a continent on the other side of the globe, it was to underpin a radically different course in the treatment of society's criminals, and co-incidentally introduce a new era in the Colony's development. What a motivator for driving achievement, for brooking no challenge!

To Elizabeth, Jane meant something very different. She was the 'other woman'; she, not Elizabeth, had Macquarie's love. It hurt, and it hurt deeply. Nevertheless, the very strong-willed Elizabeth will rarely let it get her down. She will repeat to herself, 'Then by my works I will become to him the woman without whom he is unable to live, to fulfil his dreams, and more. If I cannot have equality with Jane in his affections, I will at least have equality by way of regard and importance'. For Elizabeth, the memory of the Jane – the Jane she had never seen – was disquieting, even troubling. Though, as for Lachlan, what a motivator for driving achievement, for brooking no challenge!

Powerful as these passions were for each the Macquaries, they would lie apparently dormant to the onlooker. They were private and very personal. Passions like these have the potential to animate their hosts to do great things; the potential to destroy a man and woman in the face of failure. Yet such is their nature and intensity, their holder will offer no defence against them.

Lachlan and Elizabeth's policies for his governorship are explored in the following two chapters. Together they represent the first of the two ways to the treatment of crime and criminals explored in this book. This first way being the 'right way'. This is what they are to paint on the blank canvas represented – as they see it – by the scene from the entrance to Port Jackson (see p.36).

Chapter 4

The Age of the Macquaries:
The Colony and the Place

WE LEFT LACHLAN and Elizabeth, governor and governor's wife, waking up in Government House after a peaceful night's sleep. What did this House represent to their people, and what would its chief occupants come to mean to them? These people, many of whom that night had slept as soundly as they – well, those who had not been dreaming of a great tomorrow, or fretting over their misery of today, or were now asleep exhausted after a night's thieving, or fornicating and carousing. In this community of over twenty thousand souls, to a greater or lesser extent, in one way or another, this Couple and this Residence would dominate the lives of these people for the next twelve years.

Government House itself imposed a physical presence on the small, unprepossessing town. It was not so much its size – it was quite small and there were several bigger houses – but its placement in the amphitheatrical landscape. On the east rise of the Cove, and just apart from housing to its immediate west, it was otherwise surrounded by bushland, save for an open expanse running down to the water's edge. With the Macquaries came dramatic change, the effect of which was to lend the overall appearance of the house and the grounds a certain grandeur. The Macquaries' principal works were a two-storeyed gabled east wing, which included a large bow-fronted dining room (accommodating up to 150 diners), and an extended veranda. Outside, the grounds at the front of the house were landscaped with lawns, a carriageway, paths, garden beds and trees. Mrs. Macquarie, being Elizabeth, largely planned and surely supervised with an eagle-eye the whole operation. Earlier on, Macquarie, qua 'Mr Elizabeth', would have signed off on the proposal

with something like a 'Yes Dear'. This picture of the front of Government House and its surrounding grounds was painted some five years after the Macquaries were there. It represents the house and grounds largely as the Macquaries left them. (The garden has matured, and small changes have been made to the roofline and about the entrance – the latter insignificant in the scale and detail of the painting.)

To the general population Government House meant the seat of power, a power which could make or break their lives and from which they could not escape. It was the lion-tamer's home, except they were not lions and he was not wary of them. As we have seen, not all thought of themselves as vulnerable lambs – certainly not the thrusters – but this lion-tamer had reliable backup in the early days, in the body of his former regiment, so at first even the military instinctively deferred to him. Nevertheless, for the general citizen, including those in the upper social echelons, there was something about Government House of which they were far more conscious and concerned, namely, its capacity to admit a man and woman to membership of the social elite within the Colony. For this there was even a membership card; it took the form of a written invitation to dine at the Governor's table. Those who had one comported

'Maison du Gouverneur a Sydney. (Nouvelle Galles du Sud)' (c1826). Pl. 29. [L.] de Sainson, artist. V. Adam, engraver. [E.] Hostein, lithographer. J. Published by J. Tastu, [Paris, c1833].

themselves with puffed-up waistcoats and bodices; those who wanted to be seen as of higher social status, but were yet to gain admittance, lived in anxious hope. Among the yet-to-be-admitted group were the emancipists. But they – even the affluent and the professionals among them – did not suffer from pangs of anxious hope, since their former legal status had always rendered them inadmissible to polite society. As in the past, presumably now, or so they thought.

To the Macquaries too, Government House was the seat of power, a power of an autocratic kind. We may bridle at this, yet in fact a governor was a quasi-autocrat. For although he was subject to the law, it bequeathed him commanding powers; and although he was subject to his political masters, they were many months away, and in any case they chose to govern in most respects with a light touch. Now, there are degrees of quasi-autocracy. The Macquaries chose the hard interpretation, because of their natures and their driving need to achieve. And so, in the interests of bringing about what they believed was good and noble, they stood up to the powerful, instead of bending a little to their wishes and easing somewhat their sensitivities. They were prepared to crash through rather than ease forward, risking all rather than guaranteeing a little. Thus did Macquarie assume power in areas where his judge saw the law differently; and on potentially problematic matters often proceeded without first awaiting Britain's approval.

In light of this, it will come as no surprise that some saw megalomania, where others saw strength; some saw demonic leaders vandalizing the Colony's social fabric, where others saw a great man and woman fashioning a new, enlightened social fabric. Nor will it come as a surprise that the Macquaries faced trenchant criticism in the Colony. Remember Macarthur and Marsden? No surprise too that the British government came to conclude that one of its Government Houses was out of control. Transportation as punishment is after all diametrically opposite to punishment as reform. This all led sadly to the Macquaries' undoing at the time. Most happily though, they did enough to leave the world a legacy for the enlightened treatment of criminals today. The last of these is for later.

THE MACQUARIES' PLANS AND POLICIES FOR THE COLONY

The mindsets the Macquaries' brought to the Colony gave direction and content to their interests from which their plans for the Colony followed directly. You will recall, their highland tradition was a common source of influence, although they took different things from it. Additionally for him, there was his military career, and his experiences of how the world works. While for her, it was education and cultivation, and her religious faith. There was another most significant influence on Macquarie: William Wilberforce's life's work had inspired him to do not just good works, but something uplifting to the greater good of Mankind. Then there were their private passions as driving forces.

Thus did the Macquarie era policies emanate from a thoughtful man and woman's heart and soul. They would not have been first revealed on a cold piece of parchment but on warm breath. And those words would not have been directed dispassionately to an obedient official in a government office, but whispered between husband and wife in conjugal privacy, as one body and of one mind.

Yet, Macquarie being Macquarie and Mrs. Macquarie being Mrs. Macquarie, there would have been times when they did not speak as one. Picture this scene at Government House, husband and wife in their domesticity. It is evening. Lachlan has dined well, is feeling good about himself, and is in an expansive mood.

> Lachlan observes grandly: 'When I have completed my work the Colonial Office will appreciate what I have done. Even the King will be pleased with the new jewel added to his Crown. When we go back to England, I will be feted, and honours will be heaped upon me. And you will be so proud of me!'

We have a sufficient inkling of Elizabeth's character to appreciate that she, sober and of serious disposition, would be taken aback by this, fearing she was perhaps about to be forgotten. She must say something, she will put him on the back foot, but she will do it light-heartedly.

> 'My Dear, I have a confession to make to you! When I looked at you, I wondered what sort of husband you would make for me. I saw in you my type of man. A man who is brave, strong, and handsome, and a person of the highest integrity. But I also thought [giggling somewhat girlishly], he's a soldier, trained to obey orders, and it was my intention that these would now be my orders!'

Lachlan appears nonplussed, though for no more than an instance. Elizabeth, now amused, smiles, and warms to her task; she feels she is making a point that needs to be made.

'I do love and honour you', she follows on [her tone now earnest], 'but your work will be my work too. I have my own ideas about how you should proceed, and I shall continue to give thought to the task in hand. Indeed, I will impress the merits of my ideas upon you. When you resist, and I think you are mistaken, I will stand up to you, even chide you. This soldier's wife intends to give her soldier-husband orders!

Your vision as Governor will be, in fact, a shared vision. I, too, see your governorship as an opportunity to do good and bring about change, to bequeath a fulfilling future to people now living blighted lives as a banished people – a change which has not been envisioned by the British authorities.'

Elizabeth quickly adds, touching him gently as she speaks: 'So, there we have the terms of our endearment for what lies ahead of us.'

Macquarie is in a good mood, and not wanting to let his equanimity be disturbed. In any case, he is accustomed to his Beloved's little outbursts. And he, being older than her and most fond of her, finds them amusing. He leaves his response at a smile.

Elizabeth looks at him affectionately, and observes wistfully with a falling voice: 'I realize that the public honours will be all yours, and I will be very proud of you. But, I must say, it does seem a little unfair that I will be forgotten.'

In this imagined domestic scene, we see not the Mrs. Macquarie of her 1810 portrait. This is Mrs. Macquarie beginning to emerge as the woman her colonial portraitist will depict almost a decade later.

The purpose of this preamble and the earlier material has been to place the Macquaries in a human context. Only in this light can we fully understand their policies, the manner in which these protagonists might handle any opposition to them; and, in respect of both these matters, properly assess their lives and work.

The Macquaries' plans for the Colony as they relate to the treatment of the convicts can be categorized under six headings: (1) punitive leniency; (2) social welfare; (3) respectful and dignified treatment; (4) a civic armature of style and beauty, (5) social re-integration and elevation; and (6) reform and personal renewal. The first four are dealt with in this chapter and focus on the Colony as a home for the convict. The latter two are covered in the following chapter and focus on the convicts themselves. There is necessarily much overlap between the two. Both involve two considerations: (1) reforming the convicts as offenders; (2) renewing and uplifting the lives of convicts as fellow human beings.

Punitive leniency

When it came to punishment, Macquarie's predilection was for a light hand, a sentiment shared by Mrs. Macquarie. Harsh-handedness was not to his taste. Though he accepted there was a place for severity, he adopted it only in the more extreme cases, and then generally with great reluctance, and felt as a painful necessity. Several reasons may be discerned for his adopting this approach. Nature had blessed this ruler with human compassion and understanding. Macquarie understood Man's wrong-doing as the product of endowed human weakness, but perhaps his particular concern was weakness in the face of one of those rough-hands life deals out apparently indiscriminately. Surely, humanity demands punishment allow for these? About this, Macquarie had no doubts.

There is a second reason explaining Macquarie's preference for punitive leniency. He had witnessed the failure of punishment as a deterrent. He wanted the Colony to be a place of rehabilitation, not punishment. And for this, Macquarie was convinced, condign punishment would act to hinder many a convict's reform; it might break them, embitter them, alienate them. Moreover, in view of the malign circumstances behind the original offending of so many, and their brutalizing experiences as prisoners, the convicts could not be expected to turn their dysfunctional lives around at the instant of their arrival in the Colony. They would require, Macquarie well understood, some degree of what might be termed punitive pampering – a preparedness to tolerate lapses. There was to be considered the convicts' general youthfulness, and the fact that they had spent the recent part of their lives apart from civil society. For many, therefore, the living of a good life would require a changed mentality, a new way of life, by way of a process akin to social maturation, as in human adolescence. In this light, any short-term crime becomes a secondary consideration, a necessary price for prioritizing long-term convict reform. Certainly, he would readily concede, moderate disciplining was needed to incline many to think again, but any more would do nothing to address the needs of these damaged souls on their progress to personal renewal. This was the pre-eminent line of thinking behind Macquarie's policy of leniency.

There were for Macquarie two other reasons in respect of this: (1) the convicts, some more than others, each in their own way, even the recalcitrant, had contributed to making the Colony the place it then was and, in doing this, they had paid a great price for their offending – this must be rewarded; (2) the general harshness of their lives demanded mercy.

More generally, unless the convicts prospered – they, after all, comprised the vast majority of the population – the Colony would be mired in a punitive bog.

A governor had a number of means at his disposal to try and introduce a climate of penal moderation. First, he might appoint magistrates whom he believed shared his views. This of course took time, being dependent on the need for magistrates.

Second, for disciplinary offences, a governor might set upper limits on the number of lashes open to a magistrate to order. Macquarie set a working maximum of 50. Quite a reduction from the previous upper limit of 300. However, these limits could easily be circumvented by magistrates accumulating punishments in cases involving multiple offences. A governor might additionally exhort his magistrates to show compassion. The problem is charitable words of themselves have little power, and in effect can be laughed off. Cumulate and laugh, some magistrates did. To circumvent this response, Macquarie substituted for the less serious offenders time in a gaol-gang undertaking works around the towns.

Third, a convict's term of penal servitude could be lessened by way of the governor issuing a ticket-of-leave, or granting a conditional pardon, even a full pardon, in light of demonstrated good behaviour. Macquarie made a habit of making these significantly earlier in the convicts' terms and with greater frequency than had been the practice of any previous governor. As part of this, he introduced shorter periods before convicts became eligible for a ticket-of-leave (for example, for a seven-year term it was three years), but additionally he not infrequently broke his own rules in the direction of leniency. And his liberal interpretations of what constituted 'good behaviour' raised many a punitive eye. In fact, in Macquarie's time, over one quarter of convicts received the benefit of an early ticket-of-leave, conditional pardon or pardon.

Finally, when convicts were sentenced to be hanged or imprisoned for an offence committed in the Colony, the governor had the power to intervene. Respecting the former, he might commute; the latter, order an early release. Macquarie did both. In cases of murder, for example, his practice was to first examine whether the circumstances of the case called for mercy, his aim being to keep the ultimate sentence to a minimum. He possessed a gubernatorial sharpness of eye for mercy not seen hitherto. As for offences at the other end of the criminal calendar, he was often prepared to forgive and forget.

'Wm. Cox' (c1830).
[Published by C. Maxwell,
Sydney, c1889.]

Some regarded Macquarie's approach to punishment as a practice which
would in fact encourage, not suppress, misbehaviour and criminality. They
saw his punitive lenience as cavalier. But it was not. Rather, his predilection
for lesser punishment was the product of deep instincts fashioned by much
thought and long experience, one's first entering his consciousness on the
fields of Mull so long ago. And whenever Lachlan, under pressure from his
detractors, entertained doubts about this, Elizabeth would have reminded
him of Dr. Johnson's exhortations on the matter.

These reforms were applied across the convict population. Yet, so
often when it came to those matters involving Macquarie's intervention,

what a man or woman was, much more than the seriousness of their offending, would determine the lenience accorded to them. This was a variation of the principle applying to the conditions under which convicts would serve their terms of penal servitude.

Macquarie had his fellow-travellers in the Colony – men and women who shared his instincts when it came to the treatment of the convicts. One was the eponymous William Cox, of Windsor, who came to the Colony as an army officer before transferring to civilian life. As a farmer, he was known for his honourable treatment of his convicts. Firm but kindly, he taught them skills and a sound work ethic; he would use his good offices to help those of merit advance in this world. Pure Macquarie. Of particular interest here is Cox the magistrate, who was known for his liberal issuing of passes. Convicts could not move about the Colony at will. To pass from their own police district to another, a convict required the permission of a magistrate; the travel might be for work, or a social or recreational purpose. And, in respect of this, the magistrate exercised a wide discretion; some magistrates were parsimonious, others generous. Cox, who presided over the court at Windsor, issued his passes most liberally: they become known as 'Captain Cox's liberties'. In this portrait of the estimable William Cox (opposite), do we see a practical, no-nonsense, though firm and kindly man, a man inviting respect? If we do not, the artist has failed.

Social welfare

The Macquaries, more than any other governor and governor's wife, treated the convicts as people whose feelings mattered. This meant working assiduously within limited means to ameliorate the harshness of their present lives, and to instil within them realistic hopes of a better future for themselves and their children. More especially, there was something about the Macquaries' approach to welfare, a quality elevating it to a different plain. Something, even today, not part of our general thinking on welfare. It is the simple idea of welfare being more than material; also being at once social and of the spirit. It involves understanding that a state of debilitating poverty and material dispossession may induce feelings of lesser self-worth. Charity addresses the former, but does nothing for the latter. Indeed, when dispensed with an air of superiority or niggardliness – dispensed as charity – there is a real risk of exacerbating the recipients' spiritual malaise. There is no other explanation for Mrs. Macquarie's Female Orphan School, a building of simple elegance, indeed a certain grandeur, which nonplussed

a man who should have known better – one Samuel Marsden – as we shall see subsequently.

The School was built in an elevated position on the banks of the Parramatta River, just outside the Parramatta township itself. It was to be Mrs. Macquarie's Arcadia for these benighted girls. Recall how Mrs. Macquarie, on first walking around Sydney, was appalled and saddened on coming across the accommodation then provided for orphan girls. This had nothing to offer a girl but a life of poverty and vice, unless she was very fortunate and possessed of a strong innate sense of purpose. Mrs. Macquarie had there resolved to do something about it, although its coming to fruition took some time. It was her project from the start. She even designed the building, modelling it closely on her father's gentleman's residence, her family home, Airds House (see p.25).

We can easily envisage Elizabeth proudly showing Lachlan a sketch of her plans, with the following:

'Does not my family home, its style and size, and the happiness it knew, make an ideal model for my new girl's orphan school. As it sits across the river from the Government House at Parramatta, let it be

'View of the Female Orphan School, Near Parramatta New South Wales'. J. Lycett, artist and engraver. Published by J. Souter, London, 1825.

a building of similar proportions, and similarly situated in parklands. Will this not loudly proclaim to the girls themselves their worth in the world; and will it not send an unmistakable message to those who would patronize them?'

And in Elizabeth's final words, perhaps we can detect a note of conspiratorial gloating?

The school, commenced in 1813 and opened in 1819, catered principally for the children of convicts; its residents included true orphans, but also abandoned children, and those with one parent who was too poor to care for them. There they were to be raised to their teenage years. Along the way they would receive a basic education, largely comprising reading and writing; in addition to this, they were to acquire domestic and other skills, including, sewing and cooking, as well as gardening and light farm duties.

Nothing better represents the Macquaries' treatment of welfare as a means of not just sustaining the body, but most importantly uplifting the spirit, than does the Female Orphan School. It is the product of an instinctive response to a social problem from the mind of a particularly good and thoughtful woman, who regarded each girl as having been made in the image of God.

There were other buildings and projects coming within the Macquaries' welfare programme, but they are more conveniently dealt with in sections below.

Respectful and dignified treatment

The building which boldly bespeaks the Macquarie's respectful and dignified treatment of the convicts is the Hyde Park Barracks, opened in 1819. These Barracks housed convict men who worked for the government in and around Sydney. Previously these men had to find their own accommodation, but Macquarie determined there was a need for tighter supervision of their evenings in order to control their general behaviour, and in some cases to prevent criminal activity. More positively, Macquarie felt that with this greater control it would be easier to inculcate habits of industry within them.

Georgian in style, the building comprised a three-storeyed dormitory block with a shingled roof, along with a pediment containing a handsome clock. The design presented a simple yet striking appearance to the outside world. Inside, its commodious accommodation was to provide comfortable accommodation for 600 convicts. A far cry from

'Hyde Park Barracks'.
[J. Fowles, artist. Published by J. Fowles, Sydney, 1848.]

the slums in which most of its inhabitants would have lived back in Britain. A far cry too from the shack-like structures which the majority of the free settlers called home. The Barracks sat overlooking a new civic square at the top of the town's eastern ridge. Soon to be built opposite was the elegant St. James' Church. In this prominent and prestigious location, how these Barracks proclaimed the message of convict respect and dignity to the town.

As ever, Macquarie allowed for feelings and fairness. To avoid breaking up families, married convicts were not taken into the Barracks; this exemption applied to the better behaved convicts as well. And to compensate the convicts for their loss of freedom, their rations were increased substantially, and the clothing provided was more than ample to meet their needs. Moreover, the weekends were theirs: on Saturdays to work on their own account around the town; and on Sundays, after Church parade, to enjoy themselves outside the Barracks.

Civic armature of style and beauty

In order to appreciate this aspect of the Macquaries' work, we need to understand what picture the British government – and, more importantly, the British people – had of its convicts. It was starkly, unpalatably this. The convicts were criminals to be sent to the ends of the earth to rid God-fearing Britain of its evil-doers, its human jetsam. They otherwise would not only cause much harm but might also lead many vulnerable folk astray, infecting them with their badness. The convicts were thought of as worse than useless; rather, they were moral cankers. Thus, it was to be hoped that none of them would choose to return at the end of their sentences. This reflected the mentality of throwing out rotten apples as garbage and having them dumped in a remote tip, to rot. Now, what people think about a man or woman, that man and woman are at risk of

'Vue Des Écuries Du Gouverneur á Sydney (Nouvelle Galles du Sud)' (c1826). Pl 30. [L.] de Sainson, artist. V. Adam, engraver. H. Vander Burch, lithographer. Published by Tastu, [Paris, c1833].

thinking about themselves, especially as they reflect on this ten-thousand miles from home, and in a run-down town without domestic or civil amenity. Unless, they are very, very, strong of mind.

This the Macquaries, sensitive human beings that they were, understood; this they sought to correct, to avoid. Thus, they set about bequeathing to Sydney and the townships an armature of civic style and beauty, around which the convicts – yes, the convicts, constituting as they did the vast majority of the population – could live their lives, and of which they could be proud. 'Why would anyone construct fine buildings for us if they did not think us worthy of them, if they did not think we in this place did not have a bright future?' This, the convicts were intended to ask themselves; this the convicts did increasingly ask themselves. And each time the question was asked, the man or woman's sense of self-worth and morale were raised, a spring entered their steps, their heads were held higher, their eyes looked not at the present but into the future.

So, the Macquaries set about constructing grand ornamental buildings and attractive streetscapes far exceeding what utility required. One

'Francis Greenway'.
Self-portrait. Copied from M. Ellis, *Francis Greenway: His Life and Times* (Deluxe edition). The Shepherd Press, Sydney, 1949.

structure more than any other came to personify the Macquaries as public builders; it was their Government House stables. This elaborate, castellated, octangular building stood on the crest of the rise just to the east of Government House. Inside, the horse stalls and boxes, along with staff quarters, were arranged around a circular courtyard. The stables (see p.91), completed in 1819, were to be the first piece of what was to be a new and grand Government House complex.

Commentators have detected Mrs. Macquarie's hand in its design, since her vision for Sydney displayed a penchant for medieval forts. Whatever be the case, the architect was Francis Greenway, a man who paraded himself around Sydney, decked out most dapperly while projecting an unmistakable hauteur. This man had been trained by, and seen at first hand, the work of the great Englishman, Beau Nash. Greenway's practice was in Bath, but ended there when he chose to forge a contract after becoming bankrupt. Thus did the ship on which he was transported to the Colony also bring with it, though unimagined to anyone at the time, Regency Bath.

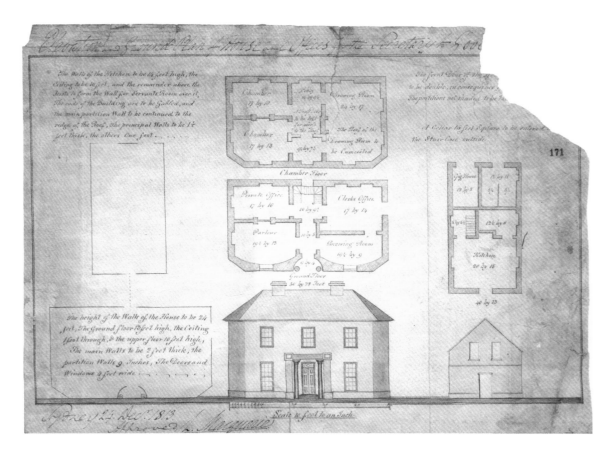

171

'**Elevation and Ground Plan of House and Offices for the Secretary to Gov[ernor]'.** Sydney, 1813. Copy from and made by the National Archives, Kew, London.

Greenway arrived in the Colony in 1814. Macquarie granted him an immediate ticket-of-leave, and then two years later appointed him to the post of Civil Architect. Greenway designed many of the Colony's finest buildings, all with an elegant simplicity. These were the first beacons of the arts as civilizing, and became objects of pride to the citizens of the infant Colony. Greenway's buildings include the Hyde Park Barracks, the lighthouse just south of the entrance to the Harbour, the church and courthouse for the new township of Windsor, and St. James' Church and the Supreme Court building in Sydney. The arrogant Greenway was a fractious, prickly, greedy ingrate, whose petulance required Macquarie to draw on his considerable reserves of tolerance. Fortunately for the Colony, Macquarie was a soldier who knew how to put up with much in the interests of a cause.

A source of much of Macquarie's dissatisfaction with the condition of the public infrastructure was the shabby and primitive accommodation set aside for the senior public officials. One of the first houses he commissioned was for his Secretary, John Campbell, in 1813. The

'A View of the Cove and Part of Sydney, New South Wales. Taken from Dawes Battery'. II. J. Wallis, artist. W. Preston, engraver. Published by R. Ackermann, London, 1820.

architect was the professionally qualified Daniel Mathew, who came to the Colony as a free settler, and took the design from Edward Gyfford's 'Designs for Elegant Cottages and Small Villas'. The plan of the house (see p.93) shows it to be a handsome gentleman's town residence, Georgian in style, its walls 24 feet in height, with a detached kitchen. How satisfied Macquarie must have been when he signed off on the plans!

These buildings were a drain on the Colony's struggling budget, but in Macquarie's eyes a necessary one to fulfil his aim of transforming a shambolic penal outpost into the elegant capital of a new country.

The Macquaries' plans for their transformed new Sydney extended to ornamental gardens and parklands, and a fashionable, elegant town square. In line with this, Mrs. Macquarie proposed a botanical garden for the town. These covered an extensive area, enveloping Farm Cove to the immediate east of Sydney Cove, and running up to the crest of

the rise above, all fenced off with a ten-foot-high stone wall. Along with this, there was promenade around the shoreline from Government House to the tip of the eastern promontory of Farm Cove. Mrs. Macquarie involved herself in both their planning and their construction, proudly seeing them opened in 1816, and feeling as a mother might at her children's graduations. Indeed, there a sense of maternal possessiveness here too. For though the gardens were open to the public by day, they were really intended for the recreation of the better classes. Yet even with this qualification, the Macquaries, particularly Mrs. Macquarie, came to regard them as a secluded space for Lachlan's and her personal relaxation and quietude when in Sydney. Understand, the governor's wife was a woman with feeling for the people but one never really feeling of them, even those who thought of themselves as of the superior class.

The image intended to display the grandeur of the Sydney the Macquaries were bequeathing the Colonists is commonly known as 'Macquarie's Sydney'. Better, were it known as 'The Macquaries' Sydney'.

Dominating the picture is an apparently massive building; in fact, it is Macquarie's hospital, comprising a central building and two separate wings, each with a veranda and covered balcony. Here, the building itself and its setting symbolize, respectively, the individual and collective scale of the Macquaries' programme of public works. Just compare it with the earlier image of Sydney in 1810 (see p.49). What a transformation in the cityscape! The hospital, opened in 1816, provided the principal medical care for the Colony's convict workforce. At the time of the Macquaries' arrival, the hospital buildings comprised no more than a collection of tents and shoddy shelters. Some have suggested that the hospital's verandas and balconies manifested an influence from Macquarie's time as a soldier in India. The sweep of this panorama proclaims a new, vibrant, prosperous city. This is an image to impress the world, in particular Britain. What might the British government have seen in this picture? How might they have thought it comported with the aims of transportation? How well might they have thought the money spent on a population of nefarious, underclass rejects?

The Macquaries' programme of beautification was not restricted to Sydney. In the first year of his governorship he established five townships in the Hawkesbury district, either side of the River, about 35 miles north-west of Sydney itself. These he named Castlereagh, Windsor, Wilberforce, Pitt Town and Richmond. Each town was to be laid out in an attractive and orderly fashion, and to comprise a church, school, courthouse, gaol and cemetery. Importantly, there was to be in these townships no lessening

of the Macquaries' architectural ideals; indeed, Greenway's St. Matthew's Church at Windsor is regarded by some as his masterpiece. As the settlers or convicts were riding or being driven along the higher ground and looked down upon the Hawkesbury with its bucolic landscapes and its picturesque villages, they would behold a pastoral idyll, the equal of anywhere in the English countryside. This is what the above image of a view looking down upon the nascent township of Wilberforce was intended to convey.

This section on the Macquaries' beautification of the Colony concludes with reference to Mrs. Macquarie's improvements to St. John's, Parramatta, completed in 1818. It is perhaps the only building for which we have an image of its appearance around the time of the Macquaries' arrival, an image of the building said to have inspired Mrs. Macquarie, and an image of the refurbished building. These are presented sequentially (see opposite). The building which so caught Mrs. Macquarie's attention was St. Mary's, the historic twelfth-century Saxon church at Reculver, Kent, in England. The feature apparently captivating her was its twin towers. Whether Mrs. Macquarie actually ever saw the church or only a picture of it is not clear.

'View of Wilberforce, on the Banks of the River Hawkesbury, New South Wales'. Published by J. Souter, London, 1825.

'View of the New Church at Parramatta'. From G. Barrington, *The History of New South Wales*. M. Jones, London, 1802.

VIEW OF THE NEW CHURCH AT PARAMATTA.

(right) **'Reculver'**. Tomkins, artist. Angus, engraver. Published by E. Harding, London, 1801.

(far right) **'Australia La Chiesa di Paramata'**. T III. [Published by G. Antonelli, Venice, 1841.]

Churlish critics have used these fine buildings as evidence of Lachlan Macquarie's desire for self-aggrandizement. There is some truth in this, but it is very much a distorted truth. The building giving lie to this is the Female Orphan School, tucked away as it is on the outskirts of rural Parramatta. No, the Macquaries' principal purpose was to serve the esteem and self-regard of the convicts themselves. Too many critics, driven by some dark motive, detect bad in an individual though goodness be so apparent in their cause. What a disservice they do to the past's capacity to inspire and elevate us in the present.

Chapter 5

The Age of the Macquaries: The Colony and the People

THIS IS THE second of two chapters dealing with the Macquaries' treatment of the convicts. The focus of the previous chapter was the Colony as a home for the convict, and dealt with punitive leniency, social welfare, respectful and dignified treatment, and a civic armature of style and beauty. The focus here is the convicts themselves, the convicts' lives being renewed and uplifted. There are two parts to this: social re-integration and elevation; reform and personal renewal.

SOCIAL RE-INTEGRATION AND ELEVATION

At the time of the Macquaries' arrival in the Colony, the free settlers duly recognized the legal distinction between convict and emancipist, but it was common among the elite and polite classes not to accord them the same moral and social status as themselves. For in their eyes both had come to the Colony in chains as criminals; the only difference was that the former were serving their sentences, the latter had served theirs and in the eyes of the law were now free. Thus, as they come across emancipists in Sydney, and in the towns and countryside, so in the backs of the free settlers' minds are these thoughts: yet do they retain the mark of Cain; yet do they remain morally tainted. You can never quite trust them; you can never quite feel safe with them; you never quite know. What you do know is that you too will fall under suspicion in the eyes of the respectable if you were to share their company, let alone share their table. Amongst the gentler of these people, this attitude though governing would remain unspoken whenever they crossed paths with an emancipist.

The sanctimonious though saw it as their duty to remind them of their moral inferiority. Indeed, the meaner among them even appeared to delight in this. They must never be allowed to feel comfortable; they must never be allowed to get a foot in the drawing rooms and offices of power. What would it say about the Colony? What mischief might it lead to?

All this was abhorrent to the Macquaries. It was contrary to every belief, every value they brought to this convict colony; it was the antithesis of what they sought to do here. Macquarie knew that good men turned to crime in adversity and in moments of madness; not all men are blessed with that strength of character which allows them to withstand the misfortunes and temptations life throws them; and Mrs. Macquarie believed in God's raising of the fallen to new life. The world view of the self-styled colonial elite and the painfully respectable was not one the Macquaries intended to preside over, to foster, to bequeath to future generations. They would smash it! He was the governor. And Mrs. Macquarie could transmogrify herself into one of those forces of nature. In the Macquaries' new society, emancipist and free settler alike would be recognized according to their talents. This would become unmistakably clear to the serving convicts and to the emancipists, and – importantly – to the free settlers. Thus did Macquarie formulate a social principle, which was to apply largely without qualification. It is known as Macquarie's Principle of Emancipation.

Lachlan Macquarie to Viscount Castlereagh. 30th April, 1810. Digital image from the National Archives, Kew, London.

I have ... taken upon myself to adopt a new Line of Conduct, Conceiving that Emancipation, when United with Rectitude and long-tried good Conduct, should lead a Man back to that Rank in Society which he had forfeited, and do away, in as far as the Case will admit, All Retrospect of former bad Conduct.[13]

Simply, the well-behaved convict upon emancipation should be treated as though he or she had never offended. There it is (p.99) , as it first appeared, written by a clerk, in a despatch from Macquarie to Viscount Castlereagh, the Secretary of State for the Colonies, dated 30th April, 1810. What an incentive to the convicts to reform and remain well-behaved! What a strategy for bringing the best out of a benighted man or woman![14]

Macquarie's application of this principle was greater than the principle itself – actually. For in stating the principle, he conveniently omitted after 'forfeited' the words 'or even be elevated to a higher rank'. Thus, in practice, the principle of emancipation represented a principle of social re-integration and elevation. This covered not only official appointments to senior positions within his administration, as well as other civic duties, but also the introduction into Society. Two emancipists, perhaps better than any others, serve as exemplars of this policy, in regard to its application and to the opposition it faced from the great and the good both inside and outside the Colony. One of the emancipists was Simeon Lord; the other, William Redfern.

EMANCIPATION AS OFFICIAL APPOINTMENTS AND DUTIES

Simeon Lord

In early 1810 Macquarie appointed one Simeon Lord and another wealthy emancipist, Andrew Thompson, along with the Rev. Samuel Marsden, as trustees and commissioners of the new turnpike road to be built between Sydney and the Hawkesbury. This road represented a major piece of infrastructure in Macquarie's programme of public works. Its equivalent today would be a major new freeway. He also proposed to appoint Lord to the magistracy when a vacancy arose. As far as Macquarie was concerned, Lord and the other emancipist had conducted themselves in the Colony with great propriety, and had over the years provided generous assistance to the government. And Lord had been an honourable employer of convicts.

Lord, born in 1771 in provincial England, was transported in his late teens for the theft of commercial (albeit small) quantities of various types of cloth. He was emancipated early, got himself into retailing, and then branched out into various business ventures, including sealing, farming, manufacturing, auctioneering, and lumbering, along with exporting. He soon became very wealthy, living in a mansion in the heart of Sydney, near the Cove. Lord the businessman was regarded by some as bruising, by others as shifty as a dingo. Macquarie, however, would argue that Lord, in doing well for himself, brought good to others. More than this, he was not just a cog in the Colony's economy, he was one of its founders. As to Lord's business ethics? Perhaps we see here the utility of the blind spot to the great social reformer. This portrait of Lord, likely to have been painted around the time of the Macquaries, represents him well: a vain, proud, flashy 'chancer', anxious to be accepted as a man who has made it.

William Redfern

William Redfern, born around 1774 – perhaps in Canada – was a naval surgeon. If ever there was a brusque, no-nonsense man, it was Redfern. To him, a spade was always a 'bloody shovel'. He abhorred cant and pomposity; he spoke to all men alike, no matter their position. His rough features matched the unkempt appearance of his dress. What he did care about, what he did worry about, what he worked tirelessly for, were the sick and infirm, along with those for whom life was a struggle, and who had been passed over and forgotten. Here was a man of the utmost fellow-feeling and compassion. He would do what had to be done and bugger the consequences. Are we really surprised at this, once we look at the 1832 portrait of him (see p.102)?

In fact, these very characteristics played a part in bringing Redfern to the Colony; these are what drove him in the Colony, and which brought him down. Redfern was transported to the Colony for the most serious offence of inciting a mutiny amongst sailors on several ships anchored at the Nore in the Thames Estuary. The sailors were protesting their conditions – low pay, poor quality rations, cruel officers, little shore leave – but the mutiny did have political overtones. Redfern was said to have been one of those inciting the men to seize the ship. It is easy to see how the sense of justice of a man such as he would have been piqued in the circumstances. And Redfern, only young at the time – 23 years of age – and by nature a very hot hot-head, would have been 'all-in'. Indeed, it would take a lot less for him to swing into action. Almost thirty years later, he took a horse whip to the editor of the Sydney Gazette for what he regarded as unfair criticism.

(opposite) **'Simeon Lord'**. Framed portrait in the Australasian Pioneers' Club. Access kindly arranged by John Lanser, curator. (Eric Sierins, photographer, 2018.)

This is the man Lachlan and Elizabeth as a couple admired perhaps more than any other in the Colony. What drew them to him was not his manner, but his treatment of the convicts and the general poor as their doctor. He served them at the hospital, he ran out-patient clinics for them, and he would ride deep into the bush to tend their needs. The personal gratitude of these people was not what he looked for, though heaven knows it was deserved. No, in these actions he was satisfying himself – you see – driven as he was by a sense of duty and a need to bestow compassion. Redfern was universally regarded as an outstanding doctor, by far the most able in the Colony. It was to Redfern, though 'bedside manner' had apparently not been part of his medical curriculum, the ladies of the elite turned as they approached childbirth. For his talent and dedication, he was held in great esteem among the people, even by the highest in the land such as men like John Macarthur.

'Dr. William Redfern' (1832). G. Mather, artist. Copied from *The Sydney Morning Herald*, 31st July, 1926 (p.11).

One of his greatest contributions was to public health. Macquarie, horrified by the calamitous rates of mortality and morbidity on one of the convoys transporting convicts to the Colony, turned to Redfern. The good doctor obliged. His extensive and most thorough report, covering matters such as ventilation and cleanliness, and the powers required by surgeons on the ships, was adopted and set the new standards of the day. They proved most efficacious and represented a benchmark of humanity.

The post of the Colony's Principal Surgeon was one D'Arcy Wentworth. When the time came for his retirement, the Macquaries had no doubt who should succeed him. On the grounds of competence and dedication, the position must be the noble William's. Accordingly, Macquarie forwarded Redfern's name to London for approval, and waited with expectation. He also thought Redfern a worthy candidate for the magistracy.

These appointments tell us much about how Macquarie conceived of his emancipation principle's application. Redfern was a naval officer; his crime involving mutiny, as a category of crime, was of the highest order of seriousness. Macquarie, the army officer, would have well understood this. Lord, by way of his two appointments – commissioner and magistrate – was not merely being returned to the station in life which his crime had forced him to forfeit. No, Lord was being raised to a level of civic status, which by virtue of his birth would not have been open to him in Britain. And when Macquarie applied his principle to Lord, he apparently had forgotten it included the word 'rectitude'.

Of course, not all convicts were potential beneficiaries of this policy. Yet did Macquarie hope to uplift the spirits of the many by raising the civic status of a few. Well, this was the pithy Macquarie explanation for his policy. Nonetheless, quite significant numbers of convicts profited by way of lesser appointments and positions, ones commensurate with their lesser skills and abilities. In these ways did Macquarie indeed raise the spirits of the many.

We should not deal with these appointments solely as facts, events striped of their humanity. The Macquaries never dealt with matters this way. If we are to appreciate the Macquaries' treatment of the convicts, we must do our best to empathize with the people behind these events. Indeed, this is why their portraits accompany this aspect of our story. Just imagine, how these two benighted men must have felt as Macquarie offered them these appointments. These two, as lads thrown into a wretched prison then, unwanted in their own country, having to endure the long voyage amid sickness and disease, physical and personal abuse, finally to be cast upon an isolated shore. And now they, though social nobodies, were on the verge of a new status, one Lord so coveted and Redfern so deserved, yet which a few years before had seemed behind their reach. Their lives would have surely flashed before them. So, join them in their surprise, their disbelief, their profound joy. Ever the more so, because these were no token appointments. For Lord, his appointment alongside a figure of the pre-eminence of the Rev. Samuel Marsden spoke for itself; as did the position of the Colony's Principal Surgeon. Could it really be true, they would have wondered?

Jury service

Equally significant as the appointments of Lord and Redfern was Macquarie's recommendation to his masters in Britain that emancipists be eligible for jury service. Just consider the enormity of what was being requested here. We hear the exclamations of the respectable. Men who had broken the law in Britain and who had been banished as wrong-doers, were to be permitted to participate in the administration of the law in the new colony! A duty which would involve them in making individual judgements about what is right and what is wrong, and in cases which would include leading free settlers! The fallen becoming judges of their moral superiors! The inherently corrupt being handed the power to corrupt the heart of justice! This proposal had a secondary significance; it involved handing civic and political power to the emancipists en masse, not just the minority of high achievers among them. To Macquarie it was a message to all convicts that with emancipation they would be the equal of the free settler. To the free settler – the elite among them especially – it was a sign that their governor might be a madman.

More generally
Macquarie well understood from his days on Mull the importance of self-worth in the living of a good life. Moreover, he well appreciated that few of the convicts had within themselves the wherewithal to raise their own morale or generate personal incentive. What rare strength of character it would take, in the light of the wretched damaged lives they brought with them and in the absence of encouragement – indeed, often in the face of the opposition many would face in the Colony.

Thus, Macquarie would go around the Colony fervently proclaiming, holding out to them, his message of hope: they, the convicts, had come to a place where virtue was rewarded and merit was extolled; under his authority, good behaviour on their part would take them far. It was a message a convict might here on many occasions; indeed, it was part of his welcoming address to all convicts on the day of their arrival in the Colony. There was a co-leader of this cheer squad, the redoubtable Mrs. Macquarie.

EMANCIPATION AS THE INTRODUCTION INTO SOCIETY

The second way in which the Macquaries applied their principle of social re-integration and elevation was by way of invitations to Government House society. There was no colonial letter awaited with greater anticipation, opened with greater excitement, bragged about more widely, than an invitation to dine at the Governor's table. The invitation confirmed in writing one's membership of the colonial elite, one's acceptance into colonial society. Invitees would hope for a summer's evening, so they might drive there in an open carriage while the hoi polloi looked up at them with envy. People like John and Elizabeth Macarthur might treat the whole event as a matter of course; most patently were not a Macarthur, but did dream of being in their set, or at least rubbing shoulders with them socially.

So, imagine the self-styled exclusives' mortification that evening in 1810 when they entered Government House to find they were dining alongside William Redfern, Simeon Lord and one or two other leading emancipists. O dear! From a present feeling of delight, now plunged into a dread of 'what next?' This, with no opportunity of expressing their thoughts and churning emotions, aside from a derogatory word, uttered sotto voce, should they happen to be beside one of their own. How painful it would have been to watch these social and moral snobs interact with their new official social equals, some feigning politeness, others testing the boundaries of impoliteness.

As for the Macquaries, well, theirs would have been a medley of emotions: as the guests arrived, an air of excited expectation; soon, profound disappointment; later upon reflection, something more. Annoyance and disgust – how could people given so many of life's blessings, be so petty and cruel to those who had faced so many of life's misfortunes? Overwhelming pain – these most worthy emancipists, who arrived individually with their heads held high, now gathered together, no proud smiles, rather their expressions projecting the greatest discomfort. Finally, malign amusement – Mrs. Macquarie in particular. O the pleasure of watching these puffed-up, would-be grandees squirming over the here and now; fretting too over what might lie in store for them! Not a little anxiety for the hosts themselves. In Lachlan and Elizabeth's minds these invitations, coming as they did so early in the Macquarie governorship, represented a soft introduction to the elite of their emancipation policy. If there was trouble already, what were the prospects for the policy's future?

The Macquaries held other social functions at Government House. These did not have the status or formality of dining at the Governor's table, though there was a certain cachet attending them – it was the 'House' after all. The social circles were wider on these occasions; some of these were private events, others public. Mrs. Macquarie held an outdoor party for the convicts (along with their overseers) who were working on the improvements she was making to the grounds of Government House and the Domain. And the birthdays of the King and Prince Regent were celebrated, these events being open to the general public.

A mark of social acceptability just below the Governor's table was the Officers' mess, this being in accordance with the officers' high social status within the Colony. Thus, Macquarie urged his fellow officers to entertain some of the leading emancipists and to invite them to their formal dinners.

Another of the means at the Macquaries' disposal was by way of personal friendships with emancipists. These were friendships they not only did nothing to hide – a little hard when you have a personal staff and live in a house as public as the Governor's – but in fact would publicly flaunt. There is no better example of this than Macquarie's decision to act as the chief mourner at the funeral of the opulent emancipist Andrew Thompson in 1810. He was one of the emancipists who, Macquarie believed, had given his services to the Colony generously and liberally, and who had contributed mightily to the Colony's economic advancement. Actions such as these were part of a deliberate ploy. By this means, the Macquaries thumbed their noses at the exclusives, and in front of the convicts. Indeed, at Government House functions and in public, Mrs. Macquarie might almost ignore a member of the elite out of her favour, while in their very presence gushing over a favourite emancipist. How embarrassing an outing could become for the self-important! This woman could be a terror. These actions sent an unmistakable message to the well-behaved convicts, both those still under penal servitude as well as the emancipists: your personal history renders you and your children no less worthy a person than the free settler and their off-spring; indeed, without limits in the Colony's social hierarchy.

Mary Reibey (c1835). Digital image from the State Library of New South Wales, Sydney (MIN 76).

One of the Macquaries' favourites was the hard-nosed business woman, Mrs. Mary Reibey. An English provincial girl, she was born in 1777, and was convicted of horse-stealing as a teenager, for which she was transported for seven years. She married Thomas, a free settler, and together they built up a business empire, spanning most aspects of the Colony's commerce. They had farms; they traded, imported, transported; there was a hotel; moreover, they brought property and developed it in the heart of Sydney. And when Thomas died soon after the Macquaries' arrival, she took their whole operation to new heights. She was not litigious like many; that was for fools. Rather, she had her own far more efficient rough-and-ready methods – on one occasion she was charged with assaulting one of her debtors. When we look at her portrait, are we surprised? How pugnacious she appears. A conqueror!

Though she is at this time no longer young, that measure of sweetness and mellowness often accompanying even the toughest person in their advancing years appears not to be much in evidence here. Of course, the Macquaries would have admired what she had made of her life and, being the Macquaries, and in light of this, overlooked her palpable faults. They would have applauded also her charitable works: she supported the work of the Church, and involved herself in a range of charities and good causes. Nevertheless, she was not received into the drawing and dining rooms of Sydney society. Convictry was her mark of Cain; moreover, she was unpolished and uncultivated, deemed by the genteel – such as they were – to be beneath them. Lachlan and Elizabeth soon saw to that.

One of Mrs. Macquarie's particular favourites was dear William Redfern, whom she always placed on the Governor's right hand at Government House dinners. Another favourite was the Macquaries' bodyguard, the emancipist Charles Whalan. Born in 1772, he was transported for poaching as a teenager. In due course he became Sergeant of the Governor's Bodyguard of the Light Horse. It was in this capacity he met the Macquaries. Here are two extracts from one of her letters to him, written after the Macquaries had left the Colony (see p.108). Witness warmth; witness sternness.[15]

> My Dear Serjeant
>   … I am having your picture framed, and intend to hang it in my Bed Room, as I expect it will put me in good humour to look on it, when I feel disposed to be otherwise, which you know is not infrequently the case with me …
>   We could not find the large Silver Salver on coming home … it was not to be sold on any account.
>   Be so good as to explain this.

The Macquaries' principle of social re-integration and elevation had four underpinnings, in addition to that of being an incentive to reform. First, on what grounds other than prejudice could it be presumed that a man or woman reformed in action was not also reformed in their soul? What would it say about a society which institutionalized such prejudice? What would it say about a society which chose to ignore their God as forgiving? Let it be clear, the Macquaries appreciated that the convicts were far from perfect, even many of the better ones – they were not naïve or beyond the range of gossip. Yet, these things are somewhat relative, are they not? The fact is, they did not have a high opinion of all the free settlers

My dear Serjeant —

I am having your picture framed, and intend to hang it in my Bed Room, as I expect it will put me in good humour to look on it, when I feel disposed to be otherwise, which you know is not unfrequently the case with me. —

We could not find the large Silver Salver on coming home, it was not to be told on any account. — Be so good as to explain this. —

either, seeing many of them as sharp, roguish and chancers, and not a few of the wealthy as exploitative. More generally, Lachlan and Elizabeth were worldly-wise: they were well aware of the behind-the-scenes lives of many of the so-called 'great and good' back home.

Second, to ignore the principle would be to ensure a two-class society, one in which as a matter of course the emancipists would follow the rules but never make them, generate the wealth but never fully enjoy it, and for ever be excluded from the Colony's society. With this, an unmistakable whiff of slavery would sully the air. It would be a Colony demeaned; one

Elizabeth Macquarie to Charles Whalan. 18th August, 1823. Digital image from the State Library of New South Wales, Sydney (ML MSS 6/1).

inviting history's condemnation. As importantly, its ethos would be the antithesis of what the Macquaries wanted it to be, how they wanted it to be seen by the world. No, their Colony was to be a place of liberation, one to be admired, one to be emulated.

Third, it was the convicts and emancipists who through their hard work had built the Colony and made it what it was today. Moreover, around 85 percent of the population comprised the convicts, the emancipists and their children, and this would hold into the foreseeable future. Surely, surely, fairness demanded that they participate in it and profit from it fully.

Fourth, some of the most talented men and women in the Colony were emancipists; to deprive the place of their talents would be to undermine its potential and future. What folly, and all for prejudice!

All four grounds of themselves tangential to reform, yet all calculated to imbue the convicts' psyches – the very grounds of their beings – with two fundamental elevating feelings: one, the Colony and its future belonged to them as emancipists; two, they, not just the free settlers, would drive the Colony forward and be its leading citizens.

We have explored the social exclusionary mentality of the elite and polite classes of the Colony's society. This attitude would have appeared to them to be sound, something not in need of explanation or justification. Indeed, this as unexamined wisdom would surely have prevented them from ever imagining that a governor might challenge it. So, when someone in the know first broke the news regarding the guest list for a forthcoming Government House dinner party, perhaps doing it with dramatic effect, at one of the society hostess's candlelight suppers, just imagine the reaction. About the same effect as a bolt of lightning: bodies shuddering; jaws dropping; plates and cutlery rattling. One can hear one of the women asking somewhat hesitatingly, 'What can we do about it?', and one of the older men replying menacingly, 'O we'll do something about it, alright!' And so they did, as we shall see.

CONVICT REFORM AND PERSONAL RENEWAL

For the Macquaries there were two aspects of convict reform and renewal. The first involved taking steps to prevent convicts relapsing into their old ways. The second involved implementing measures to renew them, transforming them into men and women with the habits of industry and a more robust morality, along with work skills for those without them and with new opportunities, both so they might improve the lives of themselves and their children. The children of the convicts were also the direct focus of the Macquaries' concern. For this group, it was about preventing these children from being drawn into crime as their parents had been back in Britain. In fact, this was a concern of theirs for the children more generally.

As we have seen, the reform and renewal of convict lives was part of the thinking behind all five of the above policies. Repeated brutal punishment might crush a man's spirit, embitter him, or compound his sense of worthlessness and hopelessness; so too, exploitative and draconian treatment by supervisors and masters. In respect of these things, it was no different for the women. And, once in this state, the convict was at far greater risk of rebelling and returning to crime. In contrast, an early ticket-of-leave for good behaviour offered a great incentive to a man or woman under penal servitude to develop good work habits and to earn money in their free time – foundational building-blocks for a new life.

One purpose of the Hyde Park Barracks was to bring the more undisciplined, rambunctious convict under greater control, so their acquiring the habits of industry through work were less likely to be interrupted by their as yet untamed proclivities for mischief or worse. And the Barracks also, along with the Female Orphan School, as fine buildings were to demonstrate to the convicts that no less elevated personages than the Governor and his wife thought they were not doomed people but individuals whom they wanted to, and thought could, amount to something. They were people worthy of respect. Again, we see the idea of personal uplift and incentive as precursors to reform.

The civic armature of style and beauty had its place in the Macquaries' quest for convict renewal. The convicts were coming out to a penal colony, a place of misery with a future of misery, or so they would have thought. Yet, what did they find? A nascent city with ever-improving prospects, which in turn would bequeath them a future. With good conduct and hard work, they could avail themselves of its offerings. Importantly, here, unlike in Britain, they had the Macquaries to champion their interests – so the even half-thoughtful among them would have realized. As the Colony was going ahead, so might they. It was a place of which they could be proud and in which they could become proud of themselves.

Finally, the Macquaries' policy of social re-integration and elevation was intended to encourage reform by sending an unmistakeable message to all – the convicts and those who would put them down – that the convicts, once emancipated would not be second-class citizens, there to do the bidding of the free settlers and serving as lackeys for the advancement of their interests. Rather, the convicts as emancipists would, being the equals of the free settlers, share in running the Colony and in enjoying the privileges and prestige of power.

Some general considerations come into play here. The preceding measures though themselves facilitative of reform are not sufficient for reform. Certainly, it is important that punishment does not crush, or that greater control is exercised over someone whose capacity to regulate their behaviour is deficient. Nonetheless, leniency of itself will not bring about reform, and control cannot be extended after a sentence has expired. These measures represent the avoidance of the negative, though offer nothing positive. Incentive along with a sense of self-worth have this latter capacity, but will come to naught unless the convict enjoys the means of responding. Thus does the convict require skills to apply and the opportunity of applying them; moreover, the convict must have within himself or herself the habits of industry and a governing morality, so that they might sustain a good life. These features of convict life were described earlier; here they are rehearsed and elaborated upon as they relate to convict reform and renewal.

When convicts arrived in the Colony, they were soon sent to work either for the government or assigned to work for a free settler or emancipist. To Macquarie, work was the principal means by which the convicts would acquire work skills and the habits of industry, and would find through these opportunities for advancement. To these ends, the system of assignment had the greatest potential. This system was a system well in place at the time of the Macquaries' arrival in the Colony. Its original introduction was on utilitarian grounds alone. For the Colony's survival and then sustainable growth, it required productive free settlers; however, to be productive the small numbers of free settlers needed a labour force. There was no alternative for this but the convicts. At that time assignment carried no connotations of renewal. This was incidental, and to be found principally in the nature and conditions of the convicts' work, and the circumstances under which they led their lives. One feature was the freedom the convicts enjoyed, most being under a degree of control representing little more than a light touch. In this way, though their opportunities of straying were somewhat curtailed, their sense of autonomy remained intact. When it came to work, the unskilled had the chance of learning skills, and thus of acquiring something to offer an employer once freed. All had the opportunity of experiencing regular work and the discipline attending it, perhaps for the first time in many years, perhaps in their lives. From mid-afternoon on weekdays and around midday on Saturday they could work in their own interests and, especially the skilled, earn very good money. As part of this, they might mix with the more law-abiding of the Colony's citizens, or at least come under their good influence. The possibility of a new life became real. In many respects, there was not much difference between the lives of the assignee and the free. What a far cry from serving their time in a congested prison hulk or gaol, filled with like-minded individuals, and with its malign brooding atmosphere of hopelessness, bitterness, rebelliousness and criminality! This was the idea of work championed by Macquarie. Nevertheless, the convicts' experience of assignment as reforming varied. While some masters – the Macquaries' fellow-travellers – treated convicts as souls to be rescued, others treated them as men and women to be exploited, and in doing this undermined their chances of reform.

Opportunity for the convict also came upon emancipation. In regard to this, Macquarie envisaged an emancipist yeomanry spread across the countryside, the convict profiting from the land and the Colony's commerce profiting from them. To this end, he actively sought out convicts with a proven record of honesty, industry and sobriety – well, in principle, but interpreted these most liberally in their favour – and offered them modest-sized land grants. Moreover, he keenly endorsed the assignment of convicts to the emancipists, as well as the free settlers. Nothing represented Macquarie's ideal than did widespread emancipist land-owning. The Colony for the Convict; the noble Convict! This was pure Macquarieism. Perhaps not surprising then, in regard to the conditions of the convicts' assignment, but especially in the liberal granting of land to them as emancipists, many free settlers resentfully thought of Macquarie as favouring the convict over them.

The idea of assignment is well represented in this accompanying image of a woman churning butter (opposite). It is, in fact, an English farmyard scene; and the woman working is neatly attired and appears contented. In fact, herein lies the image's relevance. For the woman as portrayed could well be in the Colony, a convict serving her sentence by way of assignment to a comfortable free settler. Under a good mistress, she might learn new skills, and be encouraged, be shown how, to live a new life. The point is here, she will be living a normal, decent and potentially transformative life. For many this life was far, far more salubrious than it had been in Britain; many too contemplated something even better in the future. Remember Mrs. Reibey? Remember though, there were very, very few like the redoubtable Mrs. Reibey; and for not a few even a

Woman Churning Butter.
No. 14. [W. Pyne, artist.]
Published by W. Miller,
London, 1805.

modicum of respectability remained beyond their damaged psyches. Yet the majority did make new lives for themselves. As it was for the women, so it was for the men (see p.219).

Macquarie increasingly regarded government service as having an important part to play in the reform of the convict, the strengths of assignment notwithstanding. This came about as he detected a growing attitude among the army officers and the wealthy to regard the convicts as nothing more than a cheap workforce, one there to enrich them. Moreover, with this attitude came a cold disregard for the convicts as fellow human beings who, like them, had their own dreams of a better life. These attitudes the Macquaries detested; these were attitudes they sought to eradicate, or at least do what they could to minimize their pernicious effects. Macquarie saw other advantages for the convict in government service. Each convict's progress to reform could be more closely and uniformly monitored, and they would be less subject to abuse. To Macquaries' enemies, these reasons were actually rationalizations for the workforce he needed to build his civic armature. In practice these supposed advantages proved somewhat chimerical, in any case. The government supervisors could be just as callous, just as uninterested in their charges' futures.

The final component of the Macquaries' thinking on the convicts' renewal and reform was the need to instil into them a governing morality. This was another of the Macquaries' signature policies, one which may have owed much to Mrs. Macquarie's influence. To this end, Macquarie instituted weekly Church parades for convicts in government service so that they might hear the Biblical precepts on right and wrong put before them with a Divine authority. Similarly, those assigned convicts working within three miles of a church were expected to attend worship. Its purpose was to steer and keep the convicts away from crime. For some, it was also to challenge their dissolute and licentious lives, which in many cases inclined them through association to crime, or rendered them less able to resist its temptations. The Macquaries cared about the convicts' souls; they wanted the convicts renewed in spirit. It was not enough that the convicts did not re-offend simply because they feared punishment. No, the Macquaries wanted the convicts to desist from crime because it was the wrong thing to do, because it was incompatible with the living of a good life. To strengthen this policy, Macquarie built new churches, including ones in the outlying districts, and installed clergymen in these parishes.

A part of the Macquaries' focus on reformation was their commitment to preventing crime amongst the children of the convicts, and indeed the children of the free settlers. To this end, new schools were built in Sydney and the outlying settlements. Among these was a new type of school, the Charity School, one intended for the children of the poorer people, many of whom were struggling convicts. By way of education the Macquaries aimed to save the next generation from poverty and social disadvantage. They did not want the Colony's children to face the undermining social conditions experienced by many of the convicts in their native Britain. As the Macquaries promoted church attendance for all adults, not least by setting their own example of devout attendance at Sunday worship, so did they publicly endorse Sunday School for the children. Their aim was to plant religious principles in the young minds of the next generation when they were most receptive and impressionable.

An important observation should be made here about the Macquaries' thinking on crime. As they saw the causes of much crime predominantly lying in human weakness in the face of malign social circumstances or in a personal morality wanting in the face of temptation, so these were the factors to be addressed if crime was to be prevented amongst the general population. Similarly, these were the factors to be addressed in the lives of the individual convicts if they were to be turned from crime and their lives renewed. Here we see in the Macquaries' thinking a rare conceptual consistency across their approach to prevention and their approach to renewal. It is a powerful understanding. An idea, some will think, rendering the attitudes of the day to punishment most problematic. An idea rendering the epithets 'crude', 'stop-gap', 'ineffective expedient' appropriate to punishment as a general preventative measure to much crime. This largely unappreciated idea of the Macquaries is something to which we must return in a subsequent chapter.

* * *

The present and the previous chapters have set out and explained Governor Macquarie's policies as governor for the treatment of the convicts. These policies emanated from Government House, the seat and symbol of the Governor's autocratic powers. Nonetheless, some shrewd and close observers of the Governor and his wife thought they detected another seat, another symbol, of power, one perhaps greater though out of the way. Its physical representation took the form of a chair carved into the low rocky headland on the eastern promontory of Farm Cove. It became known as Mrs. Macquarie's Chair. It was a place where Mrs. Macquarie always liked to come when in Sydney, so relieving herself of the city with its raucousness, its bodily smells, and the rough, disorderly types so much in evidence. So Macquarie, always wanting to delight his beloved Elizabeth, had the seat carved there for her pleasure. There she would come alone to relax, to read and to paint ... and to think. Now there's the rub! So whispered the suspicious observers. Some actually were convinced she would like to have been the Governor. A few thought she was their governor – in effect. And they were close to the truth. Today, afar, we see the physical chair as now empty (see p.116). But if we were to sit upon it, we should surely sense Mrs. Macquarie's ghostly presence. It

Mrs. Macquarie's Chair.
c1870. Botanic Gardens,
Sydney.

is proper that we do. Though, as we shall see, something very much more is required of us by way of a tribute to her.

It was from this chair Mrs. Macquarie would steel herself to steel Macquarie in the face of opposition; it was from this chair she would steel her body, though often it be weakened by poor health, as she joined him in battle. For opposition he indeed did face; and battle he did engage in. When some of the Colony's turbulent settlers decided they had had enough of the Macquarie policies, it was on him, not her, they directed their firepower. To their opposition we now turn, in this next chapter. Along with the leading settlers, Macquarie faced the ire of his judges. This, and the effects of all this conflict on Macquarie, are dealt with in the following chapter. Then comes a chapter on the opposition Macquarie faced from Britain. These three chapters together give an account of what is described here as the 'other way' – the 'wrong way' – of dealing with crime and of treating criminals.

Chapter 6

The Macquaries' Enemies in the Colony: Part 1

T HERE WERE THREE principal groups from whom the Macquaries faced significant – indeed, undermining – opposition within the Colony, namely, a number of the military officers, a coterie of the leading free settlers, and the judges. The first and the second are the subject of this chapter. While each one broadly supported the views of the other, each was particularly troubled by a different aspect of the Macquaries' attitudes towards and policies for the convicts. We look at the free settlers through the malignant eyes of Samuel Marsden and John Macarthur. These two larger-than-life characters were introduced earlier, the descriptions of them and the accompanying image there (see p.56) unmistakeably anticipating trouble for any governor who contested their particular interests. In regard to Marsden and Macarthur, though many others thought like them and supported them, they were the most prominent figures; more importantly, each of them had powerful sympathizers who prosecuted their cause in Britain. As for the judges, the Judge-Advocate, Ellis Bent, was the only judge in the Colony until 1814, when a Supreme Court was established with his brother Jeffery as its head. Ellis was a mild-mannered, reasonable man whose quarrel with Macquarie came early, on what for him was a matter of legal principle. The Governor also rowed with Jeffery, whose gross unreasonableness in so much of his behaviour made it impossible to determine whether he was contesting an issue on principle, for self-interest, or simply to satisfy his maniacal, querulous nature. As for the military officers, we deal with them in passing and as a group. They are less significant for this story, for while they upset Macquarie, they were never going to cause him real trouble in London. More particularly, the basis of their dissatisfaction with Macquarie carried no fundamental policy implications for the running of the Colony.

REGIMENTAL OFFICERS

The regimental officers, by virtue of their place in the Establishment, enjoyed well-founded claims to social exclusivity in the Colony. Indeed, the senior officers attended Government House functions as of right. Moreover, a man's being invited to dine with the officers in their mess represented a degree of social acceptability just below that of the Governor's table. For this reason, Macquarie urged his fellow officers to entertain some of the leading emancipists and invite them to their formal dinners. The officers as a group were somewhat loath to do this, treating it as a diminution of their high status. Nevertheless, the senior officers of the 73rd Regiment acceded to the Governor's wishes. As their former commanding officer, he enjoyed a certain cachet in their eyes; and in any case friendships from this time remained. However, when this regiment was replaced by the 46th in 1815, a number of the officers were prepared to ignore his wishes, even surreptitiously expressing their hostility towards him – one means was by declining invitations to Government House parties.

SAMUEL MARSDEN

Samuel Marsden, a Yorkshireman by birth, first met Macquarie and Mrs Macquarie in 1810. Aged 45 at the time, he was already a long-serving magistrate, and soon to be appointed the Colony's Principal Chaplain. He grew up in the Christian faith, and as a young man quickly discovered his own divine spirit was closest to what he believed to be the God of the evangelicals in the Church of England. Indeed, through these circles he was to meet the great evangelical, and the man who was to become his patron – a man whom we have already met – William Wilberforce. It was this great who succeeded in persuading the 28 year-old Marsden to accept the post of assistant chaplain in New South Wales.

Wilberforce must have seen something very special about Marsden. A certain saintliness together with a zeal to bring the sinner to repentance would have been prerequisites for the godly man's blessing. In regard to this, note, Wilberforce thought of the Colony as a black hole of sin. Perhaps as well he saw a man with the character to impose himself on

**'Revd. Sam'l. Marsden'
(c1810).** G. Terry, artist and
engraver. Copy from and
made by the National
Portrait Gallery, London
(NPG D46189).

a wild frontier; and Marsden's patent physical strength and boundless
energy would have added well to the mix. What an irony, that the
man whose life's work played a major part in inspiring Macquarie to
assume his own great cause, was the man responsible for Marsden, the
man who would do so much to undermine Macquarie's mission. The
present portrait of Marsden was completed in England not long before
he returned to Australia after a period of absence. The line of his sight
is striking, do you not think? His eyes being cast as it were upward and

over, not worldly bound but heaven bent, perhaps imagining his God looking down on him with approval. What manner of man, what personal characteristics, do we perceive? Remoteness, coldness, self-satisfaction, earnestness, joylessness, saintliness? Patently, no winning charm here! Certainly not a man to whom even the good Elizabeth would warm. But then, 'good Elizabeth' seemed quite to enjoy the company of a man with a twinkle in his eye, even a hint of roguishness, one like William Wentworth, whom we meet later.

Wilberforce's recommendation proved to be a tragic misjudgement, one perhaps betraying his naïve understanding of the human condition. The fact is, a penal colony, a place where the vast majority of the population were convicts and ex-convicts, was not the place for Samuel Marsden. So many of its inhabitants had lived much or all of their lives on the outside of, or at the margins of, respectable society. When they came to the Colony they brought this lifestyle with them. Others did come from respectable, if often lowly, circumstances, yet the weaknesses responsible for their being there remained all about. More generally, among the free settlers and the convicts alike, moral chasteness and the sanctity of marriage were not always primary precepts. For Marsden, the problem was that this culture, so evident in the Colony, activated and brought to the fore some of the irrational elements of his spirituality hitherto lurking in the recesses of his mind. Along with this, it opened up earthly flaws in his clay. In fact, it was these personal weaknesses of Marsden's which led to his dramatic and splintering confrontations with the Macquaries. There were three matters of policy on which they clashed and which are relevant to this story, namely, punishment, social elevation, and the Female Orphan School.

Marsden, the chaplain, did not come to the Colony as a pastor-shepherd, bent on gently guiding the straying back to the fold, and unconditionally committed to providing comfort to the weak. No, he came as a chaplain-missionary. When Marsden entered Port Jackson for the first time he, like the Macquaries later, saw a blank canvas (see p.36). But the image he painted on it was very different. Marsden's was of a Biblical New Jerusalem where once fallen souls would under his exhortations turn to the worship and service of the God of his imaging. He did of course win converts, but all too few to mention, and he soon realized preaching was not going to change the Colony's seedy cultural climate – this population of apparently instinctively bad men and women was not to be transformed into a community of saints. As a consequence, his zeal become zealotry. With this, the dark view of God he held – God as a harsh judge – one perhaps underpinned by a strong punitive streak deep within him, now manifested itself in his consciousness. In this way, Marsden the magistrate soon came to pursue a course unconscionable to decent men, and to justify it as Divine will: if he could not lead this population to goodness, he would make the place more moral by flogging and flogging, and flogging again, the badness out of them. This he did, and thereby wrote himself into Australian history as 'The Flogging Parson'.

Macquarie was appalled at Marsden's approach to punishment. It was anathema to him. As we have seen, he was a most reluctant flogger. It was inhumane: he was despairing of every wanton lash; and he heard the cries of the needless pain it inflicted. He understood from experience the circumstances of much of the convicts' offending, and knew flogging would do little to deter them. Rather, he understood repeated floggings as something which would serve to break their spirits or harden their rebelliousness. All these aspects of Marsden's punishments troubled and saddened him. But what particularly enraged Macquarie was that this harshness would hazard his leading the convicts along the road – a road already strewn with pitfalls – to a new and productive life. Macquarie would not take it. As the autocrat he was, he treated Marsden's refusal to change his ways as insubordination. Thus Marsden, though an independent magistrate, received a ferocious dressing down at Government House. The Parson in response would have squirmed, perhaps quivered, for he did not cope well with such personal confrontations. From what we know of Marsden, he would have done no better than splutter, with a sanctimonious air, 'I try to serve my God'. How Macquarie would have enjoyed causing him such pain then; how he would have enjoyed recalling the event to Elizabeth some time later!

Macquarie's displeasure with Marsden's use and justification of condign – indeed brutal – punishment was an on-going affair. Indeed, the contention between them was aggravated by a dispute they had in the first year of his governorship. This was the appointment of Simeon Lord and Andrew Thompson, along with Marsden, as trustees and commissioners of the new turnpike road to be built between Sydney and the Hawkesbury. Marsden was outraged when he heard of his appointment. He fumed. 'How dare Macquarie! Not only does he insult me in private, now it is in public'. As Marsden saw it, he was being asked to work with, mix with, ex-convicts who continued to live immoral lives as fornicators, and in Lord's case also as a practitioner of fast financial footwork. This, then, was an appointment which could not but besmirch the sacredness of his high ecclesiastical office and ruin his personal reputation as a holy man of God. Huffing and puffing, he told Macquarie so. Macquarie exploded. An act of insubordination, one striking at the heart of one of his signature policies. This was enough to turn a man into an implacable foe. Marsden would be no exception.

What infused Macquarie's hostility to Marsden with hatred for Marsden were the motives underlying this decision. For Marsden, with the Colony run by men of the Devil, any hope of his bringing it to a state of decency, let alone it becoming a New Jerusalem, would be obliterated. No – this would herald the start of its decline into an immoral abyss. This was the motive of Marsden the chaplain. There was also the motive of Marsden the man. Marsden, the son of a blacksmith, had risen to a position of importance from one of social humbleness. He, and people like him, revelled in and wanted to continue enjoying their new-found importance. But for this, they had to keep the majority down. Marsden had not striven to rise in the sight of God and man, to serve with the fallen. Macquarie was frustrated beyond words with what he saw as Marsden's perverted take on religion, together with his spiritual and social elitism as a divine. How these things stuck in Macquarie's craw! It was no different for Elizabeth.

Another reason for the Governor and the Chaplain's divergence of views on the elevation of the convict was their different take on reform. Macquarie looked for the good in the convict, sought to encourage and cultivate this, and understood too much could not be expected too soon in view of the past circumstances of the lives of many of them. In comparison, Marsden appeared only to see the bad, and was determined to 'convert' it out of them, or to frighten it out of them with talk of hellfire; both with the expectation of more-or-less instant results. Failing this, they were to be given up on, and treated as outcasts. For Macquarie, reform was not categorical, and a convict did not have to tick all the defining boxes all the time. Moreover, Macquarie was well aware of the private lives of many of the elite and respectable; and he could not but wonder with good reason whether his social-climbing chaplain would have refused to serve with the Prince Regent on moral grounds.

Marsden's third conflict with Macquarie centred on the building of the Female Orphan School (see p.88). Actually, the contretemps involved Mrs. Macquarie, as the School was a project most close to her heart. Both Marsden and Mrs. Macquarie agreed that the orphanage for girls should not remain in the heart of Sydney. For Marsden, it was a catalyst for much vice in the area, being so close to the docks and the Rocks. Moreover, this exposure led to many of the girls adopting prostitution as a means of

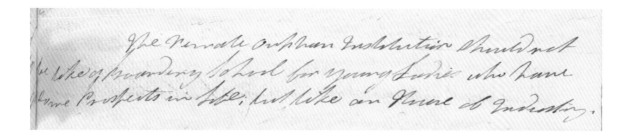

Samuel Marsden to Commissioner Bigge.
15th March, 1821. Digital image from the National Archives, Kew, London.

support once they left the orphanage. Mrs. Macquarie agreed. But she wanted more from her new orphanage. Recall, as important as it was for the girls to receive basic education and training, they must also have instilled within themselves a sense of personal worth and self-esteem, a feeling of being able to make something of their lives. Without this, they surely risked a future as victims of others' financial greed and sexual appetites. And it would certainly be hard for them to raise themselves to a better life than might have been theirs in Britain. Mrs. Macquarie would give them proof of their worth and potential; the Female Orphan School – their home – would be as grand as the Governor's country residence – her home – across the river.

Such thinking was foreign to Marsden's nature. Moreover, he did not want to understand such dangerous and foolish thinking. We hear his outraged, disbelieving expostulations. Girl's with the stain of convictry rising to pollute the Colony's moral climate! Extravagant spending on girls who inevitably would – at least should, for the Colony's moral health – remain at the lower levels of society! Such wicked waste! God will surely punish us for our iniquity! So he went, on … and on. Indeed, he later would demean himself for history in a letter to the Commissioner of the Inquiry into the Colony (see the following chapter). There he observed:

> The Female Orphan Institution should not be like a Boarding School for young Ladies who have some Prospects in Life, but like a House of Industry.

And here are those words in his own hand (see above).[16]

The Female Orphan School was a project on which Marsden worked with Mrs. Macquarie. She would have been well-acquainted with his thinking on the matter. He undoubtedly would have been the recipient of pieces of her mind. It must have been quite traumatic for him. This is apparent in another sentence from the same letter – we shall return to this in our sketch of Mrs. Macquarie's character in the final chapter. Save to say, it is almost enough to have Marsden's sternest critics feeling sorry for him. Recall, Marsden cowered in the face of personal attack, and Mrs. Macquarie shot point-blank.

Marsden, among all those who opposed Macquarie in the Colony, was the one who most raised his blood pressure, most caused him to lose sleep, most caused him to rail. He could understand the opposition of others, driven as they were by greed and other human failings. And he knew Christian ministers, like all people, were not perfect. But! How, just how, could a Christian minister base his whole ministry on such a malignant view of his fallen charges, those whom God had put in his care? We hear Macquarie bewailing, 'How on Sundays as God's representative can he lead the convicts to shining spiritual uplands, when on Mondays as a magistrate his floggings leave them prostrated and bloodied on the ground? How can he care for them when they know he regards them as lesser beings?' What, of course, cast Marsden's view so strongly into relief was his saintly Elizabeth's practice of love and understanding towards the convicts.

Marsden represented a serious threat for Macquarie. Marsden detested him as he detested Marsden. This Macquarie well knew. The problem was, Marsden did not keep his behind-the-scenes attacks on him within the Colony. Rather, he actively conveyed calumnies of all sorts and magnitudes to his powerful and like-minded sympathizers in Britain. In writing he would lament to anyone who would listen: convicts were not being adequately punished; and the immoral emancipists could look forward to being put in positions of power. Woe! While he scored no direct hits against Macquarie, his persistent lobbying on his God's behalf contributed to the creation of a climate of opinion in Britain that the Colony under Macquarie was not serving its intended purposes. Do we not hear Macquarie crying out, 'Will no one rid me of this troublesome priest?'[17] Poor Lachlan!

Marsden too was suffering. His dream of a New Jerusalem was fast fading. He was not being applauded and rewarded in the Colony for his faithful services to his God; rather, he was under cruel attack, as though from the Devil. 'Fallen Man did not understand him', he would wail. In 1814, when he could stand no more, he took himself off to New Zealand as a missionary to the Maoris. There he would minister unto the Islanders; there he would add souls to God's kingdom. To this end, Marsden put in a substantial sum of his own money, a gesture signifying his sincerity and contrary to his critics' representation of him as greedy. Moreover, Marsden's venturing into this largely unknown world was a testimony to his physical courage. Indeed, his work with the Church Missionary Society is why he is revered in many quarters today, and is represented in London's National Portrait Gallery.

As Marsden aged, a mournful fog increasingly enveloped his mind. In this life he had dedicated himself to God's will, not man's convenience, and for this he was now suffering – of this he convinced himself. What could he do but spend much time imploring his God to understand this, and to reward him with His glory in the next life? Mrs. Macquarie, when her mind was farthest from her Bible, might have hoped her God saw it differently.

None of these things would have happened if the great, though worldly-unwise, William Wilberforce had not persisted in urging Marsden to take himself to the convict Colony for its own good. Thus, most sadly: the Colony's convicts were deprived of a nurturing Principal Chaplain; a God-fearing governor was without the type of religious support he so desired for his work; other lands and peoples were deprived of the goodness and talents of a man who could have offered them much; and a good man, a man of God, largely wasted his calling, and suffered.

JOHN MACARTHUR

John Macarthur too beheld with anticipation a blank canvas upon entering Port Jackson (see p.36). Soon an idea had him licking his lips, though he would take some time to settle on the detail. This represented the second ambitious vision for the Colony antithetical to the Macquaries', though one quite different from that of Marsden's. The grounds of Marsden's vision were, as we have seen, religious, and infused with puritanism and elitism. Macarthur's were financial, fortified by greed and elitism. Macarthur dreamt of a society structured around, owned and led by, a landed gentry. In this world, the convicts' ambitions would be limited to little more than comfortable colonial serfdom. Macarthur – like Marsden – wanted the Colony to be a better society, but it would necessarily come at the expense – social and financial – of the convicts. And, it would come at the expense of the Macquaries realizing their dreams for their poor, benighted convicts – something the shrewd Macarthur well understood and anticipated.

Macarthur was a Devonian, a sometime farmer, who came to the Colony as an army officer in 1790, at the age of twenty-three. As we have seen, the pattern of this perturbator's colonial life was one of serious troublemaking. Indeed, this behaviour, as a means of resolving conflict and

'John Macarthur'. Copied from S. Macarthur Onslow (Ed.), *Some Early Records of the Macarthurs of Camden.* Angus and Robertson, Sydney, 1914.

advancing his interests, had the quality of a deeply innate characteristic rather than a rationally adopted strategy. Yet, despite a life led in the midst of self-generated, unproductive public chaos, Macarthur continued to progress his farming interests. He envisaged a future for the Colony in the production of the finest wool, and he himself as the supplier of choice to the growing and apparently insatiable English market. This dream was as broad in scope as it was bold in execution. At the beginning of the century on a visit to England he turned on his charm and applied his brilliant entrepreneurial skills. There he acquired some of the finest sheep from the royal flocks – yes, the royal flocks – along with a large grant of some of the best land in the Colony on which to graze them. His genius was to toughen these temperamental merinos by interbreeding them with a hardier beast, so producing an animal offering the finest wool, though one able to thrive in the harshness of the colonial environment. Though his part in this work was interrupted in 1809 by his exile in England, the programme continued in the hands of his extremely able, level-headed wife, Elizabeth. When the British authorities allowed him to return in 1817, Macarthur was set to become 'Father of the Australian wool industry'.

Macquarie, well knowing Macarthur's reputation, must have quivered somewhat on hearing of his return. Meeting up with him was part curiosity, part duty for Macquarie. Not so for Macarthur, who was most keen to meet up with the Governor. For the pastoralist was more enthusiastic than ever to develop his wool interests, to build up great riches for himself. For this he needed the Governor's blessing in the form of material support. Opposite is the image of the man Macquarie met, a portrait of Macarthur, gentleman pastoralist, then aged about fifty.

Now, here is a man projecting a refined, born-to-rule demeanour; a man who sees himself properly surrounded by the accoutrements of affluence and style. A man who considers you with a dignified aloofness. A man who rules by virtue of who he is; one who does not require you to vote for him. Nonetheless, scratch the image, and all the malignancy and unease portrayed in the caricature of him is still there, though now in the layer below (see p.56). All his earlier passions, his blinkered self-interest, are there – but now no longer naked. His view of the Colony as ripe for the picking is still there. His eyes have mellowed, but as a measure of the man, deceive somewhat. Now, rather than attacking those who would thwart him, impulsively, wildly, without thought for the consequences, his response will be measured, delayed, secretive; he will be prepared to play the long game, to wait for the time most favourable to his cause. About this he will be relaxed. He might even first turn on his considerable charm. Yet at heart he is every bit as dangerous; indeed, his refined methods render him more dangerous.

For many men in Macarthur's position, their primary reason for wanting to see Macquarie promptly would have been to express their warmest appreciation to the Governor and Mrs. Macquarie for their acts of kindness to his wife and family while he was in exile. Perhaps even to satisfy their curiosity as to the manner of this 'nice' first gentleman and first lady, with a view to a future friendship? But no, for outside the bosom of his loving family, Macarthur was hard-boiled and direct.

True to himself, when he met Macquarie, he soon got down to business. He boldly requested ever more hundreds of acres of prime – the best – grazing land so he might continue to escalate his production of the finest wool, along with a generous supply of cheap labour – convicts – to work it. O, and by the way, this entreaty followed his Elizabeth's having slipped into one of her social chats with Macquarie's Elizabeth an enticement: this was along the lines of how the two families could profit hugely from co-operation in the development of the wool industry.

In any case, Macquarie refused the land Macarthur coveted west of the Blue Mountains. What is more, to compound Macarthur's rage, Macquarie granted fifty-acre parcels of this pastoral Arcadia, along with assigned men, to each of five hard-working emancipists and five free-settler small farmers. That was it; Macquarie was the enemy! For the sake of the Colony, it must be ridded of him, the sooner the better. Thus, within ten years Macarthur was attacking a second governor. This time it was with subtlety and finesse. His strategy was to brief against Macquarie in the circles of power and influence in Britain; these were people he had cultivated and who regarded him as a man of merit, these were those who thought of him as the one with a vision for the Colony suited to Britain's interests. It was a vision he developed, broadened, refined and buttressed over the next few years. He would hold his idea of a plantation society over until the time was ripe.

The Macarthur vision for the Colony was really a vision for the wool industry, and this was really a plan for the future wealth and prestige of himself and his beloved family. Though this was not the way he presented it. Macarthur's starting position was that the Colony's future economic prosperity lay with the private sector. Moreover, to this end, one part of this sector stood out, namely, the wool industry, by way of its potential to export the finest wool known. In none of the other industries was there the potential for such untold wealth to be unlocked. Certainly, individuals were acquiring great individual wealth with their manufacturing, merchandising and mercantile interests – Lord was a paradigmatic example. But here the capacity for expansion was limited, as was consumer demand. In contrast, the world wanted the Colony's wool; and great virgin expanses of some of the finest grazing land lay to the south of Sydney, and to the west of the Blue Mountains. This opportunity would best be seized by way of an industry organised around large-scale estates, ones properly managed, and adequately resourced. In Macarthur's mind, each of the three elements involved the convicts, to his benefit. What about to their benefit? Hmm!

Large-scale organisation. Large-scale meant farms of at least 10,000 acres, with the number of estates being limited to forty or fifty.

Proper management. The ownership and management of these properties would be in the hands of a body of substantial and honourable men, ones experienced in primary production, who had the acumen to develop their landholdings, the assets and character to persist in the face of adversity, and the manner to bring the best out of lesser men.

Enter Macarthur and his interests. He took it as self-evident that he was the man par excellence. You see it in his portrait as the pastoralist.

Resourcing. Only the government possessed sufficient resources to meet the industry's needs. These were land and manpower. The government alone could grant large swathes of the best land to individuals; it alone controlled the assignment of the large numbers of convicts. Mind you, only men and women from the best of the convicts were wanted: those who would apply themselves to work, whose minds were on pleasing their masters not escaping from them; skilled mechanics who could keep the wheels turning and the infrastructure intact; those with the muscle to clear the land and do the heavy lifting.

As for others in the Colony with legitimate claims to convict labour – the government, along with the smaller farmers and the businesspeople, many of whom were emancipists – well, in the interests of the Colony – yes, the Colony – they would just have to make do with what was left. So be it.

There was also attached to the proposal a hidden nasty, one put there for the convenience of the landowners. It relates to the sanctioning of misbehaving assigned convicts. Macarthur wanted the power to punish minor offenders, one now invested in the magistrates, transferred to the landowners.

So, what was in it for the British government; what was in it for Macquarie? Well, the large landowners would maintain and manage the convicts at their own expense. Professionally managed work, absent idleness, would be the convicts' punishment. Moreover, the scheme would be more reformative of the convict than current practice. For in the countryside the convicts would be away from the cities with their ready temptations of crime and vice. More positively, in the solitude of rural life, the convicts could contemplate the evil and foolishness of their past ways, and commit to putting these in their pasts. All this, at no expense to the British government. And for Macquarie, as governor? A thriving wool industry supplying the ever-expanding British market, and with this generating great wealth for the Colony. What was not to like about all that? Macarthur's linking of wool and convict in a synergetic economic partnership, once again demonstrated his imagination and shrewdness as a businessman.

Did Macarthur have any qualms about his scheme: possible abuses in its operation; inherent unfairness in its conception? In regard to the former, yes; in respect of the latter, no. Macarthur did acknowledge the possibility of the abuse of these convicts as workers. It might come from an exploitative landowner, wanting too much of them; it might come from a cruel overseer, mercilessly punishing a convict behind the master's back. But Macarthur quickly dismissed these as no more than potential problems. He would allow a regime of independent and vigilant inspection. Though, as he well knew, but did not formally acknowledge, this would be difficult to implement in practice, especially on very large, far-flung estates. The reality was for Macarthur that the wool industry being in the hands of substantial and honourable men would be sufficient to ensure minimal abuse. As an aside to this, it should be noted, lest an alternative conclusion be all too hastily drawn, Macarthur was reputed to take the physical welfare of his own convicts most seriously. He fed and accommodated them well, offered them indulgences as deserved, disciplined them with the greatest restraint; in return, his reward was an apparently very contented convict workforce and good productivity.

In any case, consider what his scheme would be replacing, he would helpfully inform the authorities. Landownership now largely in the hands of adventurers and otherwise insubstantial men; men without sufficient drive, expertise or resources, who did not sufficiently work or adequately supervise their convicts, and who indulged them whether deserved or not. How could the wool industry, so mismanaged, contribute to the Colony's economic growth let alone the convicts' reform? It could not, he would claim. Indeed, he would cite the low productivity and high failure rates of these small landholders, themselves often former convicts. A malign distortion; financial self-interest trumping social justice. Macarthur well knew not a few convicts as emancipist farmers did go on and prosper. And while many little more than made a 'go' of it, yet did they live better lives than would have been theirs in Britain. Both Governor and Pastoralist took pleasure in these same facts, though how different the basis of their pleasure! Macquarie saw success, and treated this as self-evident evidence of damaged lives progressing toward renewal. Macarthur saw failure, and treated this as self-evident evidence in favour of his scheme. Self-interest ruling his mind, blinding his vision, Macarthur gave no thought to how the current arrangements might be improved in the convicts' interests.

How might the Macquaries, whose regard for the convicts and their futures was so different, have reflected on Macarthur's scheme? They might have started by asking themselves some questions. For the great mass of convicts caught up in this scheme – this will include some of the most skilled and diligent workers – what would it mean for their lives then and into the future? Let us consider this. These men and women, as convicts, would be on huge estates, west of the Blue Mountains, isolated, a large town not being within easy reach, and Sydney being out of practical reach. This would keep the convicts away from the temptations of vice and crime all too prevalent in these places – certainly. But, it would also keep them away from many of those innocent pleasures – carnivals, sporting events, lively crowds enjoying themselves – which delight and raise the human spirit, and for many make life worth living. Keep them away too from experiencing at first hand good lives in action; perhaps too from being taken under the wing of the more beneficent among the free. As important, keep them away from seeing, or at least hearing about, people once like themselves but who, upon emancipation, had worked their way up to a better quality of life and a higher status. And among the gossip, there would be talk of some of their type who were even 'mates' of the Governor and his wife. Now, there's something to raise the head and ambition of a lowly convict a little higher! How different it would be under Macarthur's proposal. With nothing to lift their spirits, no examples of elevated emancipists, no unexpected adventure just around the corner, no zest for life, how could the convicts not develop a servile mentality, not become reconciled to the present, not despair of a worthwhile future? Surely it would take a man or woman of great imagination and strength of character to envisage their emancipist self not as a worker and order-taker but as a master and order-giver, to anticipate a future not of drudgery and survival but one of interest and comfort. And, of course, there would be no encouragement from the man himself, their pastoralist supremo, John Macarthur. Moreover, against those few convicts who might dream of themselves one day becoming a Macarthur, and who had the pluck to take the first steps, there was in the proposal a last line of defence, one representing an insurmountable barrier, namely, the new emancipist would not be eligible for a manageable grant of land and the convicts he would need to work it. To Macquarie, small land grants were a mechanism to facilitate the new emancipists setting out on their independent lives. The success rate of this measure might have been less than hoped for, and might have lowered productivity somewhat, yet it makes perfect sense when the priority is the individual convict's reform, not the Colony's economic productivity. Macquarie's specific policies, and the reason for their differences from Macarthur's proposals, follow from two powerful and radical ideas as controlling, namely: first, the Colony now and into the foreseeable future is to be a place for the reform of the convict, and thence a home for their prosperity and enjoyment, a home of which to be proud, and in which they will participate fully; second, the Colony must be structured so as to favour, nay facilitate, convict reform – reform is not something to be treated as incidental, nor solely up to the convicts themselves.

Macarthur's proposal for the wool industry was a work of monumental self-interest. A bounteous supply of cheap convict labour producing an endless supply of experienced but unambitious and subservient workers as emancipists. Moreover, over the years there would be no danger of these individuals developing by accretion into a sizable body of small landowners whose presence would undermine the monopolistic interests of Macarthur and his ilk. Nor would there be a danger of emancipists achieving political power. For Macarthur's proposal envisaged this small body of substantial and honourable men growing wealthy, very wealthy, and becoming in effect a powerful ruling aristocracy.

There was more to Macarthur's vision of a servile, serving convictry than financial self-regard and power for its own sake. It was also about control, and it arose from Macarthur's very malign view of the convicts and their character. To him, convicts were by nature recalcitrant, and in the circumstances of the Colony were treacherous. Indeed, they represented a potential threat to good order and a danger to those who would keep them in their proper place. Freedom must be theirs eventually – this the law requires. Let it then be a cautious freedom, one never allowing them the power open to the free settler. The following three opinions of Macarthur's well illustrate his sentiments regarding the convicts, their character, and what he considered to be the consequences for policy.

On the state of convict discipline and control, from a letter he personally wrote to the Commissioner of the Inquiry into the Colony:[18]

I feel great hesitation in offering any suggestions respecting the regulating and rewarding the Convicts for their services, because no arrangement, however wise, can, in in my opinion, effect any material change for the better, whilst the practice is persevered in, of indiscriminately granting land to Convicts, and whilst the most active and vicious, are permitted to roam through the country, tempting the servants, by their ill example to neglect their Master's business, and seducing them to commit depredation upon any property within their reach.

On the idea of emancipists serving on juries, from his evidence to the Commission of Inquiry:

> … I think it would be an act of the greatest temerity to remove the Legal incapacity of men to sit as Jurors, who have been Convicts – Most of these unfortunate individuals cherish the highest degree of Malignance towards those, who have not suffered similar degradation with themselves, and Nothing affords them a sincerer gratification then to sink either by contrivances or Calumnies, respectable Men to their own level …[19]

And who, according to Macarthur, was to blame for the policies and practices so inimical to the future prosperity of the wool industry, and so conducive to the current disorder in the Colony? And what was the gravamen of Macarthur's complaint? To him the answers were plain and simple:

[a] democratic feeling has already taken deep root in the Colony, in consequence of the absurd and mischievous policy, pursued by Governor Macquarrie [sic] – and as there is already a strong combination amongst that class of persons, it cannot be too soon opposed with vigour.[20]

Recall, Macarthur had determined to hold his policy until the time was ripe. This he judged to be Britain's Commission of Inquiry into the Colony. The preceding three opinions together reveal, in all their darkness, Macarthur's bigotry, elitism, and malign view of the convicts.

How dramatic is the gap between the Macquaries' perspective of the convicts' character from that of Macarthur's: the convict as morally worthy, as against the convict as manifestly bad! How dramatic is the gap between the Macquaries' perspective of the convicts' future from that of Macarthur's: citizen go-getter as against civilian automaton!

Macarthur's personal, egregious character flaws explain much. Take first his avarice, one to be satisfied at the expense of all others. Related to this, was the moral malady from which many such people suffer, namely, the perception that only money really matters. Thus, the focus of government support should be large-scale wool production, because it offered the greatest economic benefit. No thought for the growing Colony benefiting from having other activity, such as manufacturing. No thought of a society with large numbers of little people beavering away under their own initiative perhaps being a more psychologically healthy one. As for the public sphere, Macarthur viewed Macquarie's policy of expending large sums of money and large numbers of skilled labour on fine, ornamental public buildings and attractive streetscapes as absurd, indeed negligent. It perhaps never occurred to Macarthur – gentleman in presentation, but at his core a rough diamond – that architectural beauty might give pleasure to benighted men and women, make them proud, buoy their spirits, raise their levels of activity. Then there was his manifest elitism clouding his view: wisdom and honour were to be found exclusively at the big end of town; thus, it is with them the Colony's controlling power should reside. Finally, there was his deep-seated prejudice against the convict. If the picture he painted of them had been anything like true, most convict work would have been at the end of a lash, the many convicts would not have enjoyed almost total freedom during their penal servitude, and the Colony would not have been moving forwards to ever-sunnier uplands.

Yet we miss the force of Macarthur's ideas if we see them only from this perspective. The fact is, Macarthur's proposals presented an arguable view of how the Colony might be structured socially so as to best satisfy the British view of it as a place of punishment and a permanent home for those it hoped would never again set foot in their green and pleasant land. How attractive to the British government, ever anxious to reduce the financial burden on them of this most convenient, albeit insignificant, little outpost! Not only this, but something they wanted – a guaranteed and plentiful supply of the finest wool – to boot.

Poor Lachlan and Elizabeth's passion to see their beloved convicts enjoying, profiting from, and running the Colony was under attack from not one but two leading thrusters, Samuel Marsden and John Macarthur. For Marsden, a powerful vice-infested convictry would pollute the Colony's moral fabric to its very core and precipitate its social decline. For Macarthur, the growth of a powerful convictry would be at the expense of the Colony's economic growth and prosperity; at the expense too of his acquiring of wealth. You see, Marsden would not allow himself to comprehend that the convicts, like he himself, had be made in the image of God. And Macarthur did not care that the convicts, like he himself, might want to get on in this world and experience those consequent higher human emotions. Both Marsden and Macarthur were dangerous opponents. In regard to Macquarie's future, they were equally potent by way of their British connections. In regard to that which the Macquaries held to be good, Macarthur represented the greater danger – Macarthur's proposals were enticing; Marsden's views could easily be dismissed as eccentric.

There was another significant opponent of the Macquaries and their treatment of the convicts. It was the judge, Ellis Bent. His significance lay largely in the content of his views he held rather than in the potency of his opposition. If Marsden and Macarthur were dense thorn bushes, then Bent was more a single prickle. Though as a prickle, he enhances our picture of Macquarie the man. To him we now turn.

Chapter 7

The Macquaries' Enemies in the Colony: Part 2

T HIS IS THE second of the two chapters on the Macquaries' enemies in the Colony and the nature of their opposition. In the former chapter it was the divine, Samuel Marsden, and the pastoralist, John Macarthur. Here we deal with the ire of a man of the law, Ellis Bent. This chapter concludes with a discussion of the effects of all this conflict on the Governor, Lachlan Macquarie.

ELLIS BENT

The Judge-Advocate during the first five years of Macquarie's governorship was one, Ellis Bent. Born in 1783, the son of a gentleman, and Cambridge educated, he was admitted to the Bar in 1805. In a few short years he established himself as a barrister of some eminence. This brought him to the favourable attention of Castlereagh, whom we have already met. Castlereagh thought it was time a properly trained lawyer filled the important post of Judge-Advocate in the Colony. He turned to Bent, who duly obliged. We see him from around Macquarie's time in this portrait (opposite).

Bent and Macquarie, and their respective wives, both journeyed to the Colony on the same ship. Bent was, as this image suggests, a most affable man. On the long voyage the two couples necessarily mixed a lot, and indeed found mutual enjoyment in one another's company. The Macquaries must have anticipated with delight the friendship continuing in the Colony, for a remote convict colony might appear a very lonely place to a governor and his wife. A governor who was seen be seen to

Ellis Bent (c1800). Digital image from the National Library of Australia, Canberra (PIC Screen 41 #R119).

play favourites courted conflict; in any case, in such a place there might be few whose status was sufficiently elevated to command, let alone be congenial to, the company of a gubernatorial couple. Macquarie showed his pleasure in having Bent as the Colony's Judge-Advocate by building him a very fine town house. Also boding well for Bent's tenure was his being possessed of a benign and balanced nature, one without egregious character flaws. Unlike Marsden, he was not a moral crusader, who thought of his punishments as a means to others' goodness. Unlike Macarthur, he was not one overwhelmed by blind self-interest, who would callously cruel the lives of others to achieve his ends. Unlike both of these men, he was not a larger-than-life character, who was driven to impose himself on the Colony. More positively, his instincts were comfortable in a policy climate favouring the humane treatment of the convicts. Does not Bent's expression, as captured by the artist, bespeak these things? Yet in the relationship between Bent and Macquarie, which promised so much professionally to the Colony, and personally to Macquarie, fine cracks soon appeared, followed by widening fissures, then tears. So how did this come about?

The role of Judge-Advocate was a big one, with its multiplicity of duties together encompassing many facets of colonial life. The holder of the position was responsible for the administration of justice. He presided over the Governor's Court in criminal matters and over the civil court; he was responsible for the magistrates stationed around the Colony; and it was his duty to decide the legal validity, together with the clarity and consistency, of ordinances drawn up by the Governor. In the first two of these, he played a major role in the punishment of offenders; in the last of these he had the final say in the running of much of colonial life. That there was the potential for conflict between a governor and his judge-advocate is patent. But its actual happening will be almost inevitable when an autocratic governor with zealous views about the running of the colony, including the punishment of offenders, meets a legally sure-footed and conscientious judge-advocate, one raised in the tradition of judicial independence. Now, we know Macquarie was the quintessential former. And we can readily appreciate a man like Bent, an English barrister of growing eminence, now exercising judicial functions, might be in the character of the latter. In regard to this, bear in mind, while Bent performed judicial functions, he was not actually a judge – his independence was limited. This inch was Macquarie's ell.

The most contentious matter between the two of relevance to this story arose from the power residing with a governor to pardon offenders, including convicts, undergoing punishment. To Bent's legalistic mind, it was a power to be exercised lightly and rarely. Such a case might be one in which continued punishment would cause undue suffering to an offender, and which was not foreseeable at the time of sentencing. The problem was this was at odds with Macquarie's personal utilitarian view of the pardon: namely, a mechanism by which a governor could lessen what he considered to be in the circumstances of the case too harsh a punishment on the judge's part, and properly for his use as often as he saw the need arising. By way of this practice, Macquarie would overrule sentences in cases where he considered an offender's reform should take priority over their punishment. By 1815 it all became too much for Bent, who felt something needed to be said. In a despatch to the Secretary of State for the Colonies, Earl Bathurst, he lamented:

> It is not seldom that I meet in the streets of Sydney with persons, upon whom but shortly before I have been under the necessity of passing the sentence of death, or of some other punishment intended to be exemplary.[21]

Here is Bent's complaint (above), extracted directly from that despatch.[22]

The second matter of contention related to whether ex-convicts should be allowed to participate in the administration of justice. You will recall Macquarie thought a reformed emancipist should resume their place in society forfeited by virtue of their offending. In its application, Macquarie's mind ventured into areas where reasonable men in London thought a reasonable man would not go. They were wrong. Macquarie saw no barrier to lawyers, once convicts and now emancipists, appearing for parties in the courts. To disallow them their rightful means of a livelihood would surely represent a malign prejudice. Bent was not comfortable with the idea. Nonetheless, he was prepared to allow their appearing in civil matters and in the lesser role of agent, at least until there were some lawyers in the Colony who had come free. His reasoning rested on practical considerations: without legally trained people guiding the parties, court business would become cumbersome. Now, this pragmatism was at odds with Macquarie's principled argument. Conflict was inevitable once two or three free lawyers came to the Colony. In fact, it came earlier. A free lawyer did come in 1814; yet, he came not to practise in the courts but to rule over them, as head of the newly created Supreme Court. He was trouble.

His name was Jeffery Bent, and he was the older brother of Ellis. Haughty and arrogant, he was aloof and keen to be seen as not one of the people. His behaviour and demands were all calculated to serve the elevation of himself and his Court. As part of this thinking, he would not allow ex-convict lawyers to practise in his Court. He would rather close his Court, the inconvenience to innocent parties notwithstanding, until properly trained barristers arrived as free settlers. He would give not an inch to the peculiar nature and special needs of the place. Now, there was a case to be made for avoiding any practice potentially undermining the status of the law, especially in a convict colony. But Bent was principally driven by the motive of self. There was also a catalyst at work here; it was Bent's instinctively querulous nature. What made Jeffery Bent a more problematic character for Macquarie was his malign influence over his wavering younger brother. At Jeffery's instigation, Ellis also closed the Governor's Court to ex-convict lawyers.

One matter on which the two brothers thought similarly, and about which Ellis Bent was certain long before his brother's arrival, was the inappropriateness of ex-convicts serving as magistrates. How could there be about such men an air of certain honour and moral gravitas? When the law was not administered with such honour and gravitas, how could it weigh upon the mind of the would-be villain? This, one might have heard Bent ask rhetorically in conversation with Macquarie.

The third matter of contention between Ellis Bent and Macquarie is to be found in the judge-advocate's duty of vetting ordinances proposed by the governor. The problem was, Bent often thought some of Macquarie's rules were inconsistent with the law or covered matters outside a governor's powers.

Broad and deep grew the conflict between them. Ellis Bent became increasingly restive over Macquarie's countermanding of his punishments. Macquarie become increasingly restive over what he saw as Bent's interfering with his vision for the Colony and in his running of his (yes 'his') Colony. Restiveness kindles hostility, quiet reason becomes strident, pettiness replaces dignity, the three together begetting estrangement.

To Ellis Bent, the former two actions by Macquarie undermined the majesty of the law; they surely risked public safety and civil obedience. And, in respect of the third matter, he was no more than carrying out his duty to restrain an autocrat – a would-be supremo – from breaching the boundaries imposed on him by the law of England. To Macquarie, however, his own actions represented nothing more than the measures necessary to implement his humane and honourable vision privileging convict reform and convict participation in the running of the Colony – the place was, after all, their home.

In this conflict between the two, Jeffery Bent did not have to expend too much energy fanning his brother's dissent – actually, in Macquarie's mind, this dissent represented rebellion. The problem was anticipated above. This honourable and intelligent man, educated in the English law and being inured to legal conventions at the highest level, was always at risk of experiencing conflict in performing conventional judicial work though without full judicial independence. Without a driven, no-nonsense reformer like Macquarie as governor, this potential conflict might have remained academic and lain dormant. But Bent did have Macquarie. This brought into rough relief the delicate legal question: in what respects and to what extent did the Judge-Advocate enjoy independence in light of the words in his commission, 'observe and follow the orders and directions of the Governor'? This Bent respected, but surely the intent of these words was not to render him a petty functionary. Do we not feel sympathy for this conscientious and honourable man in this predicament? How much easier it would have been for him to have served Macquarie as a lazy lickspittle!

By 1815 Macquarie could take no more. He laid the resolution of the conflict at the feet of the British government: the choice before them was the Bents' recall or his resignation. The Government sided with their Governor. In this sort of colonial conflict, this was the default position, for they well understood the governorship in any remote colony could be perilous. There had already been one rebellion in the Colony; they did not want a second. This is not to say the Government thought Macquarie was right. In fact, his free and ready use of the pardon, while it did not entail the actual flouting of the law, did represent an abuse of the spirit of the law and conventional practice.

Jeffery Bent, once back in England, and ever true to his nature, worked at blackening Macquarie's name. He adduced evidence – first colouring it – of what he believed to be Macquarie's unsuitability for the governorship, and then pressed, and pressed again and again, the need for his recall. In this, he joined forces with Marsden and Macarthur's henchmen. Their aim, a voice unable to be silenced, a force unable to be resisted; their motive, pure malice. All three willingly became cyphers for the wild and not-so wild malcontents of New South Wales.

Ellis Bent did not see again the land which had made him. He fell ill in 1815, and died feeling unfulfilled, unappreciated, and deeply sad. He would not achieve high judicial office, as would have been his reasonable expectation. His sincere and learned efforts to advance the authority of the courts in a place of legal uncertainty had come to naught. Worse still, history might remember him as the judge-advocate recalled for misperformance of the duties of office.

Again, it would be easy to paint Ellis Bent as another of the 'baddies', who thwarted the enlightened work of a good man for simple self-interest or at least for no good reason. Nothing could be further from the truth. Rather, inclining Bent to decisions inconvenient to Macquarie was his view of the pre-eminence of the rule of law, a product not of personal malice but of professional understanding.

MACQUARIE: A MAN UNDER PRESSURE

In this maelstrom of free settler and judicial felt and manufactured discontent, two good people were feeling the pressure. A pressure most unexpected. For Lachlan and Elizabeth had come to the Colony with what to them was self-evidently a noble vision coupled with the highest ideals. The Colony was to be a place concerned with the reform and advancement of the convicts, a place where they would no longer bear their mark as an English Cain. Here they could make a new start in life, their past errors being overlooked. They as convicts would be free from the economic oppression which had broken the spirits of some, driven others to be defenceless against temptation, even surly rebellion, and indeed propelled so many of them into crime. And others – the wilfully dishonest – now with the opportunity of putting their offending behind them. Now behave, take advantage of their new world, and theirs would be an expectation of at least the simple comforts and enjoyments of life.And those with ambition and ability might anticipate rising in society to levels not open to them back home. All, free citizens being happy with their lot and enjoying a sense of individual worth and self-respect. This vision of the Macquaries was as broad as it was long. For they foresaw this approach would release the convicts' reserves of talent, underpin the Colony's economic growth, and transform it from a place in which one would not want to be seen into a place where one might be proud to live. Thus, one day would the humble convict's psyche rise from despair, broaden from personal contentment to incorporate national pride.

'Splendid Jem, once a dashing hero in the Metropolis, recognized by Tom amongst the Convicts in the Dock Yard at Chatham'. R. Cruikshank, artist and engraver. [Published by G. Vertue, London, 1830.]

Behind the Macquaries' dream for the convicts was a powerful mental image of them as poor benighted souls. We are given access to their image by way of the accompanying vivid picture of convicts being readied to embark for New South Wales. In it, the convicts appear as colourless and lifeless, without identity and stripped of their individuality, surrounded by onlookers disporting themselves colourfully and gaily. In England, though no longer part of it. This was the mental picture of two people with everything who were capable of fellow-feeling with those who had nothing. It is an image demanding action of its host. 'Introduce these wretches to a welcoming community, bring them to life, allow them self-expression, put colour in their lives, let them flourish', it would have cried out to Lachlan and Elizabeth.

When driven by such a vision and such an image, with their attendant emotions, even the most pragmatic of men and women are at risk of proceeding as though a spell of naïvety has been cast upon them. So it was with the Macquaries. Even though Macquarie had served and lived in Government House in India, he approached his duties in New South Wales as though not appreciating the rigours of such an office. It was a tough role even for lazy maintainers, let alone reforming idealists like Macquarie who cared about the place and its people. Moreover, it did not appear to occur to either of them that decent, thoughtful, humane people would not applaud their mission. Well, in their less elevated moments they could entertain the likelihood of some apathy, even the odd disgruntled murmuring. But hostile and thwarting opposition – never.

The physical and mental stress upon Macquarie, and on Mrs. Macquarie occasioned by their intense intimacy, developed over the term of his governorship from a degree below awareness to a level at times just short of intolerable. As a start, consider the facts of a governor's everyday range of duties. Thought of in today's terms, he was governor-general, prime minister, the collective ministry, and head of a number of government departments; moreover, in all likelihood he was saddled with a junior civil service unsuited by aptitude and temperament to the job. A good governor's secretary could lighten many of the burdens, but only up to a point, for it was the governor who made the big calls and bore ultimate responsibility. In any one day, the governor might meet with his judge-advocate, propose new ordinances regulating the control of spirits, entertain the captain and officers of a visiting foreign vessel, visit the opening of a new school, begin drafting a detailed despatch of thirty or so pages to the British government reporting on the state of the colony. On and on it went, long day after long day. There were too the frustrations of office: a governor might wait for twelve months for a reply to one of his despatches, and then find his proposal not approved; or there might be criticism of some of his earlier decisions. Then, of course, there would be the daily diet of criticism from the locals, as there is for any government. All this to bear, and only his wife with whom to share it. Moreover, none of the gaiety of London life to leaven the burdens of office; no overseas holidays away from it all.

After about five years, in the normal course of events, gubernatorial duties might be expected to produce weariness in a man, coupled with a longing for home. But no more. For the Macquaries it was this, but there was more at work, as we know. They had this burning desire to change the lot of the convict, one arising from deep within their beings and

No Doubt, many of the Free Settlers, (if not All) would prefer (if it were left to their Choice) never to admit, Persons who had been Convicts to any Situation of Equality with themselves, But in my humble Opinion, in Coming to New South Wales, they Should Consider that they are Coming to a Convict Country, and if they are too proud or too delicate in their Feelings to associate with the Population of the Country, they Should Consider it in time, and bend their Course to some other Country, in which their Prejudices in this Respect would meet with no Opposition.

Lachlan Macquarie to Earl Bathurst. 28th June, 1813. Digital image from the National Archives, Kew, London.

intensified by that powerful image of the convicts as pitiful beings. What made the Macquaries peculiarly vulnerable to opposition and failure were the nature and depth of their motives. Recall, there was his vow to his beloved Jane in death to raise the socially oppressed who without his help would not know happiness in life. With this ran the driven man, the product of years of frustrated ambition, and now conscious age rendered this his last chance. And for Elizabeth, her emotionally held belief that to win her place in her beloved Lachlan's heart she must prove herself integral to his mission; there was her God to please as well. These are motives found only in peoples' hearts and souls. Powerful stuff!

Nothing reveals the strength of Macquarie's convictions about his emancipist policy, his potential for over-reaction when faced with opposition to it, better than this despatch to the Secretary of State for the Colonies, Earl Bathurst, in 1813. Its tone is particularly telling, written as it was in the earlier stages of his governorship when he is seeing and enjoying success, any opposition largely being either behind the scenes or muted. There is nothing dispassionate about it; it has been written with great warmth. Thus, he wrote:

> No Doubt, many of the Free Settlers (if not all) would prefer (if it were left to <u>their</u> choice) never to admit persons who had been Convicts to any Situation of Equality with themselves. But in My Humble Opinion in Coming to New South Wales they Should Consider that they are Coming to a Convict Country, and if they are too proud or

Some Illiberal Men there Certainly are in this Country Who would destine a fellow Creature Who had once deflected from the Path of Virtue to an Eternal Badge of Infamy, and however a Subsequent Conduct of Rectitude might be expected to throw a Veil over past Errors, Yet in the Eyes of Such persons, No Reform - No Amendment however Sincere, will be admitted as Sufficient for this purpose. I am happy in feeling a Spirit of Charity in Me which Shall ever Make Me despise Such Unjust and illiberal Sentiments -

too delicate in their feelings to associate with the Population of the Country, they Should Consider it in time and bend their Course to some other Country, in which their Prejudices in this Respect would meet with no Opposition.[23]

And there it is (see p.145), as Bathurst would have seen it.[24]

Then, around fifteen months later, he wrote again to Bathurst with similar passion, similarly troubled.

> Some Illiberal Men there Certainly are in this Country, Who Would destine a fellow Creature, Who had once deflected from the Path of Virtue, to an Eternal Badge of Infamy, and however a Subsequent Conduct of Rectitude Might be expected to throw a Veil over past Errors, Yet in the Eyes of such persons no Reform, No Amendment however Sincere, Will be admitted as Sufficient for this purpose. I am happy in feeling a Spirit of Charity in Me, which shall ever Make Me despise such Unjust and illiberal Sentiments.[25]

Again, here it is (above), as Bathurst would have read it.[26]

In this state of mind, Macquarie was particularly emotionally susceptible – indeed increasingly susceptible – to physical and mental maladies in the face of entrenched and sustained opposition when it came. As we have seen, come it did. There was Marsden's denouncing the Colony as, not a foundation of reformation, but a quicksand of immorality. Then there were the self-appointed landed gentry, who wanted all the best land and most talented mechanics and artificers for themselves, at the expense of the convicts and of the Colony. Along with this, there were the army officers refusing to entertain or be entertained alongside the emancipists, even the Macquaries' favourite emancipists. Military men not acceding to the wishes of one who was their superior! To have to put up with such blindness, such selfishness, such insubordination was more than trying for a man with Macquarie's disposition. In fact, he treated all these things as varieties of insubordination. Now, there was little which irked Macquarie more, lacerated his vanity more, than insubordination. Recall too, the Bents. Ellis's trumping of patent beneficence with legal niceties – well, as Macquarie saw it. And the constant pettiness of Jeffery's behaviour; his refusal to stand when the Macquaries entered the Church for divine service. All so tiresome! Another Macquarie trait was at work here, compounding the problem. Though an army officer, the Governor was not an instinctive warrior; to the contrary, he liked to like and be liked. In this respect, his falling out with Ellis Bent – this in particular – left him somewhat wounded, for the two families had become firm friends.

These slings and arrows continued, indeed intensified in the second five years of his governorship. The on-going friction between himself and Marsden did not abate, culminating in 1818 with Marsden being summoned to Government House, stripped of his magisterial appointment, and being told never to enter the House again. Then in 1817 Macarthur returned, his wings apparently clipped, but as Macquarie well knew, as potentially dangerous as ever. Added to these immediate problems was the uncertainty of what was going on in the background. What were these two men, along with Bent – no doubt others – saying behind his back in Britain? To what degree did they brief with impact? These unsettling questions were constantly recurring. As to the answer, Macquarie could only guess; he could only hope for the best. Yet, with the passage of time, he found it increasingly difficult to entertain the best.

Then came the policy reversals Macquarie began receiving from the British government – one shattering blow after another. All future pardons to be approved in Britain; expenditure to be restricted to what was essential to the maintenance (cf. ornamentation) of the Colony; no ex-convict lawyer to practise in the courts; greater caution to be exercised in the application of his emancipist policy. And there were others. To this transformer of men and women's lives, and indeed of the towns and general infrastructure as part of this, these censures were mortifying. They struck at the raison d'être of his governorship. Also, with them came, to this now overly sensitive man, the worry of what might be their underlying significance.

Such criticism from outside will cut especially deeply into the drive and self-esteem of the idealist and reformer. Yet such people face something equally debilitating – perhaps more undermining – the little voice of self-criticism from within. It recurs with irritating frequency. It cannot be avoided, it cannot be berated, it cannot be excised. Its force comes from its being to some degree grounded in reality. It is loudest in a man or woman's darkest moments, when they are not capable of seeing their handiwork in a dream-like glow. This was Macquarie's experience. Few convicts took sainthood upon themselves in their new country. Even those who flourished personally, added immeasurably to the Colony's growth and prosperity, and themselves rose to the top. The fact was, some among these men were the financially devious and the enjoyers of life's vices. Lower down the scale, not a sufficient number of convicts granted land went on to enjoy the degree of success necessary to realize Macquarie's ambition of a countryside populated with a thriving convict yeomanry. Others carried on a modestly successful, apparently regular business, yet involved themselves in illicit trading behind the scenes. Still others – a minority let it be clear – lived unchanged lives, even fell further. Or take the new hospital, as part of Macquarie's determination to improve the health and welfare of the people, especially that of the convicts and the poor. From the outside, locals and visitors delighted in the building's elegance and grandness. Unfortunately, within a few short years, this became a place only for the desperate. It was overcrowded and unhygienic; the care from many of the convict and other nurses was slovenly. Visitors would proceed up a grand staircase to find a stinking commode at the top – the builders had neglected to install privies. Now, though these things be individually true, read together they grossly belie the wonders Macquarie had wrought in the Colony, even without allowance being made for the inimical circumstances in which it had all been achieved. They, in fact, represented no more than what they represented individually, that is, isolated cracks in a grand edifice. The problem for Macquarie was his increasing incapacity to appreciate his Colony's flaws in their true light. Too often on cloudless days he did not bask in the sun's rays but troubled over its sunspots.

For Macquarie, the combined effect of these multiple sets of pressures assumed monumental proportions. Macquarie's person – his body and mind – was as though a castle subject to sustained assault, whose walls were about to be breached, whose integrity was about to fracture.

Surely only the emotionally imaginative are capable of conjuring up in their minds the intensity of the stress which was Macquarie's at this time. Added to this, stress cumulates over time. Its effects, in most cases hidden at the beginning, start to manifest themselves publicly, first only to the astute observer, soon becoming apparent to all eyes. This is how it happened for Macquarie. Around 1815-1816 some people, particularly those close to him, thought he had begun to act oddly. To others he appeared somewhat distracted, removed in his personal dealings. Yet others went further, feeling iciness had replaced geniality. Those close to him even sensed an incipient paranoia; he appeared to be seeing himself as a man surrounded by people hoping for a misstep on his part, with his consequent fall. Here now was a deeply troubled, frustrated man. What followed grieved his friends and admirers: all too often they were seeing in him not nobility of thought, but baseness of action. Where once there had been understanding and softness, there was now all too often judgement and harshness; where once there had been affability, there was now irascibility. It was all so contrary to his inherent nature. The problem here for Macquarie was not only the stress. For exacerbating the effects of the pressures arising from his work was his deteriorating health: he was increasingly experiencing debilitation and suffering pain from various illnesses, including a bowel complaint for which treatment was proving largely ineffective.

This was the period – the second half of his governorship – when Macquarie needed emotional support of the rescuing, empowering kind. Fellow-travellers like William Cox had been, and would continue to be, important as he sought to introduce his controversial ideas and entrench them within the Colony's fabric. But Macquarie needed more. This 'more' was the young William Charles Wentworth, born in 1790, in Australian waters. He had all Macquarie wanted in an intimate. His father – D'Arcy Wentworth, in fact – was a twig on one of the branches of the great aristocratic Fitzwilliam tree. His mother, Catherine Crowley, by this time deceased, had been transported as a convict. Wentworth himself was a large, ungainly, patrician figure of imposing presence and authoritative speech; nonetheless, his earthiness was apparent. He commanded his high intelligence, English legal training, and broad upper-class English education to great effect. This, along with the hint of greatness which Macquarie would have discerned within him, promised much more in the future. This portrait of Wentworth (see p.149), then probably in his late thirties, conforms with this character sketch.

Contrast this portrait of Wentworth with a later caricature of Macquarie (see p.230); the potential for a mutually enriching bond between the two is understandable. And realized it was, by way of a personal relationship – a relationship deeper than friendship – and a cause. For William Wentworth adored Macquarie and treated him as a father-figure. In turn, Mrs. Macquarie took it upon herself to be a mother-figure to William. In a letter to this son, written after she had returned to

Britain and he had left boyhood far behind, she counselled him to get his hair cut, and to look after his general appearance so as to appear a dandy. Imagine how Elizabeth would have bossed Lachlan around!

Wentworth's fellow-travelling activities were both practical and symbolic. An instance of the former included his membership of a three-man party which discovered a route across the Blue Mountains, this being the first step in Macquarie realizing his vision of a great southern Arcadia. Illustrative of the latter was his attendance at Simeon Lord's marriage and his signature on the marriage certificate. This was particularly significant, because Macquarie had been rebuffed in his attempts to elevate Lord within colonial society. For though Lord was now free of the shackles of convictry, to the self-appointed respectable among the free settlers he, despite his manifest good works, remained an unscrupulous wheeler-dealer of grotesque proportions.

Wentworth's 'more' – the 'more' Macquarie so much needed – manifested itself in various forms. There was, of course, his unfailing and constant encouragement and displays of filial affection, which resonated warmly in Macquarie's core. Then there was his undignified 'pipe'[27] directed anonymously against the then resident regiment's colonel, one George Molle, whom Wentworth believed had been disloyal to Macquarie. This involved Molle's conniving in his officers' bawdy portrayals of Macquarie, and in their attempts to subvert aspects of his emancipist policy. This 'pipe' ridiculed Molle, questioning his bravery, character, and his social skills as an officer. Wentworth certainly knew how to cause pain with his pen. The fact is, William, like his father, had a wild streak. When raw nerves were touched, it was though the dogs of war were instinctively unleashed within him. And Molle, by this action, had touched one of those nerves.

Another of Wentworth's raw nerves was the plight of the emancipists and their attempted subjugation at the hands of the exclusives. You see, his father D'Arcy Wentworth, now practised as a trained doctor, but in his past had practised as an unskilled highwayman. By this means he reluctantly found himself on a ship transporting convicts. It could have been worse. But for the intervention of his noble and powerful family, he would have gone as a convict and in the squalor of the ship's bowels. As it was he travelled a free man and in some style. It could have been worse for Catherine Crowley, his mother, too. For she had got together with D'Arcy and travelled with him. No flies on Catherine! What rankled William was the exclusives shunning of his father – in his view, very much their social superior – who was left to live out his days a somewhat forlorn figure on the margins of society. This is what gave Wentworth his cause, namely, the championing of Macquarie's emancipist policy, which he began in earnest around the time of the Macquaries' departure and pursued with a passion unique to himself, and which in no small measure contributed to earning him the epithet, 'The Native Son'.

Wentworth never forgot Macquarie. The governor who had treated his father, D'Arcy, as his social equal, and ensured he was a frequently seen guest at Government House functions. In Macquarie's last sad days, we will find Wentworth joining Macquarie in spirit as he lauds the man and his work with his pen.

Though Wentworth did much to bring comfort to the ever-increasingly troubled Macquarie, and did help him maintain his reforming spirit, it was not enough to avert breaches in his Governor's equanimity. Three events attest to Macquarie's mental descent, two standing out in this respect. The one for which he perhaps stands most culpable and, in any case to this day is seen by many as his greatest shame, is his ordering the military to launch a punitive assault upon a large group of Aborigines in 1816. This followed a series of particularly ferocious, and indeed fatal, raids they had made against settlers on farms around Appin, on the south-western outskirts of the settlement. The soldiers were to quell the Aboriginal people in the area; as part of this they were to shoot any who resisted and hang the worst of the offenders. What happened was a massacre. Not only were Macquarie's literal instructions interpreted very liberally, they were obscenely exceeded. For in the attack, Aboriginal men were found to have been deliberately driven over a cliff to their death, and fourteen bodies were later found strewn around the area. Several others were subsequently hanged, and their remains displayed as a warning. The problem here is not Macquarie's order for these Aboriginal raids to be quelled – he had a sworn duty to protect the Colony's people and their property – rather it is the way he went about it. Here his orders to the military were similar to those he had given a year or so earlier when a group of rebels rose up with the intent of taking over the Colony. Surely the two were very different. For at Appin these Aboriginal men were only defending themselves against what they correctly saw as the white man's theft of their lands, something essential to their survival. So why did this operation unfold in this way? It is hard to think there was not something about Macquarie's manner that day taken to indicate the Governor's patience had expired and he would not be displeased were the military to use more than minimal force. If this, as is likely, the case, it would not reflect the real Macquarie, but a Macquarie whose mind was fracturing.

It is not just that Macquarie by nature was not a harsh man – let alone a brutal man. Rather, it contrasted so dramatically with what had been up to this time his most enlightened attitude – enlightened for the times – towards the Indigenous peoples. For he accepted the facts of Aboriginal dispossession by the British as being responsible for the destruction of their way of life, and for the state of social degradation in which many now found themselves. Indeed, of all the governors he alone had taken steps, token though they were, to acknowledge this wrong (witness, for example, the Aboriginal farm he established, and the land he set aside for ceremonial purposes, both not far from Sydney town itself).

Then there was the infamous Domain incident. Though open by day, the Domain was closed at night; this was the time when people would enter for nefarious purposes and in the process damage the surrounding wall and the gardens. One day in 1816, two men and two women entered the garden illegally, at least one innocently – it was Henshall, the ex-convict who had minted Macquarie's new currency, who had decided to take a short-cut to work one morning. On hearing of these breaches, Macquarie exploded, this being the first part of an egregiously disproportionate response. He ordered the men be flogged and the women imprisoned; moreover, he forbad the four first being put before a court. By virtue of this action, Macquarie had taken the law into his own hands. Blinded by rage, he had temporarily lost the capacity to see how these actions would be manna from heaven to his enemies.

One final example: nothing illustrates Macquarie's changed temperament better than two incidents relating to the punishment of bushrangers. In 1814 in Tasmania, Lieutenant-Governor Davey's summary execution of bushrangers exasperated Macquarie. In response to a similar event in 1821, he told Davey to use plenty of rope.

Despite these and other incidents, ones reflecting the dark state of Macquarie's mind, he along with Mrs. Macquarie retained their enlightened vision and maintained their will to enact it (remember, for instance, the Female Orphan School which was opened in 1819). This notwithstanding, let it be clear, throughout this time – certainly on Macquarie's part – it was a fading vision and a weakening will. Lachlan and Elizabeth accepted too that the toll the governorship was taking on both their lives necessitated its end be sooner than later. At these times both became deeply troubled over what might lie in store for their convicts – those poor blighted souls – not only those of the present generation but those yet to reach these shores. We must feel great sympathy for them – must we not? A few years earlier it had been so different. The Macquaries and their party had ascended his newly cut road across the Blue Mountains, some forty or so miles from the heart of Sydney. They had looked to the east towards Sydney, and saw verdant and gently undulating countryside, tracts of land now cleared along the Hawkesbury River, and the growing town of Parramatta. To the west lay a vast unexplored plain, one ripe for agricultural prosperity, one in which the convicts would enjoy a majority share. Lachlan looked out and saw a great nation in the making, one brought about by the work and talents of Britain's cast-outs. Elizabeth first looked up at her husband and saw a great man; then she looked inwards and was proud of the woman who had helped make him. Both glowed!

The beginning of the end
In 1819, Macquarie was informed by his British masters of the appointment of a Commissioner to inquire into all aspects of the state and administration of the Colony. On being informed of this news, Macquarie showed now rare delight, confident he and his work would be vindicated.

Macquarie expected the Commissioner would be an intelligent person and practised in examining evidence carefully and coming to a balanced judgement. He would be able to see what sort of lives the convicts now enjoy, and how this was underpinning the progress of the Colony. He would know what sort of lives these people would have been living had they remained in Britain. He would be able to understand – at least, upon explanation – the connection between the social conditions in which they now live here and once lived there, how they are treated here and were treated there, the opportunities they have here and the lack of opportunities for them there, all this as it relates to their changed lives.

Indeed, Macquarie gained great heart from the fact that the Commissioner would spend an extended period in the Colony. He understood how it would be beyond most imaginations to conjure up from an armchair in Britain exactly what was happening, what was at work, in his Colony. It would be so counter-intuitive to respectable people, especially in light of their common-sense beliefs about the reasons for the convicts' offending, and their entrenched view of the convict as a being of low moral and social worth. Moreover, it was so contrary too to conventional wisdom about the efficacy of punishment as a deterrent. Once here, the worth of what he was achieving would be so plain to see.

Behind Macquarie's thinking – wishing – was a blinding desperation. Perhaps Mrs. Macquarie, shrewd woman that she was, saw it differently.

Perhaps she understood the Commissioner's report would depend on what sort of man he was, not on his intelligence. For many intelligent people do not see, will not allow themselves to see, the obvious, the good in something, if it is contrary to their instincts or interests. Perhaps she knew all too well that how he would see things would depend on whether he had a heart, on whether he could put his prejudices about people different from himself to one side, on whether he was capable of entertaining in his mind something different from what he had thought before.

Yet, Macquarie would not have heard any expressions of doubt. The splendid optimist in him, so finely captured in Opie's 1804 portrait (see p.23), was not yet dead. Nor were those deep personal needs, lurking just below the surface of his mind, and underpinning what most exercised his thinking. A prosperous future for the convicts! Glory for him! Indeed, we imagine his long-gone, unforced smile re-appearing in public, along with the former spring in his step – sadly, the one not quite as broad, the other not quite as high. Any joy was not to be for long.

We now turn to consider, through the minds of the people involved, how the Inquiry into the Macquaries' Colony came about, and then explore the Commissioner's findings.

Chapter 8

The Opponents of 'Macquarieism' in Britain

THE MACQUARIES' ENEMIES in the Colony, at least those within the elite, regarded themselves as the Colony's natural leaders, the men of destiny responsible for its fate. Governors come and go, you understand, they themselves are necessarily the ruling constant. Yet, for all their insufferable self-importance, all their huff-and-puff, all their power within their own little fiefdoms, all their local conniving, they themselves could do nothing to change the course Macquarie was charting for the Colony. In the Colony, each in their own way could be uncooperative (a magistrate might ignore the Governor's exhortations for leniency); or might cause him pain (a disgruntled settler might make him the subject of an anonymous dirty ditty). These things they actually did, as we have seen; but with these actions they were at their limits. Power resided in London with the British government alone. All they could do to bring about change was to use their contacts to turn the minds of those with power in Britain against Macquarie and, more especially, against his mission. This they set out to do. This they did, with persistence and growing vehemence, starting not too long into Macquarie's reign. But with what success? They were certainly heard in the British parliament; and a Commission of Inquiry into the Colony was established by the Government. The Colonists' trumpeter in parliament was Henry Bennet. The Secretary of State for the Colonies, Earl Bathurst, was the man who set up the Inquiry. His Commissioner of choice was one, John Thomas Bigge. Macquarie's traducers treated this as an early success. But would Bathurst and Bigge bring them satisfaction? Would the Inquiry deliver them victory?

'**The Hon'ble. Henry Grey Bennet M.P.'**. Pl. 10. Proof. A. Wivel, artist. W. Holl, engraver. Published by A. Wivel, London, 1823.

HENRY BENNET

Henry Bennet, a Whig reformer, was one of the vocal members of the House of Commons. This son of an aristocrat, this Cambridge educated barrister, was a most amiable man, yet he manifested a capacity to bore his company – a characteristic not uncommon in men and women who present as both earnest and honourable. This portrait of him says it all: a decent, dull, unprepossessing Everyman. There is no sparkle about the image; there was no sparkle about Bennet.

To those who did not share his convictions, or who just found them inconvenient, Bennet took on the character of a pest. It was his misfortune to lack any disarming charm, to have no resort to a winning smile. Ability and the tenacity of a dog with a bone were his only armaments.

Nonetheless, there was much to commend Bennet; he was a champion of social justice. The poor and oppressed's disadvantage and suffering were his passion. Not surprisingly, Macquarie and his Colony caught this reformer's eye, along with the broader matters of crime and the transportation of criminals. He was in his mid-thirties at the time. It was 1816 when Bennet led a parliamentary debate on transportation, concluding with a damning verdict. To the criminal classes in Britain, the contemplation of transportation held no terror, was not thought of as punishing, and thus did not have the capacity to deter them. Moreover, convicts once sent to the Colony entered a world of vice and depravity, one antithetical to their reform, worse still, conducive to their further decline into criminality. Then, in case all this did not sway his audience, he pulled out the old chestnut, that is, the economic argument, the draining expense of the system. Surely, he did plea, would it not be prudent to allocate Britain's scarce financial resources to alternative criminal justice measures? Then, to the sharp ear, he undermined the force of his own argument when he let slip that he was relying on data from 1810. Was that not the year of Macquarie's arrival in the Colony? Whoops! Moreover, those in the know, as we are, would detect in Bennet's preoccupation with the Colony's moral degradation, the channelling of the Macquarie-hating Marsden. What Bennet had done, and would do again, was get caught in one of the zealot's traps: the irresistible urge to seize upon any information supportive of their cause with little regard for its veracity. His informer, Marsden, let himself be caught in the other trap: the preparedness to exaggerate.

In 1817 Bennet returned to his attack on the Colony, this time focussing on its Governor, having been briefed by the late Ellis Bent's vindictive brother, Jeffery Bent, a man who had dedicated his immediate future to hunting Macquarie to destruction. To buttress his case, he presented a petition from some of the Colony's citizens. This petition complained about what they regarded as Macquarie's arbitrary and illegal use of punishment; it was prompted by the 'Domain' incident. This document was drafted in the sternest of terms – Bent had seen to that. He also saw to it that his brother's complaints about Macquarie's lenience were not forgotten. Around this time Parliament was warned about there being an insubordinate convictry: crime, serious crime such as robbery included, was out of control. Well, how could it not be thus, in the face of the Governor's lenience!

Bennet's tireless campaign continued unabated. At the beginning of 1819 he moved the appointment of a parliamentary committee to inquire into the government of the Colony. It was defeated. But a countering Government motion by Castlereagh soon followed, and was successful. This motion called for a parliamentary committee to inquire into the best method of providing for the punishment and reformation of offenders, including whether the Colony had outgrown its intended purpose. In doing this, the kind and thoughtful statesman had the pride and feelings of his appointee in mind. He was not a zealot, simply a good man.

Throughout this period, Bennet did not confine his operation to the parliament. He worked behind the scenes and in public. In regard to the latter, he published two letters taking the form of short treatises, one to Viscount Sidmouth (the then Home Secretary) in 1819, and second a year later to Earl Bathurst. These represented in effect vicious attacks on Macquarie the man as well as Macquarie the administrator. Arbitrary government, petty corruption in the granting of tickets-of-leave, a milieu of immorality, a discontented populace, the playing of favourites when it came to land grants and significant appointments, and the oppression – even persecution – of those bold enough to challenge the status quo. In regard to the last of these, perhaps two men in particular comes to mind!

Bennet was the enemy of transportation as a system, and of Macquarie as a governor. But he was not an enemy of Macquarie's ideals. For Bennet was a champion of humanity, and he sought the convicts' reform, not their punishment for its own sake. Law-and-order platitudes were not part of his thinking, and not to his taste. To him, the idea that more severe punishment could prevent crime was an affront to common sense and decency. There was a place for punishment to be sure, but it should be inflicted only when necessary, carefully targeted, and then administered parsimoniously.

Moreover, Bennet was a man who empathized with those who suffered under Britain's system of justice. He felt their penal pain; with passion he campaigned indignantly on their behalf. Public labour in chain gangs, for instance, he proclaimed as spectacles for the gaze of the idle and the taunts of the cruel, which inevitably – understandably – brought out malevolence and suppressed rage on the faces of these sad souls. Or the case of a women in prison awaiting transportation who, when the time came to leave, had the baby she was suckling brutally snatched from her breast. How troubled was Bennet over what to him were abominable horrors! How hard he campaigned for something better!

Bennet the good man was, most unfortunately for the Macquaries and their mission, a limited man. He could see what was wrong with transportation, but he could not conjure up in his mind its potential to transform lives. Bennet was not one of those people who can discern a pattern in an apparently disordered set of dots.

When, a little later in 1819, the Government announced its decision to appoint a commissioner to inquire into the Colony, two groups 10,000 miles apart celebrated, though the emotions each felt were of a very different kind. Bennet and his fellow-travellers in Britain were pleased, treating it as a victory for criminal justice; the vindictive malcontents in the Colony glowed with mean satisfaction, now savouring the real possibility of Macquarie's humiliating demise. Nonetheless, the two groups did not now sit back and await their preferred outcomes. The Government must not be let to go cold on the need for reform; moreover, whatever was in the Commissioner's Report, the Government must see it their way and act upon it. To this end did they continue to do their best to influence the minds of Ministers, of Parliament, and of the British public. Indeed, Bennet's letters to Sidmouth and Bathurst followed in this period. And Jeffery Bent in England, and Marsden from the Colony, campaigned and lobbied assiduously through their channels of influence. As for Macarthur, he had his truly cunning plan. All the while they braced themselves and awaited with an air of expectancy for the Commission of Inquiry.

To understand why the Inquiry took the direction it in fact took, it is necessary to get inside the heads of Bathurst, the Government minister, and Bigge, the Inquiry's commissioner. The fact is, what a government wants and whom it appoints in large measure together determine the findings and conclusions of inquiries of this nature.

HENRY BATHURST, 3RD EARL BATHURST

Bennet represented a danger to the Macquaries' work because this politician's understanding of what was best for the transported convicts was blinded by his incapacity to appreciate that their lives were being transformed there, let alone understand how or why this might be so. The threat from the aristocrat Bathurst, a moderate Tory, lay in different personal weaknesses. For this man, though one of Britain's most senior cabinet ministers, was indecisive, and he lacked the political courage of his convictions. Indeed, this threat had the potential to be fatal to the Macquaries' work, for Bathurst almost alone held the Governor's future on the tip of his pen. To the Secretary of State for the Colonies as an enemy of Macquarieism, we now turn.

'Henry, Earl Bathurst'.
J. Wright, artist. H. Meyer, engraver. From an original picture by T. Phillips. Published by T. Cadell & W. Davies, London, 1810.

Much about Bathurst's character is to be seen in his mien. So, perhaps an amiable, even-tempered figure, one at peace with the world, who would do all in his power to keep it this way. Surely a man who had never entertained a passion for a cause. There was nothing of the martyr in him – certainly not the sort of man a governor would want in his praetorian guard. Nonetheless, Bathurst did possess qualities inclining him to be protective of his governors. Is there not a certain softness to be discerned in his eyes? Indeed, he did possess a capacity to empathize with those whose circumstances were very different from his own. In Bathurst's political record are his efforts to ameliorate the lives of slaves in

British possessions. Nothing radical though! No Wilberforce, he! Perhaps not surprisingly, then, Bathurst had cautiously approved Macquarie's emancipation principle, though other significant figures spoke against it at the time. Moreover, as Colonial Secretary, he tried to understand the difficulties faced by governors in far-flung colonies and, in light of this, did his best to mitigate public attacks against them. But time would show there were soon-reached limits to this.

Dealing with complaints about a colonial governor and his administration was stock-in-trade for Britain's Colonial Office. They would come locally from Britons with some sort of real or self-appointed interest in a colony's affairs. Some of these matters would, as a matter of course, find their way into the Parliament. Then there were the complaints regarding some real or imagined grievance and coming directly from residents in the colonies themselves. These would be dealt with routinely and represented nothing more than low-level background noise. But with Macquarie and his Colony it was different. At first there was nothing unusual about the disquiet. Then by 1816 a crescendo of discontent was in the making. The conductor was Bennet, of course. Yet the noise came not only from parliamentarians in debate; it also came from the chattering classes in the coffee houses of London, worse still from the press. The administration in a mess; the Colony a waste of money; the need for an inquiry!

Bathurst by virtue of his character was vulnerable: first he flapped; then he dithered; then, in effect, he let others decide for him. The political hubbub unsettled him; he could no longer relax in his club with his chums at the end of the day. But how should he respond? Was there really a problem in the Colony? And, if so, did the fault lie with Macquarie or the system? In either case, how should he act, yet not ruin Macquarie? So, behind the scenes Bathurst urged upon Macquarie an at-least noticeable change in his course. And what was the response? None. He found himself pigheadedly ignored. Poor Bathurst! Foolish Macquarie! For Bathurst, now overwhelmed and exasperated, found a backbone in a man formed of very different clay, the then Home Secretary, Viscount Sidmouth. This portrait of him has been calculated to present him in all his aloof glory.

This Oxford educated barrister's political identification was Tory, and he viewed the world, particularly those he regarded as lesser beings, through hard and deeply conservative eyes. Though religious, he would have been most uncomfortable had he found himself accompanying Jesus of Nazareth on one of his walks among life's losers. Rather, he was more at ease with the type who thought relief for the poor would only facilitate

'Rt. Hon'ble. Lord Sidmouth'. W. Beechey, artist. E. Scriven, engraver. Published by J. Bell & Co., 1808.

their multiplying. More than opposing social reform, this otherwise likable and mild man regarded it with suspicion and hostility. He was not a man who, having looked down, sorrowed, and thence looked up and tried to envision a fairer world. O no! No joy for Macquarie here.

Sidmouth first ensured the Home Office hounded Bathurst with tales of Macquarie's punitive lenience and predilection for expensive ornamental architecture. Then did the hard men in the Government bellow unremittingly in Bathurst's ears: 'When will you understand, Britain's crime rate will not lessen while Macquarie's convicts go unpunished, many enjoying a far superior quality of life to that of

Britain's lower orders?' Transportation must be dreaded: to these people it must represent life extinguished not, as it does now under Macquarie's benign hand, life's new beginning. Along with this, the hard men falsely construed Macquarie's financial management as profligate, especially in light of Britain's budgetary woes. What these men, though, were by social cast incapable of seeing, unwilling to admit, was the real cause of Britain's crime wave, namely, the social and economic circumstances of the day, the malign effects of which were borne so harshly, so unfairly, by the lower orders.

At last Bathurst saw the light; it had suddenly become so clear, so necessary to act decisively. Transportation was no longer serving as an object of apprehension in Britain or a means of reformation in the Colony – the latter a secondary consideration. Transportation must be rendered once again 'an Object of real Terror'; this was the goal necessarily outweighing all others, including the economic and social growth of the Colony. Concrete action soon followed mental resolve. And so it was, in the first months of 1819, that Bathurst appointed a Commission of Inquiry to investigate and report on these matters in respect of transportation and Macquarie's administration. In taking this action, Bathurst was not following his disposition as a man, but his instincts as a politician. For my Lord Bathurst the peer could be ignoble in his thinking: prepared to do what he had to do; prepared to put expediency before principle, in order to please and make things go smoothly. He was not a statesman.

When governments set up inquiries they often have a result in mind. This certainly was the case here. The point of the present Inquiry was to investigate whether the Colony could be made to serve the principal objectives for which it had been established. In these circumstances, the selection of the commissioner becomes critical. He must be a man whose ability and stature are sufficient to the task and the conclusions. As importantly, he must be a man who will see the problem as the government understands it, and who accordingly will fashion a solution consistent with the government's thinking on the matter. This was the hour for a forerunner of the fictional, civil-servant fixer par excellence, Sir Humphrey Appleby, to shine. Hear him telling Bathurst that he has just the right man for the job: the forty-odd year-old John Thomas Bigge. 'Sir, an excellent man!' The official explains his decision to Bathurst, describing Bigge thus:

> ... a lawyer by training but, more importantly, a black-letter lawyer
> by nature. A highly educated man, indeed a cultivated man, but

Macquarie 'Stitched-up'.
Copied from J. Lynn, and A. Jay (Eds.), *Yes Minister: The Diaries of a Cabinet Minister by the Rt Hon. James Hacker MP.* Vol.1. BBC, London, 1981 (paperback). (Cover photograph, Don Smith.)

nonetheless one narrow of vision. A man who will be incapable of understanding how any device not of the law could be effective as a means of social control. He will turn instinctively to punishment. Moreover, his work as a judge has shown him to be a cold man; a man by nature favouring a clinical analysis of problems. He will not condescend to talk with the convicts themselves. There is no danger of compassion and humanity moderating his thinking. He can be relied on not to shy away from very harsh measures, no matter how much personal pain they might cause, how much they might blight the convicts' future lives. He is an Establishment arch-conservative, a snob, a believer in social hierarchy, who sees social mobility as a cancer, and will think of the convicts as scum.

Sir, you could rely on Bigge instinctively seeing the place as you would want and reaching the recommendations you seek. Macquarie's understanding of how the convict should be treated will be beyond his ken; Macquarie's policies will be anathema to him. And there is no chance of Bigge warming to Macquarie, and being tempted to try and please him even a little.

Bathurst was convinced; he made the appointment as advised. Now, the deed having been done, Bathurst once again could go about his work with equanimity and enjoy the company of his chums without a cloud in his sky.

The dynamics and emotions of this interaction are vividly conveyed in the accompanying image. Be amused, be troubled, as you recall the cunning, smug expression of Sir Humphrey Appleby, the deeply conservative Departmental Secretary (Nigel Hawthorne) – right – having just advised a now most pleased James Hacker, the affable Minister (Paul Eddington) – left – on a matter troubling him.[28]

JOHN THOMAS BIGGE

There are three aspects to be considered here: Bigge the man; Bigge's Inquiry; and Bigge's report to the British government. Each is dealt with in turn.

John Bigge: The man

The British Colonial Secretary's man in the Colony arrived early in the second-half of 1819. Commissioner Bigge carried with him both formal and advisory instructions from Bathurst as to how he should proceed with his Inquiry. His principal aim was to determine what changes needed to be made to restore Macquarie's colony to its original purpose, a place of punishment, of dread, one serving as a deterrent to crime in Britain. In the future, convict punishment was to trump considerations of the convicts' reclamation. At least part of the problem, Bigge was to understand, lay with the Governor's foolish punitive lenience and general indulgence to the convicts. Under Macquarie, the Colony had become not a place of dread for the criminal underclass; rather, it was all too often fantasized by them as a place of opportunity. Bigge, in fashioning his reforms, laboured under two constraints; the need to: first, significantly reduce the financial drain of the Colony on Britain; and second, maintain for the free settlers a climate of normalcy in regard to their needs and rights, and the Colony's general amenity for them. Yet amongst this sternness we find a glimpse of Bathurst's own preferred self. Despite the 'aggravation' Macquarie's intransigence had caused him, and his frustration with the man, Bathurst cautioned Bigge to treat any adverse criticism he might entertain of Macquarie with delicacy. The Inquiry itself was to proceed by way tours of inspection around the Colony, formal interviews, and on-and-off-the-record briefings. His two keenest witnesses were John Macarthur and one Samuel Marsden.

Bigge to this point in his life had followed the expected course of one such as he; one who was high-born and endowed with wealth, who was clever, diligent and serious. First Oxford, then the Bar, this leading on to the chief justiceship of Trinidad at the time of this present appointment. This was the background of the man who would judge Macquarie and his work. It lay with Bigge to determine whether the Colony would remain a convict colony; and, if so, the principles to govern gubernatorial policy in respect of the convicts, their punishment and general treatment. Moreover, Macquarie well knew – indeed, this became a matter of increasing concern to him as the light within his soul faded – Bigge would determine whether his governorship would receive high praise; whether the Establishment would bestow on him glory and welcome him into their midst as a great man. Recall, for Macquarie, these dreams arose from needs lying deep within his psyche.

How anxious Macquarie must have been to meet Bigge and try to discern what spirits animated his clay! How then upon first sight might

John Bigge (c1819).
T. Uwins, artist. Digital image from the State Library of New South Wales, Sydney (PM 153).

Macquarie have read Bigge? To speculate about this, we must turn to Bigge's portrait, shown above.

Prissy and 'toffy', to be sure. And is not in his pose a certain detachment apparent, one not of the judicial kind but of one who practises aloofness from his own species? Perhaps too we might detect a man who floats above the world, one having no more than a narrow engagement with it. A man too who has not experienced fighting any of nature's baser temptations. And a man who regards much of his world as too dirty to touch.

The Bigge inquiry

Macquarie's first tète-à-tètes with Bigge would have confirmed these impressions. And Macquarie would soon have accepted the Inquirer was too different to be companionable. Nonetheless, the critical matter was the convicts' futures, and whether Bigge would become a fellow-traveller. This is what really exercised Macquarie's mind, and what with Elizabeth he agonized over. In regard to this question, Bigge's professional background of itself would have offered hope. A senior legal officer, trained to assess evidence and its significance, sworn to be objective, fair, and impartial, one ruled by reason, and able to understand two sides of an argument, and a man of the highest integrity. Nonetheless, it is one thing to demonstrate these qualities as a judge in court, quite another to exhibit them in the role of potential social reformer. Indeed, especially for one whose political identification is high Tory. Moreover, there was more about Bigge to worry Macquarie. It soon would have become apparent to the worldly-wise Governor that although Bigge had travelled the world, he had experienced little of life; he was not a man who had soiled his hands by venturing beyond the cultivated. Nature had not allowed him the advantage of carrying the gene of ordinariness. Macquarie in his desperation for vindication clung to Bigge's presumed professional character. Bathurst's Sir Humphrey had put his faith in his personal characteristics, confident this new experience for Bigge would leave his soundness intact.

Macquarie welcomed Bigge fulsomely, in public by way of ceremony and in private by fussing over him. But not for long. His early sanguinity on hearing of the appointment of a visiting commissioner, and this particular commissioner, soon gave way to fretting. While Macquarie had welcomed the Inquiry, he bridled when becoming aware of the circumstances under which it was to be conducted. He and his work were to be judged by a man nearly twenty years his junior. Worse still, he was to accord Bigge precedence next to himself; moreover, Bathurst warned him against contesting any immediate changes Bigge might recommend while in the Colony. How affronting and humiliating for this proud autocrat, and in his own fiefdom! This put Macquarie in the wrong frame of mind, compromising his initial resolve to schmooze Bigge. In their first meetings, instead of presenting himself as relaxed and open, he appeared edgy and defensive, as though primed to fire. Soon followed friction between the two. Soon followed a heart-felt plea from Macquarie to Bigge on the convicts' behalf, the mental picture of the benighted convicts dockside still haunting his mind (see p.143).

Let me therefore entreat of You, Most Solemnly, Most earnestly, and most fervently to reflect on the great Effect the Commission with which You are Invested is Capable of accelerating and Securing the Prosperity and Happiness of these People, or giving a mortal Wound

Let me therefore intreat of You, most Solemnly, most earnestly and most fervently to reflect on the great Effect the Commission with Which You are Invested is Capable of accelerating and Securing the Prosperity and Happiness of these People, or giving a mortal Wound to their Breasts and dearest Interests.

Let not the Disposition with which Nature Seems to have Endowed You for doing good, be overwhelmed by an over Strained Delicacy or too Refined a Sense of Moral Feeling.

Avert the Blow You appear to be too much inclined to Inflict on these Unhappy Beings – (if You make them So!) and let the Souls now in being, as well as Millions yet Unborn, bless the Day on which You landed on their Shores, and gave them – (when they deserve it –) what You So much admire, Freedom –.!

Lachlan Macquarie to Commissioner Bigge. 6th November, 1819. Digital image from the National Archives, Kew, London.

to their Breasts and dearest Interests …

Let not the Disposition, with which Nature Seems to have Endowed you for doing good, be overwhelmed by an over Strained Delicacy, or too Refined a Sense of Moral Feeling …

Avert the Blow You appear to be too much inclined to Inflict on these unhappy Beings (if You make them so!); and let the Souls now in being as well as Millions yet unborn, bless the Day on which you landed on their Shores, and gave them (when they deserve it) what you so much admire Freedom![29]

Read the copy of this plea sent to Bathurst (above). Do we not hear Bathurst thinking to himself, 'the poor fellow, he just cannot accept it is all over for him'?[30]

These are the words of a very worried Governor. They reveal how Macquarie saw his role in the Colony, and the passion with which he held this view. We discern too a man who could put himself into the heads and hearts of men and women very different from himself.

Nonetheless, it was not long before Bigge challenged Macquarie on a matter very close to the Governor's heart. Macquarie informed Bigge of his intention to appoint William Redfern to the magistracy. To Macquarie, his unstinting and exhausting service as a doctor for over twenty years, service for which he had won the admiration of all – convict and exclusive alike – demanded no public honour less. Bigge's opposition was withering: these works must count for naught in light of the man's part in a most heinous mutiny; such an appointment would contaminate the magistracy. Yet Macquarie did proceed, for both principled and venial reasons. To accord victory to the exclusives would embolden their attacks upon the emancipists; in any case, he Macquarie, was not being seen to submit to a whipper-snapper like Bigge. Moreover, there was an accelerant in the mix: recall, William was a Macquarie favourite. As a result – sadly – Macquarie let himself down by being rude to Bigge, such was the warmth this issue generated in his heart.

What followed over the course of the Inquiry were the constant irritants of Bigge's observations, which to Macquarie revealed his deep disregard for the convicts' welfare and reform, and their long-term futures. Ornamental architecture as a means of engendering a sense of worthiness among the emancipists! Increased rations to convicts on entering the Barracks as compensation for their then less freedom! The supposed hard labour of lime-burning at Newcastle – a site of secondary punishment for the most refractory convicts – involving no more suffering than for free men doing the same work in England! And amongst the general population of serving convicts, a detectable spring in their step, even an uppity air! So did observations by Bigge become questions for Macquarie. Where is the punishment? Where is the cost-cutting? Why will you not heed my warnings, accede to my requests? In regard to this, frustrating for Macquarie was his realization of what underlay these heartless observations. Macquarie discerned in them the man's most stunted understanding of human nature and shallowness of humanity. These together rendered him unfit for the task, of this Macquarie now had no doubt. These things made Macquarie at once very, very cross, and very, very sad.

Alongside this there was the constant niggling; the two even contested the appropriate site for the new Tasmanian township of Launceston. The fact is, almost from the beginning grew a mutual awareness of there being an irreconcilable difference between them. Thus, Macquarie continued to realize his vision for the place and his beloved convicts; thus, Bigge worked assiduously on his Inquiry and ideas for a very different convict Colony. Two moons, orbits apart, circling the same planet.

Bigge completed his field work in early 1821. Upon the eve of his departure he was accorded all due ceremony by a dignified governor. As the Commissioner sailed down Port Jackson on his return to England, he looked back upon Sydney for the last time. His was not the elevated, ethereal look of a man who was envisioning the unfolding of a New Jerusalem; rather, it was of a man relieved to be leaving a place of coarseness and darkness, and a people – free and bond – he did not want to mix with or understand. Now, he would turn to preparing his report for Bathurst and the British government.

The Macquaries were certain they would be back in Britain when Bigge's report was made public. Remaining in the Colony, though, were two men awaiting Bigge's recommendations with great expectations. The redoubtable John Macarthur ignobly craved it would lay a foundation for a wealthy landed-gentry, with the Macarthur family at its pinnacle. Along with him, another man sought with equal intensity something humbler though equally base; the devout Samuel Marsden, who never grasped his Maker's message, continued to pray with vengeance in his heart for Macquarie's downfall.

The Bigge Report

What is referred to as the Bigge Report takes the form of three volumes. The first of these, 'Report of the Commissioner of Inquiry on the State of the Colony of New South Wales, and its Government, Management of Convicts, their Character and Habits', was presented to Bathurst in mid-1822. This is the volume primarily dealing with Macquarie's work as it relates to his treatment of the convicts. For the lawyer Bigge, three entrenched understandings informed his Inquiry, in respect of punishment: (1) the odiousness of a person's crime trumped any latent goodness which might lie within them; (2) an offender's reform, though not unimportant, paled beside the condemnation of wrong-doing, and deterrence; (3) criminal behaviour is rational, its control therefore necessarily requires legal not social means.

Deterrence and condemnation required harshness; this followed as a logical consequence of these understandings. Harshness was now to apply, not only to the recalcitrant, but to all convicts from the time they set foot on the Colony's shores. The convicts' experience while under servitude was to be one of unremitting labour, the sternest discipline and suffocating control. To this end, as far as practicable, convicts would be moved from government work and assignment in Sydney and the bigger centres to the countryside. There, the majority of the most skilled and diligent were to be assigned to men of social merit with large pastoral holdings, who would be responsible for their upkeep. Away from the temptations inherent in town life, and with much time on their hands for reflective thought, they might contemplate the error of their ways. As for the remainder, they would work in gangs clearing the bush, opening up land for farming. The work-shy and obstreperous among them risked being sent north and coerced into back-breaking land-clearing for settlements, in oppressive heat and under onerous working conditions. Even the educated convicts did not escape the attention of Bigge's beady eye. They were to spend a term in a remote camp, before undertaking services befitting their skills as book-keepers, teachers, and the like.

As for the practice of free time, when convicts could earn wages as means towards an independent future with at least a modicum of prosperity – Bigge recommended its abolition. Moreover, in a measure hitting the gentleman convicts the hardest, any financial assets a convict brought to the Colony were to be forfeited until they won their freedom.

In Bigge's mind, the sum of these measures was not enough to eradicate from the Colony what to him was the troubling air of lenience about the place. His unfeeling heart allowed him to turn the screw some more. Macquarie's not-infrequent practice granting very early release, and his associated low requisite standard of good behaviour, must be quashed. Moreover, the existing presumptive terms to be served before eligibility for a ticket-of-leave should be extended. Along with this, there should no longer be an implied right to a 'ticket'; 'good behaviour' must mean what it says, and not constitute a muddled, middling 'on-balance' judgement. Further to this, Bigge recommended that conditional and full pardons become a rarity. There was more at stake here than the effect on the capacity of punishment to condemn and deter. Equally troubling and problematic, this lenience engendered in the convicts a premature optimism of the best being just around the corner, this in turn fostering an infectious cockiness among them. So agonized Bigge.

It would not have occurred to the other-worldly Bigge that these measures – longer and tougher sentences largely served in social isolation – would break some convicts' spirits or engender within their hearts a sullen resentfulness, even outright rebelliousness. Or that together these measures risked cruelling a convict's chances of developing the incentive and the wherewithal so essential for reform. All Bigge thought about was ensuring that the convicts' term of penal servitude was not a time during which they could prepare, supported by an animating optimism, for a life after release worth living. How unlike Macquarie!

Under Bigge's proposals, this would be the new punitive lot of all convicts. Yet the convicts were spared one indignity Bigge had contemplated for them. He was of the opinion that all convicts undergoing punishment should be dressed in a distinctive garb. This difference would be their shame on display, it would render them objects of gawking and sneering, all acting to keep them in their place. Mercifully the convicts were spared this indignity. But it not happen because Bigge's heartstrings had been successfully tugged. O no! Rather, it was because the upper class – the class whose sensibilities he understood so well – implored him to abandon the idea. You see, to comport with their affectations, their servants – mostly convicts – wore livery. To deprive them of this would be to do them a most mortifying mischief.

For those convicts who continued to wreak their depredations on the population – the apparent incorrigibles – Bigge had something new and obscenely nasty in his mental toolkit of punishments. It involved his proposal for new sites of secondary punishment and how he thought of them. These were not just to be places where punishment took clear priority over reform and renewal. Not simply to be places where punishment was administered solely with the aim of deterring the inmates once and for all from future offending. No, in these places the inmates' both present and future were to be of no concern whatsoever. Rather, the purpose of punishment was to be the deterrence of the convicts in the mainstream of colonial life. To this end, these new places of punishment were to be by repute so punitively grotesque as to elicit terror in the mind of the would-be re-offender upon mere mention of their very name. What Bigge did not envisage was that this ethos would become to those who ran them an unwritten licence for cruelty. The euphemism 'to hell with the convicts', at first a throw-away line descriptive of the spirit of the proposal, would come to describe what was actually involved in being sent to these prisons. The worst of these were (arguably) Norfolk Island and Port Arthur, where the 'cat-o'-nine tails' reigned supreme. Today these places symbolize the horrors of Britain's system of transportation for its criminals. Perhaps here we have another instance of Bigge's naïve trust in the law. Certainly, he would not have conceived how a governor and a commandant, having within themselves, respectively, an incipient ruthlessness and latent sadism, could find themselves in such positions of power, let alone how each, remote from their immediate master, and emboldened by the newly sanctioned purpose and spirit of the Colony, could preside over such abominations. There is in all this a salutatory lesson for us today: the blind belief in the efficacy of deterrent punishment, so long as it is severe enough, tinctured as it often is with a malevolent vengeance in a punitive climate of public opinion, constitutes a very slippery down-hill road to cruelty.

These preceding proposals of Bigge's address the important matter of how the Colony might be refashioned to provide a credible deterrence to crime in Britain and to convict re-offending in the Colony, and according to the most cost-effective arrangements. Yet the Commissioner, when in the Colony, though soon satisfied with the progress of his thinking on these matters, remained most anxious. What continued to trouble him was Macquarie's vision of the Colony as a country for the convicts. There was something instinctively unnatural about it, surely? Indeed, with the upmost clarity would Bigge have perceived its inherent fatal flaws. It flouted the class laws upon which all well-ordered societies must found themselves for their own moral integrity and prosperity. Moreover, it involved putting emancipists in high office: hidden white ants in the Colony's moral fabric; public celebrants of the wages of sin. Thus must Macquarie's progress towards the realization of this dream to date be destroyed; thus must measures be put in place to ensure it does not happen again.

Accordingly, Macquarie's emancipist policy became one of Bigge's prime targets. Take, for instance, the raising of Simeon Lord – a man born of the lower orders, a former convict, and reputed to engage in sharp business practices – to the high office of magistrate. To Bigge this appointment bespoke the two mischiefs in Macquarie's thinking on this matter. Such offices require men of stature, whom the lower orders look up to with awe, whose status they accept as beyond reach. Moreover, these offices demand men of the highest character; take away this, and their bearers' exhortations to those in the dock become risible. The inevitable outcome will be the undermining of the controlling authority of the criminal law in the minds of the turbulent and more generally the criminal classes. Such people are not going to be told what not to do by one of their own, are they? You will recall, on his arrival Bigge had opposed Redfern's magisterial appointment, but his request was ignored by Macquarie. Nevertheless, Bathurst sided with Bigge, and Redfern was ignominiously relieved of this post. And in a second blow – the knock-out blow – Bathurst even refused to appoint Redfern to the post of Principal Surgeon. Following this, in the face of Bigge's request to remove Lord from the magistracy, Macquarie meekly acquiesced. Macquarie's emancipist policy as an instrument of social engineering was now dead. Emancipists would no longer play a leading part in running the Colony.

Macquarie's policy of active land grants was another of Bigge's prime targets. Bigge did not want the creation of a convict yeomanry, a large body of small land owners, proud and prosperous, perhaps even one day forming a political base. Rather, his idea was to put agriculture in the hands of the wealthy and respectable, now and in the future, who would constitute a landed gentry, and in turn become a ruling class. Along with this, he aimed to lay the foundation for a convictry, once free, becoming nothing more than a paid, dependent serving and servile class. Indeed, Bigge's recommendations that the convicts' period of penal servitude be largely under the control of the large land-owners, served remotely, they living apart from the general community, and no longer enjoying the freedom to earn money, were made with these ends in mind. Bigge's intention was to try and ensure that few convicts upon release would possess the mentality or means needed for occupational independence, let alone leadership. Accordingly, he added three other complementary recommendations: first, holders of tickets-of-leave not be permitted to own land; second, no land grants be made to convicts upon emancipation, with the possible exception of those who already were men of means; third, no convicts be assigned to emancipists, whether they be landholders or running their own businesses. Another aspect of Macquarie's bright vision would be extinguished. Few convicts would now rise from a lower class to a higher one.

The idea of ornamental architecture and attractive streetscapes, expensive and serving no utilitarian purpose, was to Bigge both preposterous and wilful. In this regard, the building Bigge became most lathered about was Macquarie's Government House stables (see p.91). Bigge saw the problem everywhere; moreover, it was proceeding apace, to the enthusiastic beat of Macquarie's baton. Bigge would readily dismiss the programme's elevating effect on the convict. Can you not imagine Bigge exclaiming to himself with a sneering snort, 'All this for wicked wastrels beyond cultivation!' In any case, he would argue, the convicts were not sent to the Colony to be elevated but to be punished, to keep their heads down, not to hold them up high. Moreover, fine architecture requires money – money Britain does not have. Bigge reinforced his opposition by drawing attention to some of the practical needs of the

Colony. In respect of this, he noted, many public buildings (the hospital at Liverpool, for instance) and private dwellings were in a ramshackle state. Bigge's observation, devoid of a broader policy context, was not without some merit. But do we see him railing against the construction of the grand Nelson's column in early nineteenth-century London on these grounds?

Thus, Bigge reported to Bathurst. Imagine him – this passionless man, one not given to empathizing with the common man and woman – commission completed, now relaxed and detached, without a thought for the fate of the countless lives whose fate lay in his Report. Yet, we confidently suppose, many a grand hope for his own future. Perhaps he contemplated an appointment to high judicial office in England from a grateful Government. Meanwhile four men – Bathurst, Macarthur, Marsden and Macquarie – were awaiting the release of this document with much self-interest.

It is 1822. We enter Bathurst's office just as he completes his reading of the first volume of Bigge's Report. There is on his face the satisfaction of a man who has just been told what he wants to hear. His 'Sir Humphrey' advised him well. Quickly he becomes expressionless. Then he grimaces, with a pang, not physical in origin but mental. He now must face the admirable and likable Lachlan Macquarie, now dejected and worn out, soon to be broken.

Upon the release of the Bigge Report, Macarthur, though far away from the seat of power, had won. How joyously he would have celebrated and prepared to prosper! In fact, he would have been quietly optimistic. For he had spent many a pleasant hour with Bigge during the Commissioner's time in the Colony, and Bigge had appeared most receptive to his ideas. Bigge in turn remembered Macarthur with some delight, having found him a most impressive character, though not without his faults. The man had charm; and his having risen to affluence, and the elevation of his London social circle, told Bigge much about him was admirable. Besides, Macarthur had provided him with a wise and practical plan for the future of the Colony and the punishment of its convicts; he had offered Britain what it wanted from the Colony at a much-reduced cost. That it would herald riches for Macarthur himself troubled Bigge not a tittle. Rather, the thought pleased him, for Macarthur was surely the sort of man he wanted for the convicts' superintendence and the Colony needed for its prosperity.

Marsden, however, did not fare well. Bigge, far from being won over by him, found him an unimpressive man. There was an all-too-obvious social coarseness about him – a characteristic off-putting to the most-refined Bigge. Moreover, Bigge had found little of merit in his submissions. The Commissioner had not wanted to waste time listening to indulgent and destructive rants; he was there to listen to constructive proposals. Besides, Bigge's sense of fairness recoiled at Marsden's vindictiveness and patent prejudices, as when he spoke of Macquarie. Thus, Bigge in his Report, had little compunction in setting down the colonists', and indeed his own, criticisms of Marsden. For Marsden, his experience with Bigge lingered as a painful memory. Woe! Thus did Marsden once again feel himself a victim of his God's traducers. In response, as he had done so often before when he felt misunderstood, he turned to his Maker for comfort in this present life and glory in the next life.

All the while Macquarie, now in Britain, there growing ever weaker physically and more fragile mentally, braced himself to the task of winning the glory he surely so richly deserved yet risked being so cruelly denied. And Elizabeth, herself far from robust, braced her fail body to care for her beloved husband, and to bring some measure of peace and pleasure to his last days. To these events we return in the final chapter.

Part 2

A history tale for today

Chapter 9

The Macquaries' Treatment of the Convicts as an Enlightenment

THE HISTORY OF the Macquaries and their convicts is now behind us. Though of interest in itself, here it serves a secondary purpose. In this book two very big claims are being made for the Macquaries' work in their convict Colony. The first it that the sentiments underlying Lachlan and Elizabeth's treatment of the convicts, and the essence of the policies they begat, represent not simple humanity but something much greater, something seismically different from the climate of opinion up until that time. That 'something much greater' is nothing less than an enlightenment in the treatment of crime and criminals. To regard the Macquaries' work as representing no more than humanity in practice is to view it as though through shaded glass, oblivious to its glorious radiance. To regard the Macquaries' beliefs and polices as irresponsible, woolly-headed, sentimental softness should be labelled as uncivilized thinking.

The second big claim in this book for the Macquaries' approach to the convicts is that these policies represent no less than a history tale for today. The sad fact is, the Macquaries' thinking, today, two hundred years later, still represents a great enlightenment in the treatment of crime and criminals. For in countries around the world, a punitive mentality informs conventional wisdom, harsh punishment alone satisfies the people.

This chapter introduces the idea of enlightened criminal justice; then follows the claim of the Macquaries' views and practices as enlightened, ones to be contrasted with Britain's unenlightened treatment of the convicts. As part of this, it is important to consider evidence for the success of the Macquaries' policies as crime-preventive measures. Let it be clear, this discussion has no academic pretensions; indeed, such an approach is deliberately eschewed here. Rather, it is guided primarily by way of two most thoughtful observers: one a brilliant and humane 'toff'; the other a clever, reformed 'baddie' – whose writings are relevant to our appreciation of the Macquaries' work.

THE IDEA OF ENLIGHTENED CRIMINAL JUSTICE

Meet Winston Churchill as you have probably not seen him or heard him before. In fact, the image is Spy's take on him in a 1900 number of 'Vanity Fair'. Not the pugnacious, seething lion about to pounce, presented in Yousuf Karsh's famous 1941 wartime photographic portrayal of the old man. Nor the indomitable Churchill calling you to join him in the trenches of war. Rather, we see him as an attention-seeking, self-promoting, hedonistic dandy about town. Yet his earnest, almost anxious expression, framed by his furrowed brow, tells us here perhaps is a man of depth. These contrasting two features, taken together, perhaps project a man prepared to be different, to think differently. It is instructive to appreciate, this is a man who a few years earlier as a soldier had taken part in the historic British cavalry charge at the Battle of Omdurman; and he had recently as a reporter been a prisoner of war in South Africa. These were the years he identified publicly as a liberal, soon declaring himself by his membership of London's National Liberal Club. Yet while he enjoyed the company of the chattering and the glittering classes as they floated above life, his life experiences had rendered him match-hardened. This swashbuckler was no 'out of touch' 'softie'.

This was also the period when he was honing his natural talents as a man of letters, one of rare calibre. Grounded beliefs, not fashionable talk, exercised his pen, and informed his speech. And so, it was in 1910, the young tribune, answering questions in the House of Commons as Britain's young Home Secretary, uttered these majestic and most memorable of words:

> The mood and temper of the public in regard to the treatment of crime and criminals is one of the most unfailing tests of the civilisation of any country ... [A] constant heart-searching by all charged with the duty of punishment, a desire and eagerness to rehabilitate in the world of industry all those who have paid their dues in the hard coinage of punishment, tireless efforts towards the discovery of curative and regenerating processes, and an unfaltering faith that there is a

treasure, if you can only find it, in the heart of every man – these are the symbols which in the treatment of crime and criminals mark and measure the stored-up strength of a nation, and are the sign and proof of the living virtue in it.[31]

Immediately before, Churchill had informed the House of his having made a general grant of remissions totalling 500 years across the prison population. As a part of this, he reassured the House that there had been no consequential 'evil results' from this measure or subsequent offending by these prisoners. He clearly had felt the need to reassure the law-and-order champions and rumour-mongers among the Members. Churchill knew such questioning would always arise in the minds of the hard-liners. Yet, with this statement the Great Man reveals his understanding there was a need for more than reassurance in these circumstances. There was a need to raise Parliament's thinking from the specific to the general, from pragmatism to principle, from the darkened valleys to the glistening white mountain tops. A need to turn Members minds away from politics, to instead offer them statesmanship.

The young Churchill's proclamation of what enlightenment in regard to criminal justice policy entails is without peer. Here we use this statement as a yardstick to assess the Macquaries' policies and to compare them with those of the British government. First, we must consider what he is saying to us. To this end, and in the character of this book, we are not going to 'deconstruct' Churchill's statement, nor will we be 'drilling down' into it, using fancy concepts as tools. Here the aim is social elevation not academic evisceration. Read them again – these mighty sentences: take them for what they are, contemplate them, in the expectation of Churchill's claim speaking to you.

Churchill's test of civilization in respect of criminal justice comprises in effect three elements: first, the use of punishment; second, rehabilitation as a part of criminal justice; and third, the moral worth of offenders. His call for 'a constant-heart searching' in the use of punishment appears to be a cry for punishments to be no more severe than is necessary to prevent offending. The clue is in the preamble: namely, his reassurance that the early release of offenders had no evil effects. What follows implicitly is that the sentences imposed on these prisoners need not have been so harsh. More generally, Churchill is asserting the principle of parsimony in punishment. Now, this is addressed to all those 'charged with the duty of punishment'. So, who should be listening? Well, all those who have a say in the severity of society's punishment of its offenders. But who does this include? Churchill's immediate concern is his fellow parliamentarians, the men and women responsible for setting maximum and (sometimes) mandatory minimum terms of imprisonment. He would have also had in mind the judges who impose punishments on offenders within these limits. No doubt too, he would have wanted to catch the ears of the public. Yes, you and me! For among us are the people who cry out for tougher sentencing, in turn influencing ballot-sensitive politicians, whose legislation the courts are bound to follow.

The second element – rehabilitation – is there because, to this young stateman, offender reform is integral to criminal justice. To appreciate what is being said here, the implicit is as significant as the spelt-out. To Churchill, an offender's reform is not the sole responsibility of the offender himself or herself – perhaps read this sentence again, so different is it from most people's thinking. This follows from what he believes to be society's responsibility, and which he sets out clearly. First, 'a desire and eagerness to rehabilitate in the world of industry all those who have paid their dues in the hard coinage of punishment'. Its meaning could not be clearer. The reform of offenders should be a community priority and duty. An eager desire will surely manifest itself in demands for rehabilitation programmes aimed at integrating offenders back into community life, along with an expressed discontent, a demand for something better by way of rehabilitation, where these are not effective. The second part, 'tireless – yes, 'tireless' – efforts towards the discovery of curative and regenerating processes', involves two components. First, implicit in this is the idea of criminals ceasing their offending because they are changed men and women – perhaps because the anger within them is no more, perhaps because they now enjoy a legitimate source of income, perhaps because they now appreciate the hurt their offending causes innocent others – the key here is the word 'regenerating'. This is very different from the prevention of re-offending by way of the deterrent effects of harsh punishment or the confining effects of long periods of imprisonment. Second, Churchill, with the word 'discovery', shows he appreciates the need for more understanding about these things; and with 'eagerness' is calling the people to push for serious research into offender reform and renewal.

The third element of Churchill's proclamation is perhaps its crowning glory. Read it again: 'an unfaltering faith that there is a treasure, if you can only find it, in the heart of every man'. Its meaning and what it requires of us – we who in our own eyes are the law-abiding good – is so counter-intuitive to our common sense as to appear absurd, so unpalatable to our feelings and moral sensibilities as to approach offensiveness. Treasure in people who have done bad, in some cases very bad things – surely not? Some good among the better of them, perhaps, but treasure? Treasure is to be admired, sought after, envied, protected, cared for – well, treasured, is it not? Yes, yes, yes! Within the criminal there lies the potential for them to be useful citizens and to live good lives. Indeed, they have the potential to be just like us, and to become profitably accepted among us as one of us. Churchill's message could not be clearer. Accordingly, our punishments should not be profligate but moderate, our reform measures not desultory but most vital, and our encouragement in this respect not passive but unfaltering. Thus proclaims the young tribune.

What makes Churchill's criteria so important, so compelling our attention, is his grand claim for them, namely, whether our system of punishment satisfies these criteria determines whether or not we can properly regard ourselves as a civilized nation. Something to set one back and start thinking – surely. Thus, we must ask ourselves, 'What about them is intrinsic to civilization?' Perhaps it is in their representing the antithesis of the human instinct of vengeance as a reasonable response to having ourselves been wronged, or of having seen others wronged. Vengeance unbridled, especially in regard to the very serious offender, proclaims no punishment as too great, no offender's future as of consequence, and no offender as not best kept apart from law-abiding society. Even for the more serious everyday-offender: there is personal abuse, shame and humiliation, harsh punishment, then a future to be lived on the margins of society as though a moral leper, all justified as their deserts, all delivered in a vindictive spirit – you see it in the headlines, you hear it in the tone of the mob's voice. Churchill's criteria are also intrinsic to civilization because they call upon those human qualities and actions we regard more generally as admirable, as estimable, as praiseworthy in a fellow human being. These are personal actions such as forgiveness, charity, the outstretched helping-hand, humane forgetfulness, acceptance, understanding, empathy, all these and others, and especially when manifested in the face of a natural inclination to the contrary. They represent something more than everyday decency; they are less common, residing at the pinnacle of our humanity. And when starkly absent in a person, do we not see ugliness, perhaps some dark forces at work in their unconscious? These are qualities telling us something about ourselves; and because we are the life in a nation, they tell us something about our nation. No doubt the young Churchill had these things in mind when he claimed his criteria to be a measure of the 'living virtue' in a nation.

THE MACQUARIES' POLICIES AS ENLIGHTENED

Before any claim may properly be made for the Macquaries' treatment of the convicts as enlightened, three questions must be addressed. First, does this treatment satisfy Churchill's three measures of civilized punishment? Second, in these respects, was the Macquaries' treatment of the convicts dramatically different from the thinking of the day on this question, as it was to be found in the British government's approach to crime and criminals? Third, do policies consistent with Churchill's sentiments actually deal with crime effectively? As much as we might wish to stand and admire his ideals, seduced by the majesty of his words, these must surely be regarded as hollow – indeed, unsound – if we would do this at the expense of people being realistically in fear of their person and their property. Thus, we ask, 'Did Macquarie's policies work?' Not until these three questions have been addressed, will we be able to determine the true status to be accorded to the Macquaries' treatment of the convicts. Whether they represent at best nothing more than morally admirable, though muddle-headedly soft – even dangerous – policies. Or whether they represent something truly grand, something most worthy of being celebrated and practised today. To each of these matters, this discussion now turns.

The Churchill test

The Macquaries' policies for the treatment of the convicts, together with their justification of them, were set out principally in Chapters 4 and 5. Indeed, we need only a reminder of some of the features of these policies and justifications to appreciate they represent the quintessence of each aspect of Churchill's understanding of civilized punishment. Punitive leniency was Macquarie's predilection; under him, the behavioural threshold for harsh punishment was high. Recall, his attempt to circumvent severe floggings, together with his widely regarded profligate issuing of early tickets-of-leave, not to mention conditional and absolute pardons. The rationale here was utilitarian – convict spirits left intact – and principled – mercy in recognition of the harshness life had already thrown at them. Does this not represent the product of Churchill's 'constant heart-searching'?

Moreover, in respect of aspects of convict reform, Macquarie was also textbook Churchill. Thus, Macquarie's convicts who had tilled the land, built the houses and the ships, and had made wonderful efforts in agriculture and in manufacturing[32] are Churchill's prisoners 'who have paid their dues in the hard coinage of punishment'. Indeed, Macquarie's preference was to prioritize reform over punishment for all but the egregiously badly-behaved convict. For, as we have seen, what a man or woman was, much more than the seriousness of their offending, would determine the length of their term of penal servitude. This principle's operation was to be seen in the Macquaries' rejection of harsh punishment and their investment in measures encouraging and facilitating convict renewal and reform – Churchill's 'curative and regenerating processes'. Thus, the ornamental architecture, Government House entertainments, and high appointments signalled the Colony's future as a place where the well-behaved convict mattered as a person and might live well; training and a preference for no more than a lightly controlling hand during penal servitude, with community contact, prepared them for this; while land grants and employment set them on the path to achieving success.

As to there being 'a treasure … in the heart of every man', Macquarie had discerned this with utmost clarity from his early days. Remember, as a senior army officer he had seen at first hand unstinting endeavour and heroism from criminals who had chosen army combat abroad as an alternative to punishment at home in Britain. Indeed, Macquarie's firm conviction in the truth of treasure being within the convict heart sustained his emphasis on rehabilitation, and underpinned his emancipation policy. Yet, in one respect, Macquarie often went further. In some cases, he exercised humane forgetfulness in applying his emancipist principle. On such occasions, it appeared Macquarie saw only the treasure within the man or woman. Nonetheless, he did sometimes fall short of satisfying Churchill's criteria. Not, let it be clear, as a matter of belief; rather, it was as a matter of uncharacteristic behaviour. Recall this sad fact: as weariness from sustained exertion and from the opposition he faced got the better of him, so did his good nature and generous spirit wane. In turn, Macquarie's belief in the inherent worthiness of his charges faltered from time to time. Where once a convict's slip on the road to renewal might be overlooked, now it might meet with intolerance and painful censure. The convict heart as with treasure was something in which Mrs. Macquarie fervently believed too. There is no better illustration of this than in her letter to the emancipist, Charles Whalan; remember, his picture is to be hung in her bedroom as a tonic when her spirits are low.

Britain's policy as unenlightened

Now to the second question relevant to our exploration of the Macquaries' work as enlightened: how does the British treatment of its criminals at the time stand up against the tripartite Churchill test? First, consider a 'constant heart-searching' in respect of the punishment of offenders. The convicts were sent to the Colony as punishment in order to deter criminal activity at Home. It was based on the Government's blind belief in the efficacy of punishment as a deterrent. And when transportation did not result in less crime in Britain, the assumed solution was the harsher treatment and punishment of the general convict. The thought that punishment might not deter the greater proportion of offenders appeared never to enter the British mind. Moreover, this mind appeared not to contemplate – perhaps would not allow itself to contemplate – the possibility of other causes – social causes – lying behind Britain's increasing crime rates. And there was certainly no 'constant heart-searching' by the British government over possible penal abominations resulting from their policy of ever-harsher punishments for those who re-offended in the Colony. Bathurst's 'Object of real Terror' as the guiding standard for appropriate punishment was the antithesis of what Churchill had in mind, namely, moderation and parsimony.

Second, the British government by way of its form of punishment – transportation – absolved itself of any immediate responsibility for convict reform and renewal. Once there, some convicts might reform, but let it be in their own hands. If convicts did not have it within themselves to change, so be it. Then, post-Bigge, punishment as 'real Terror' rendered reform more difficult for all, and out of the question for the majority of the recalcitrant. In respect of the former, because it involved the abandonment of many of the incentives, opportunities and other means conducive to personal reform, measures in many instances introduced by the Macquaries, certainly alone championed by them. In respect of the latter, because it brutalized both the body and the mind. With the British policies, more than no 'desire and eagerness' or something less than 'tireless efforts'; rather, a wilful disregard for the convicts and their futures as fellow human beings.

As to an 'unfaltering faith' in the convict heart concealing 'treasure' ripe for the discovery – well, the converse was true of the British government. In this circle of men there was actually an unfaltering belief in there being no treasure in the convict heart. This is to be seen in each aspect of Government policy. An important reason for transportation, as we know, was the removal of the convict from society. For the convict was perceived as a moral canker, not only causing the good to suffer, but – this is what made the convict truly frightening – having the potential to corrupt the good. This justified – indeed demanded – the convict being excised in the interests of British society's long-term welfare. Then, when the convict was safely in the remote Colony, this idea informed the British government's treatment of them. This is why reform meant no more than crime prevention through deterrence; this is why the idea of reform was not taken to encompass human renewal. Surely, without treasure the latter could not be realized? From this, according to sensible reasoning, evil would forever lurk dangerously in the heart of every convict, however apparently satisfactory their manifest behaviour. Thus, must they never be placed in positions of power with its attendant temptations; thus, though free, they must they remain second-class citizens, subordinate and subject to the great and the good of the Colony.

Evidence for the success of the Macquaries' policies

One final question remains for the claim that the Macquaries' policies were enlightened. The question is: 'Were these policies effective in reforming and renewing the convict?' More than the prevention of crime through fear of punishment (deterrence) or by means of confinement (imprisonment) is required here. For the Macquaries' aim was higher, namely, to transform wretched law-breakers into productive citizens, who would contribute to their new world according to their ability. This question is not easily addressed; indeed, any answer will rest on an uncertain foundation. The relevant hard evidence is just not there, a limitation applying to the three types of evidence to be adduced here. The first comprises official figures on crime in the Colony around Macquarie's time. The second involves deductions we ourselves may make in light of what is known about convict attitudes to transportation at the time. The third constitutes observations, made by significant others resident in the Colony, on the circumstances of the transports' lives both as convicts and as emancipists in the Colony. The first measure is apparently objective; the second and third are patently subjective. While the latter two speak indirectly to re-offending (the British standard), they alone offer evidence relevant to personal renewal (the Macquarie standard).

First, consider what might be concluded from official figures. To the untrained, these may be treated as objective, yet in reality are anything but reliable. In this light, one example suffices. Back to Henry Bennet, in the House of Commons in 1816, railing at the level of moral degeneracy in the Colony under Macquarie, yet relying on 1810 data. What is important here is the sequel to this episode. In response, the Government debunked his claim, citing that recent returns had in fact revealed a decrease in criminal activity there. This, taken at face value, must be treated as quite remarkable. For Macquarie was not offering a quick political fix, but a long-term social policy. Not all convicts who would reform could be expected to turn their lives around overnight. This aside, just what can be properly concluded from such information must remain open. We would need to know whether the circumstances under which these figures and the earlier comparison figures were recorded were similar. Thus, we might ask whether the police were equally resourced and zealous in both periods; whether on the latter occasion a convict clerk might have left crimes unrecorded in the interests of a boss who had been good to him; and so on.

Also, relevant here is the matter of how the children of the convicts fared here as against what might have been their fates had their parents remained in Britain. In fact, the broad picture presents them as a largely crime-free generation; more than this, they were said to be hard-working and ambitious. In view of the criminogenic circumstances in which many of them would have been raised in Britain, almost certainly the portrayal of their lives would have been very different had they been brought up not in the Colony but there.

Secondly, we turn to what deductions might be made from what is known about convict attitudes at the time. Again, as the evidence pertinent to this enquiry is somewhat woolly, so we rely on only two pieces, though when taken together perhaps sufficient to set one back and thinking. First, recall, among the people of Britain a sentiment had developed of the Colony under Macquarie's governorship as a land of rapidly increasing opportunity. Moreover, this view was strongest among the very people for whom transportation had been set up as a deterrent to crime. In the minds of these very people, Macquarie's Colony was a place not of social subjugation and degradation, but one where with a little good fortune they might lift themselves out of their wretchedness. As transports, they would not be leaving a fulfilling life in a land which had been good to them. Britain had in fact rejected them long before they embarked, so they would reason. It had uncaringly left them blighted by impoverished circumstances. The southern colony, many were dreaming, offered them something much better. This was the reason, of course, why transportation in its current form was said in official circles to be losing its capacity to act as a significant deterrent to crime. Second, and related to this, the Colony in Macquarie's time did in fact flourish economically and socially, and it was the period when a palpable sense of individual purpose and national pride first developed among its citizens, bond, freed, and free alike. It is surely inconceivable that these two things would have occurred had the Colony been mired in the wretchedness of a rampant criminal culture, one arising from punitive softness, and without life-enhancing measures. It is inconceivable to imagine this happening if the convicts themselves had not been flourishing, since it was they who largely constituted the Colony's population.

Finally, consider what observations on the convicts, made by significant others resident in the Colony, might tell us. One significant other who

Dr. William Bland (c1847).
Richard Read, artist.
Digital image from the
State Library of New South
Wales, Sydney (P2/250).

wrote persuasively on the rehabilitation of convicts and the conditions of their penal servitude is Dr. William Bland. This thoughtful man was in a rare position to exercise insight. At the time of writing about this he had been resident in the Colony over thirty years. He was not beset by a deeply held moral prejudice against convicts – like Marsden – nor did he seek to wilfully use them – like Macarthur. The portrait above introduces us to him.

William Bland, a most able medical practitioner, arrived in Sydney in 1814, aged twenty-five. In fact, he came as a convict. His crime had been to wound a man mortally in a duel. His portrait presents him as a man of urbanity and wealth, cultivation and learning, one who appreciates the good things in life and wants to project style. Perhaps too a man who takes himself seriously and who is to be trifled with at risk. What might come as a surprise in light of this is the selflessness and warmth which he displayed towards the poor and the sick. Indeed, Bland was a philanthropist, a supporter of the arts, education, the Church, and other causes he deemed worthy. He was also politically active, being an enthusiastic supporter of William Wentworth and his emancipist cause. This political bent led to him becoming one of the first elected Legislative Councillors in the Colony. Macquarie would have approved of his support for Wentworth. And his championing of a yeomanry against the interests of the landed gentry was pure Macquarie. As was his commitment to charitable causes. Yet whether Macquarie would have ever forgiven Bland and come to like him is another matter. For Bland had written a 'pipe'[33] against Macquarie and had caused it to become public. In this pipe he had ridiculed the Governor's penchant for naming parts of the Colony after himself. Yet what interests us particularly here is Bland's active support for convict rehabilitation. He, like Macquarie, looked for treasure in the heart of every man. He, like Macquarie, believed it could be brought out of a man or woman by the conditions of penal servitude in the Colony. On this basis did Bland become a champion of transportation. His focus in this respect was the system of assignment. This he believed, when properly regulated, had the capacity to bring about renewal in a man or woman. It had the potential to offer convicts the incentive, opportunity and means of transforming their lives from ones characterized by wretchedness and destructiveness to ones of fulfilment and usefulness.

Bland set out his views on transportation, and its potential to raise the fallen convict, in an open letter to a British parliamentarian in 1849. This was based on three tenets. First, Bland believed in the worth of most of the convicts as human beings. Thus, he wrote:

> ... the British criminal, perhaps in nine cases out of ten, differs in no one moral or intellectual property, from any other individual in his own sphere of life.[34]

Second, he discerned social disadvantage as the main driver of crime. He continued, a man became a criminal:

> ... not from any original peculiar predisposition, but from the force of circumstances alone. The chief of which, it will be found, are pauperism

and wretchedness; among the more desperate characters, want of education; and with nearly all, the contaminating and perpetuating operation of example and habit.[35]

What must be noted here is Bland's inclusion of the 'more desperate characters' in his analysis. This becomes of particular importance when we contemplate applying Bland's thinking to the treatment of criminals today. In view of this quite deliberately made conclusion, it cannot be claimed that the convicts he was referring to were no more than petty offenders. Third, he argued, this second conclusion has implications for measures aimed at reforming the offender: '(t)he cure for crime, will obviously [sic] depend, in great measure, on the removal of its causes'[36]. Indeed, for Bland and those of like mind, this was just what the system of assignment had the potential to do and, in practice, did achieve in great measure.

The probative value of Bland's analysis as evidence must be regarded as high. Bland lived in the midst of the assignment system; indeed, he had done so for over three decades at the time of writing. It beggars belief that this intelligent man, most active in community affairs, could get his assessment of the convicts as reformed and worthwhile citizens, and the constructive role assignment played in this, so wrong. Indeed, many of his patients would have been convicts and emancipists. In this position, he was rarely placed to know their inner man, their inner woman, and in this way to hear their now inner bubbling spirits. Moreover, his views could not be dismissed as the product of high-minded remoteness. Every day he would have been surrounded by convicts and assignees as he went about town. Do we really suppose this fine-liver, good man though he be, would have put up with depredations upon his person and his property? Might not such experiences, had they in fact been more than background noise, have constrained him to abandon his faith in assignment as the principal means of treating the convict, and reluctantly turned his mind to imprisonment or other harsh measures in order to achieve security and peace of mind?

Bland's analysis points to the effectiveness of Macquarie's policies and, importantly, their underlying rationale. In his writing, Bland was defending the potential of the system of assignment as rehabilitative and transformative. It mattered not in this regard that in one case the convict was repairing a ship at the dockyards, or a working as a mechanic on a settler's farm, or as a maid at Government House or in the home of a wealthy settler. What mattered was this taking place in the community and outside a tightly constraining punitive framework. This was only somewhat less true for the convicts housed in the Barracks, though they constituted only a sub-group of the convicts.

The preceding three strands of evidence – official figures, the attitude of the criminal class to transportation, and observations about assignment by unbiased colonists – all point to Macquarie's policies as effective in reforming the convict. All three are relevant to reform as non-offending; the latter two address reform as personal renewal. Each patently comes on its own uncertain foundation, yet its acceptance seems to sit more comfortably in the mind than would the tortured and improbable rebuttals necessary for the contrary position.

Surely then, the Macquaries' policies for the convict and their new home must be regarded as representing the quintessence of enlightenment. Not only do these policies comfortably satisfy Churchill's tripartite test of civilization, they represent the antithesis of British thinking at the time, and they worked. Today, the Macquaries' treatment of the convicts deserves to be celebrated as a glistening jewel in the sweeping tapestry of criminal justice history. The principles underlying their policies should to be accepted as guiding for the punishment and treatment of society's criminals today. Thus, we must ask, 'How might a criminal justice system fashioned according to these principles appear? This is the subject of the next chapter.

Chapter 10

Lachlan and Elizabeth Macquarie's Legacy in Criminal Justice

THE MACQUARIES LEFT the Britain of their day with an achievement and a challenge. This was their legacy. The achievement was that great body of convicts who, had they remained in Britain, would not have gone on to live productive and happy lives. The challenge they left Britain was to understand and value the principles at work in their treatment of these convicts, and thence to adapt this treatment to the social circumstances there and to the evolving circumstances in the Colony. Yet, since the former was not recognized, nor was the challenge. Worse than this, the Macquaries' work was dismissed – actually, ridiculed in many quarters – as a muddle-headed folly. And the current aim of punishment as deterrence was unquestioned, though it was acknowledged that the deterrent policy-setting required cranking up from 'harsh' to 'draconian'. Along with this went the belief that the causes of crime lay within the individual, and the consequent view of the convict as a moral canker. Exactly the same thinking and attitudes about crime and criminals remain pervasive today in Britain and Australia, and to a greater or lesser extent around the world. More criminals sent to prison for longer, the public demands of its politicians. And the latter, ever ready to please, have duly obliged.[37] Yet, is not this punitiveness the antithesis of Churchill's definition of civilized punishment? And was not the Macquaries' treatment of the convicts found to accord with Churchill's test of civilization in respect of the treatment of crime and criminals? And was it not effective in reforming and renewing the lives of doomed men and women? In recognition of this, the Macquaries' treatment of the convicts is held up here as a history tale for today: a shining light signalling the need for drastic changes in our current approach toward the punishment of criminals; a guiding light, a policy blueprint for how we should proceed with this. The first part of this chapter starts the process of imagining a modern, more enlightened, system of punishment, one according with the Macquaries' principles, one prioritizing rehabilitation. The second part then discusses one of the great barriers to this becoming a reality; it is, political ordinariness.

THE SENTENCING SYSTEM RE-IMAGINED

In this re-imagining of society's current approach to punishment, we first consider observations made by two senior Australian judges pertinent to this. Then follows an overview of what this would mean when it comes to the sentencing of many of the offenders – many of the more serious offenders included – appearing before our courts for punishment. Finally, we contemplate the implications of this re-imagined system for the public's perception – your perception – of punishment. Throughout this discussion, its compatibility with the Macquaries' way and the Macquaries' thinking will be to the fore.

Judicial observations

Many people will instinctively recoil at the mention of a sentencing system prioritizing rehabilitation over punishment. This, because rehabilitation signals lenience in their minds. Yet, an observation, made by a Victorian Supreme Court judge almost fifty years ago, may cause some who favour harsh punishment to think more deeply. The judge was the late Sir John Starke, a distinguished Supreme Court judge, most respected Chair of the State's Parole Board, and in his day the doyen of the Criminal Bar.

'Big Jack', a towering figure professionally and physically, was not known for an unfailing gentleness of manner. Along with this he was possessed of the capacity for outrage in the face of what he regarded as despicable wrong-doing. Indeed, his rage when manifested truly bore the descriptions 'astronomical' and 'apocalyptic'.[38] Yet, on that fearsome face, tears might readily fall. One of those occasions was during a visit to a prison for young adult offenders. There he had freely engaged a number of the inmates in casual conversation. One of them was a recidivist thief and burglar, with a penchant for escaping from legal custody. As Sir John was leaving, he referred to that 'lad', and observed with tears in his eyes: 'A bloody tragedy; we know his likely future. Dealt a better hand in life, he has it in him to win a Victoria Cross'. Sir John did admire pluck. The fact is, as far as offenders were concerned, his understanding of them was unrivalled; he knew their potentialities and failings as individuals from first-hand experience. This came not only from his long period of service on the Parole Board, and work as a barrister, but also his being the beneficiary – rare for one so elevated – of a profound common touch.

In light of this, what he had to say about the sentencing of offenders bears studied thought. None better, in respect of this, than an observation he made in the Court of Criminal Appeal in 1974. This case involved serious offending – a series of robberies. As for the actual offending: the targets were all business premises; the four offenders wore disguises, brought with them a sawn-off shotgun, drove a stolen car, and threatened and roughed-up the victims. The offenders themselves ranged in age from 19 to 29 years; two had no prior convictions, a third presented an extensive record. (This case is known as *Williscroft*.) There, Justice Starke opined:

Sir John Starke. This image is from a portrait on display in the Supreme Court of Victoria, Melbourne. A digital copy was kindly provided by Luisa Moscato, archivist, Melbourne Grammar School. This image, of poor quality, was transformed by Jim Morris of Classic Colour Copying, Melbourne.

> It is often taken for granted that if leniency for the purpose of rehabilitation is extended to a prisoner when the judge is passing sentence, that this leniency bestows a benefit on the individual alone. Nothing, in my opinion, is further from the truth. Reformation should be the primary objective of the criminal law. The greater the success that can be achieved in this direction, the greater the benefit to the community.[39]

The prioritizing rehabilitation over punishment is pure Macquarie. The military allusion by this second world-war veteran, Macquarie also.

Observations such as these, when they become public, are apt to evoke amongst the majority of the community first cries of dismay, then outrage, they believing themselves to be victims of judicial softness. Here 'soft' is used in the pejorative sense, namely, weakness. Look, then, at Sir John Starke's face; do you see weakness? No, this judge's softness was born of informed compassion. Perhaps then, his is an observation which should incline us to reconsider the importance and worth of making offender rehabilitation a priority of punishment, of fashioning our sentencing system to accord with it.

What form, then, might this 'other way' take? And why should we accord this alternative serious consideration? Fast-forward forty years.

Tuesday, 18th September, 2012 was to be just another working-day in the life of the Victorian Court of Appeal. By day's end, 'just another working-day' is how it would have appeared to most if not all the participating court officials and lawyers. But it was far from this. For the President of the Court – Justice Chris Maxwell – had uttered, in the course of delivering a judgment there that day, something profound, something which should unsettle all thoughtful people. In the facts of the case there was nothing out of the ordinary. It involved a particularly nasty home invasion, one motivated by perceived grievances. Two men entered the house, while AH (the offender then before the Court) remained in their car. The resident, a woman, was bound and threatened with a hammer and knife. The experience was terrifying for her, but she was not otherwise hurt; goods to the value of $25,000 were stolen. AH, who had been sentenced to a minimum of three-and-a-half-years imprisonment for his part in this offence, was appealing on the grounds of this sentence being manifestly excessive. After dealing with the barrister's arguments in light of the facts of the case, the Court confirmed the original sentence. To this point, just another case; ho hum. Then … the President's concluding observations! They would have appeared as a bolt from the blue, though they played no part in the decision. It would have seemed as though he had put down his script and was then speaking from the heart. Thus:

> In so concluding, we [the Court of Appeal] do not overlook the powerful submission advanced by senior counsel for AH concerning the severe disadvantages from which AH has suffered lifelong. According to the unchallenged expert evidence, intelligence testing revealed AH to be in the '"extremely low" (borderline) range'. He has 'poor impulse control, low frustration tolerance and [a] sense of being overwhelmed by multiple or complex demands'. He had an 'impoverished education', staying at school only until year 8. His home life was unhappy. His parents separated when he was two or three years old. He suffered physical abuse from his stepfather and was neglected by his mother who (according to AH) 'was addicted to prescription pills, always off her face, passed out, didn't care'.
>
> At the time of sentencing, AH was diagnosed as suffering from clinical depression. According to the forensic psychologist … AH

had suffered depression for many years, with his drug problem 'only aggravating this underlying problem'. AH had begun to use heroin at the age of 13. This habit had continued for more than a decade. AH was also a long-term marijuana user.

Counsel for AH submitted that 'those with few choices make bad choices'. Moreover, counsel submitted, repeated lengthy terms of imprisonment were unlikely to assist AH in overcoming any of these serious disabilities. Public money spent on imprisoning people like AH would be much better used, he contended, if it were directed at tackling the causes of disadvantage.

Sadly, the profile and life history of AH is all too familiar in the criminal courts. The submissions made by counsel raise issues of fundamental importance concerning the social context of criminal behaviour and the inefficacy of imprisonment as a response. The orthodox approach to criminal responsibility, however, requires that a person like AH is viewed as morally as well as legally responsible for the choices he makes.

In the present case, AH chose to instigate and participate in — in the ways we have described — a very serious offence. It was not said on his behalf that he fell into one of those categories — mental illness or intellectual disability — where moral culpability for criminal behaviour is mitigated. That being so, the judge was obliged to sentence AH within the sentencing parameters fixed by Parliament, and in accordance with established sentencing principles.[40]

What might have motivated this digression? Perhaps this case had brought the Court's humanity to the fore. Perhaps, the President thought, this was the right case to raise a matter long troubling him? This speculation aside, perhaps in the facts of this case thoughtful people might be prompted to think deeply about criminal punishment. How in certain types of criminal case the Court, though a court of justice, is forced by the law to preside over injustice. What is fair and appropriate according to the criminal law, is not always fair and appropriate when thought of as a matter of social justice. As Macquarie had challenged the Colony and the British government to consider another way of treating the convicts, so the President here should be taken to be challenging the public to consider a way other than punishment as primary in the sentencing of many of our criminals. Kaapay and Kuyan.

Justice Maxwell, who delivered this joint judgment on behalf of the Court,[41] is seen in this accompanying photograph (opposite), taken soon

Justice Chris Maxwell.
Photograph kindly
provided by Justice
Maxwell.

after his appointment as President of the Court of Appeal in 2005. Here he sits in his chambers in front of a work of art depicting a scene from Randolph Stow's 'Midnite', a children's story about – perhaps most appositely for a judge – a young colonial bushranger.

As we have seen, when the public perceives judicial lenience – as without doubt this observation would be regarded by many – they attribute the problem to judicial softness. Yet, the general public has a second pejorative explanation, one they regard as compounding the first. Judges are 'out of touch'. Though pithy in expression, it carries multiple connotations. Judges live in their own bubble, not really knowing what is going on in the community; judges live in a capsule, protected from life's every-day lurking dangers. Yet, the idea of the judiciary as 'out of touch' is a demonstrable absurdity, one most confidently relied on by those who are in their own way out-of-touch. The fact is, where two or three judges are gathered together for a quiet drink, their collective cup of inside knowledge – on crime, business affairs, interpersonal conflict, whatever – overflows. They deal with these matters every day in court, and they did so once as solicitors and barristers at the heart of these matters. And, yes, they and their families live their lives with its ever-present challenges and dangers in the community. Thus does the particular relevance of this portrait of Justice Maxwell lie in the scene behind him. For it was done by children at his daughter's then school, St. Kilda Park Primary School. As he determines what is most appropriate by way of punishment for the various types of offender appealing the harshness of their sentences, his daughter is there before him.

We now imagine the President of the Court of Appeal, his sentiments in AH then to the fore, itching to leaven the current way of punishment with the 'other way', the way of rehabilitative punishment. The stage was set in 2014 with the Victorian Government's introduction of a new non-custodial sentencing option known as the 'Community Corrections Order' (CCO).

The CCO was introduced as a flexible sentencing option. Around this time, it could be imposed as a stand-alone sentence or in combination with a fine or a term of imprisonment of up to two years. The essence of this order lies in the conditions which may attached to it by a court; these include: rehabilitation programmes, which may be residential; unpaid community work; supervision by a corrections officer; the payment of a bond; along with various conditions restricting an offender's liberty, such as a night curfew, bans on the offender associating with certain people or entering certain geographical locations.

What Justice Maxwell required now was the right case. In due course it came, when the Court of Appeal was asked to provide guidance to sentencing judges on how courts might best use the CCO. The President pounced – well, so we may easily suppose. The case is known as *Boulton*.[42]

In a lengthy joint judgment delivered by the President on behalf of the Court,[43] the question was: 'Can the CCO's conditions be fashioned in appropriate cases to maximally facilitate the offender's rehabilitation whilst adequately punishing them?'[44] After a lengthy discussion, the Court deemed a CCO of sufficient length (with or without an added sentence of imprisonment of up to two years) to be most appropriate for this, even in some relatively serious cases which would previously have attracted quite substantial terms of imprisonment. The Court entertained the possibility of cases involving offences such as aggravated burglary and intentionally causing serious injury, and some kinds of rape, certain categories of homicide, and some forms of sexual offences involving minors, all potentially falling within the scope of a CCO. Critical to this was whether, having regard to the gravity of the offence and the personal circumstances of the offender, a properly conditioned CCO might at once be severe enough not to affront the requirements of just and proportionate punishment, while affording the best prospects for the offender's rehabilitation. The latter would require the conditions attached to the CCO to be appropriate to the causal factors underlying the offending in the particular case. In the punitive climate of public opinion, this judgment must be regarded as extraordinarily innovative – indeed, a bold call. It had the potential to change the landscape of sentencing in Victoria.

This and the previous two judgments are surely most enlightened, ones of rare quality. Though delivered from the heart, they were the product of the head. Indeed, most influential on the President's thinking in the first of the latter two judgments was an article by a neuropsychologist and a neurologist.[45] That article examines the relationship between significant socio-economic disadvantage, its consequential debilitating effects on an individual's impulse control and judgement, as well as on an individual's capacity and opportunity to adapt to and take part in formal education, these in turn together being predisposing factors to criminal behaviour. In light of this understanding of the role played by personal and social disadvantage in criminal offending, we may see punishment and rehabilitation as crime preventive measures differently, as now though wearing inverting glasses, thus respectively not as wisdom and foolishness but as foolishness and wisdom.

In Starke and Maxwell, Lachlan and Elizabeth Macquarie would prepare to greet fellow-travellers; in these judgments, Winston Churchill would behold 'living virtue'. So, what was their fate? To this we return later in this chapter. First, there is the matter of the system in practice.

The re-imagined system in practice

As part of considering what this re-imagined system would mean for the sentencing of offenders in practice, it is helpful first to have a clear picture of what the current punitive system means for someone like the offender AH.

Yet, before proceeding, in order to establish the relevance and importance of what follows, one question must be addressed: why a system approach as a response to AH? why not a proposal involving no more than amendments to the current sentencing system allowing for a case like AH? The answer is as simple as it is incontestable. As Justice Maxwell observed, AH the man as a type of offender is not exceptional but 'all too familiar in the criminal courts'. Indeed, research in Australia has repeatedly demonstrated that among the general prison population a very substantial percentage of inmates bear at least three indices of serious disadvantage, including: poverty; unemployment; physical, sexual and psychological abuse; little education or skills training; a psychiatric disorder; homelessness; alcoholism; drug addiction; intellectual disability; a chaotic, undisciplined and affectionless upbringing; early institutionalization; and so on. There findings are even starker for Australia's imprisoned Aboriginal offenders. Though disadvantage commonly appears in the individual offender as a basket of factors, even one of these factors in certain circumstances may be sufficiently powerful to divert the course of a life – the change being almost imperceptible at first, then increasing signs of problematic behaviour; without intervention, this life soon in an uncontrolled spiral. Important for the wider relevance of the present story, these things hold true in countries around the world, for both the general population of prisoners and the marginalised minorities within the prison population.[46]

In light of this, and now alive to the importance of the matter, we return to the immediate issue at hand. How does this traditional sentencing system deal with the likes of AH? Well, it imposes a substantial term of imprisonment with the intention of condemning him as a moral being and his behaviour as a serious wrong, of deterring him from re-offending and others – men and women – like him from offending similarly, though this severe punishment will inhibit his chances of reform.

In so proceeding, it forces the sentencing judge to say – implicitly – to someone like AH: 'Your background explains, but it does not excuse, your offending'. Let this be spelt out for effect: 'I recognize your background has been appalling, I recognize it would bring tears to the eyes of many, I recognize you would not have offended but for this background, but for your manifest and deep-seated psychological problems. Yet, I am going to blame and condemn you;[47] and I am going to punish you, as though are psychologically sound and emotionally strong; as though you are the product of the most loving parents, the best education, and the strictest upbringing; as though you committed this offence motivated by greed, with much thought and planning, and as a rationally and wilfully chosen alternative to a law-abiding means. I accept this sentence will do nothing to help you become law-abiding, indeed it may even exacerbate your personal problems; indeed, it may confirm you in your offending'. And the system requires the judge to do this without batting an eye, blushing or blanching, and certainly not issuing an express apology for the system itself. In practice, sentencing judges in their humanity will often acknowledge the offender's personal history as warranting a small discount on their sentence, but in the traditional punitive sentencing system this will necessarily be little more than tokenistic.

This is a perspective of the traditional sentencing system from the perspective of the re-imagined rehabilitative system. Contemplate alongside this, a perspective of the re-imagined system from the perspective of the traditional system. For a sentencing system in essence rehabilitative, and providing for this principally in the community – note, the Community Corrections Order is just one of a number of possible variations of what such a scheme might look like – the consequential problem is patent. This is, for even a moderately serious offence, any practical combination of measures to be served in the community (unpaid community work, conditions restricting the offender's liberty, and so on) cannot be rendered as punishing as the term of imprisonment deemed necessary by a public wanting harsh punishment. Though it is open to the judge as part of a CCO to bolster its punitive punch with a term of imprisonment, this – certainly a substantial term – will often be in the offender's circumstances antithetical to their rehabilitation. The fact is, the integration of a sentencing option intended to deliver rehabilitative outcomes within a framework designed to distribute harsh punishments proportionate to the seriousness of the offending can never be; the conceptual incompatibility involved is as determining as any law of nature. Recall Bigge's question, which in dismay he asked Macquarie, as he inspected conditions of the convicts' lives, 'Where is the punishment?'

There are two other aspects relevant to the comparison of these two contrasting approaches to sentencing. In the traditional punitive system, for the general run of cases, offence seriousness not the type of offender is primary, for it determines the severity of the sanction. Hence, the framing sentencing question is: how serious is this offence? In this re-imagined system, the offender is all important. Hence the framing questions will be: what type of offender is before the court; what programme of rehabilitative measures would maximize this offender's chances of reform? In this approach, this programme of rehabilitative measures will constitute the offender's punishment. For some offenders, punishment (*qua* punitive punishment) may properly be construed as one of the rehabilitative measures. However, even in these cases, its quantum will not be determined by the seriousness of the offence; rather, the major determinant will be the rehabilitative needs of the offender. The second aspect relevant to the comparison of these two contrasting approaches to sentencing follows from the first. Since the severity of punishment depends in large measure on the rehabilitative programme, different offenders committing the same offence will not always be punished with equal severity. Nonetheless, offence proportionality would play a secondary role, guarding against excessive severity as a consequence of rehabilitative enthusiasm, and guarding against a degree of leniency such as to trivialize a serious offence.

It was the offender AH who set us thinking about this rehabilitative alternative. Here he represents offenders – men and women – who suffer multiple personal and social deficits, which together predominantly account for their criminal behaviour. In some cases, as intimated above, one of these factors will account principally for the offender's behaviour. This may be true for certain types of drug addict. Another will be the offender whose intelligence level falls just above that defining intellectual disability. There will be other categories of offender relevant to this rehabilitative approach. The clinical identification of them falls beyond the scope of this discussion. What is critical to our thinking here with respect to this alternative approach to punishment is that these types of offender will have little chance of turning their lives around in the absence of remedial intervention from some external source. Is it not sensible, then, that we deal with them constructively? Their crimes are principally the crimes of the street (burglaries, muggings, assault, and the like). They, as offenders, appear not like us, the respectable. They are the face of the fear of crime.

Yet often judges, when enquiring into the circumstances of the of offender before the court, will be faced with a very different type of person (and offending). These will be men and women whose crimes are principally the product of moral turpitude, carried out for their own personal benefit and satisfaction, and which manifest a calculated disregard for the interests and rights of others. These types of crime often will constitute fraudulent behaviour. And their modus operandi may involve bold planning or simply sly opportunism. They not infrequently will be committed behind the scenes by those who think of themselves, and are regarded by others, as respectable. Yet they may include brazen, calculatingly brutal, crimes. In this type of case, punitive punishment will be properly the main aim of sentencing, being of a degree of severity to accord with the seriousness of the offending and to serve as a deterrent. This is to be contrasted with the role of punishment for the category of offender dealt with in the previous paragraphs; there it was primarily rehabilitative.[48]

This second type of offending was one with which we know Macquarie himself was familiar, which he understood all too well, which had sullied his own character, and which informed his benevolent treatment of the general convict. It is represented in the image (opposite), one – well, something like it – no doubt haunting Lachlan's own conscience.

In this re-imagined system of sentencing, substantial terms of imprisonment would still have their place; these would be principally for the most serious offenders, the truly dangerous, the egregiously recalcitrant, and for those whose offending involves a grave moral turpitude. Yet overall the scale of imprisonment would be much reduced; the financial resources it currently gobbles up, redirected. Then perhaps the sentences for the majority of offenders would involve programmes addressing their personal and social needs, both those circumstances underlying their offending and those with the potential to undermine their rehabilitation – programmes, well resourced, ones undertaken for the most part in the community within a tight supervisory framework of demands and constraints, less often in association with a moderate or even a short term of imprisonment.

A LAWYER and his AGENT.

The parallels between what is imagined here, following Sir John Starke and Justice Maxwell's observations, and Macquarie's understanding of rehabilitative punishment are unmistakable. Recall, the convicts' punishment for their British criminality was their period of penal servitude, this involving unpaid work for the government and the free settlers, along with restrictions on their freedom within the community. As far as Macquarie was concerned, this punishment was not separate from the convicts' reform; rather, it was very much part of it. This punishment was to be as constructive as practicable, and its harshness and duration curtailed so as to not inhibit the convicts' reform and renewal. Fundamental to using the Macquaries' principles as a guide to the punishment of criminals today – the most serious offences and the dangerous offenders aside – is the understanding of this relationship between punishment and reform. Here is an explicit statement of those principles distilled from Macquarie's practice:

1) What is of prime importance is the convicts' futures, not their past lives.
2) Proportionality between the seriousness of a convict's offending and the severity of their punishment will generally assume little significance.
3) This emphasis on a convict's reform is initially not much dependent on their prospects of responding favourably; rather, what matters is their being in need of reform as a convict.
4) In order to reform, most convicts will require help. Many will need to learn new skills to ready them for employment. Some even will be in want of socialization – those who have never fully acquired or who have lost the art of self-regulating their lives. Re-socialization – this is what is required here – is very much facilitated by allowing the convicts to serve their term of punishment in the community. In this way, the convict is able in effect to practise routine and discipline, to socialize with the free as a means of breaking their criminal associations – such normalizing influences, albeit under a supervisory regime, offer the best chance of reform.
5) In view of this type of personal history, lapses by a convict should be accorded a good measure of toleration.
6) Punishments must not be so harsh as to crush offenders.
7) The goal of reform should not merely be the cessation of offending, but lives renewed, regenerated, uplifted, enjoyed.

There is an eighth principle, namely: the convicts, on completing their punishment and thence being of good behaviour, must have open to them all the privileges, benefits and responsibilities of the free, it being as though they had never offended. The relevance of this principle will arise in the following section.

This re-imagined sentencing scheme reflects an appreciation of the principles underlying the Macquaries' treatment of the convicts. It offers, as did theirs, a different approach to the treatment of crime and criminals. In Churchill's terms, something like it would speak well of our society as civilized; in the scope of our history, it would represent enlightenment. In respect of this, be not surprised then that its realization would involve not a tweaking but a transformation of the present traditional punitive system; a transformation not a tweaking too for our thinking about crime and punishment as a community.

Implications of this re-imagined system for the public's perception of punishment

Our present punitive sentencing system offers the public much. Victims have the satisfaction of seeing their tormentor condemned, shamed, shut away and suffering penal pain. The general public experiences relief when society's predators – the violent, the sexual, the roaming dishonest – are locked up. They feel that little bit safer. These criminals are not free to do their dastardly deeds; at least some of them, and some of their kind, will now be deterred from doing likewise. Indeed, the public's very satisfaction with what the punitive system does for them – better, has the potential to do for them – gives rise to their greatest dissatisfaction with the present system. How better it would be were many more offenders sent to prison and for far longer periods of time. 'Why not?', they and their cheerleaders cry out; and in recent times they have done this to great effect. As for sentences not involving imprisonment, or involving short terms of imprisonment, these, in all but the least serious cases, leave them feeling very discontent, even angry. Crimes they regard as serious receiving little condemnation; their safety being compromised; criminals leaving court not shrouded in opprobrium but free to laugh at their victims, and then re-offend.

From the perspective of a punitive system, imprisonment represents punishment's gold standard. Anything less is not appropriate for even crimes of moderate seriousness. It is not real punishment: its pains are too easily borne to deter, its message too soft to shame. The rehabilitative alternative, absent as its measures are of any significant punitive sting, leaves the law-abiding vulnerable and crime trivialized. Indeed, the general public can in its own mind sensibly hold this view only because it does not appreciate the large presence of offenders like AH in the prison system. It does not occur to them that men and women like AH do not think like them and are not deterred by punishment, no matter its severity. They do not understand – indeed, appear to find it hard to entertain – these types of people are not so much rational masters of their circumstances, as more foolish victims of them.

This surely prompts the question: how contrasting might the views on punishment of the public be were they to embrace the alternative of rehabilitative punishment? Perhaps serious doubts might arise in their minds about the potency of harsh punishment as a deterrent. Perhaps they might start to feel uncomfortable when they go to dismiss someone like AH as evil and worthless, as a person to be locked away and forgotten about, as someone whose future is not worth thinking about. Then, they would be forced to entertain, for certain categories of offender, something like the rehabilitative scheme proposed here. Then, they might come to appreciate that programmes of reform, with their therapeutic demands and restrictions on liberty, and over an extended period, will have substantial punitive pain for the likes of AH. In light of this, the public might accept the offender's participation in proper rehabilitation, as an alternative to punitive imprisonment, as sufficient to appropriately condemn the offender's behaviour. They might accept these things, though realizing the associated punitive pain will never match what is required, for even a moderately serious offence, under proportionate punishment. As part of this, they would grasp that there is a choice to be made: the AH's of this world cannot be both punished harshly and profitably participate in programmes aimed at their reform. The conclusion would become inescapable: they must choose one way or the other.

How different it would be under the rehabilitative way! How transformed community debate about crime and punishment would be when imprisonment was no longer the gold standard! Then, when an offender was not imprisoned, the public's cry would not be that another criminal has escaped real punishment. Or, when imprisonment was actually imposed on an offender, the cry would not be, 'Why not a longer term of imprisonment for this criminal?' Rather, it would be, 'Why not rehabilitative punishment for this offender?' Then too, our focus would no longer be on expanding prison capacity; rather, it would be redirected to the better resourcing of treatment programmes and of the supervision of offenders in the community. We would no longer ignore the failures of imprisonment; and we would no longer cry out about the apparent failures of rehabilitation. Indeed, we would want to learn from these failures so rehabilitation might enjoy greater success. How differently, too, we would treat offenders like AH. We as a society no longer damning them, but seeking to understand their circumstances. No longer thundering to put them down because of the bad in them, but striving to raise them up because of the potential good in them. No longer stamping them with an eternal mark of Cain; rather, upon their reform, offering them all the privileges, benefits and responsibilities of the free and as though they had never offended.

What a contrast to our present punitive culture. How civilized; how Churchill! How enlightened; how Lachlan and Elizabeth!

The idea of a system of justice which is primarily rehabilitative, one in which imprisonment is no longer the gold standard, will not come about, will not even find a place in the political debate of the day, unless it finds champions and leaders. Expert practitioners from various sections of the field, to be sure, but principally this ideal will require championing by political leaders. They will need to explain to the people the rehabilitative alternative's potential to improve community safety long-term. For this, the public will need to understand the personal characteristics of many – perhaps the majority – of offenders, as Justice Maxwell did in the Court's judgment in *AH*. The public will need to understand the punitive and condemnatory features of a rehabilitative justice system; they will need to understand the trade-offs involved. The public will need to appreciate they cannot have it both ways. And the champions and leaders will frame the debate with a consideration most fundamental: Churchill's understanding of the treatment of criminals as a measure of society's civilization.

So, what are chances of this in the foreseeable future? For the answer, we must return to the Victorian Court of Appeal's judgments in *AH* and in *Boulton* and learn of their fate.

The fate of the judgments in *AH* and *Boulton*

The glory of *AH* perhaps unnoticed; or if noticed, unappreciated – inconsequential, a thought bubble. For *Boulton* it was very different. Certainly, the virtue in the judgment was not appreciated. But its consequentiality was – oh yes! When it comes to sensing a diminution in the pains of imprisonment, the punitive punishers carry very finely tuned antennae. When it comes to the powerful personal and social determinants underlying much criminal behaviour, and their inhibiting effect on the efficacy of punishment as a deterrent, the punitive step forth, some blindly unaware of, others negligently indifferent to, the path they are on. Not surprisingly, then, less than six months after *Boulton*, these people were doing some of their finest destructive work.

The Court of Appeal well understood that the success of the Community Corrections Order, as they had envisaged its use, would depend on there being a well-funded programme to inform the public about the CCO, its nature, application, and its place in the system of punishment. Of especial concern to the Court, particularly in the current punitive climate, was that the public might not appreciate the CCO's very real capacity for substantial punishment. Indeed, even a reasonable person, on hearing a superficial account of this sanction, might not appreciate its potential to bite hard. The Government chose not to heed the Court's advice. The inevitable avalanche of strident criticism soon followed from the tabloid press, the public, the Opposition: 'Soft on crime', 'Thugs at large', they thundered! The Government, far from defending the Court's decision, and explaining the wisdom of its decision, actually ran for cover. 'Not us', they cried defensively! In turn, they swiftly introduced legislation aimed at significantly restricting the sanction's use in cases of serious crime – imprisonment it should be – even though the perpetrators of these crimes in many instances might be expected to profit – along with the general community, as a consequence – from the CCO's rehabilitative conditions. A dark shadow now covered the Court of Appeal's enlightenment. The punitive punishers celebrated – many of the good among them perhaps largely oblivious to what they had wished for, to what they had just done.[49]

One would have hoped the Government of the day would have explained *Boulton* to the public – its potentially very onerous punitive bite, its condemnatory features, its potential contribution to their safety though the rehabilitative component – and, when it came under inevitable criticism, they would have been quick to defend it. One might have even hoped for bipartisan support. Naïve hopes – clearly! What followed was not politicians appealing to the public's rational sense, but to their basest instincts. What a far cry from Churchill's understanding, Churchill's leadership!

Yet are we faced with this confronting fact: it is on politicians we are forced to rely for something better in the treatment of crime and criminals. In this we find a barrier to a more enlightened treatment of crime and criminals, a barrier not within us but outside us, namely, political ordinariness.

POLITICAL ORDINARINESS

When people are faced with hurdles, they often will need help to surmount them. In some cases, even unaware their progress is being impeded, they will need to be alerted to their very presence. In these circumstances, people require guiding and supportive hands at their side. In respect of an enlightened approach to the punishment of offenders, the role of principal guide and helper necessarily falls to our parliamentary leaders. So, we must ask, 'Are our current parliamentary leaders, politicians or statesmen, Bathursts or Churchills?' Sadly, the answer must be the former.

How do we distinguish a politician from a statesman? Politicians fan popular causes for expedience; statesmen champion unpopular causes on principle. In regard to the treatment of crime and criminals, it is patently this way. In many countries around the globe, strong majorities

John Major. T. Leighton, photographer. Copy from and made by the National Portrait Gallery, London (NPG x38237).

of the public subscribe to the view that the punishment of criminals is to a greater or lesser extent too lenient. Up until about (say) thirty years ago, this view represented little more than background noise in the public consciousness. Cries for tougher punishments would come to the fore in the face of an egregious crime of violence, or a newspaper editorial claiming crime – especially violent crime – was out of control. These cries were always founded on the same underlying belief: crime had become a scourge because punishments were not harsh enough to serve as a deterrent to criminals. Yet, these would quickly die away, when the public's attention was captured by other news. And so, the cycle continued. Until … until politicians realized crime had the potential to be a gem of a vote-winner. Wait for one of these events, then tell the public you have heard them. Tick. Tell them you share their fears. Tick. Label criminals as scum, low-life, undeserving of sympathy. Tick. Tell the public 'crims' only understand one language. Tick. Promise to build more prisons and to lock up all the 'crims'. Tick. No need to explain or produce evidence; all you need is a catchy, trite slogan like, 'Do the crime, do the time'. No need for a long-term plan; you can imply the effect of what you propose will be immediate. As to the actual effect of what you propose on the crime rate, or any possibility of unintended consequences … well, you'll be elected by then. Too easy! Just fan the discontent by proclaiming your slogan around the country, and let the voters do the rest. Go home each night, feeling pleased with yourself. The law-and-order politician at his and her typical. Do not dismiss this description as a caricature; too many politicians are like this. In respect of the treatment of crime and criminals, they exemplify political ordinariness.

Who then are these people? For the most part, it matters not. For they are people whose intellect largely manifests itself as cunning, and they commonly rank low on the scale of verbal articulation. It is as well we do not try to understand their words, because there is little to be discerned in them. Nonetheless, not all those who favour tougher punishments, who fan public opinion, are inarticulate. These are the people who, by means of a pithy phrase, actually give us a clue to their thinking, even invoke our reasoning. No world figure, when it comes to criminal justice, better illustrates this than John Major – British Prime Minister, 1990-1997.

Few would remember him as a significant political leader. Rather, perhaps we are inclined to think of him as he appears in this portrait of him (see p.213): an Everyman; a generally decent man, who appears to exude the common person's common sense, and is mild of manner and action; a man though who is no soft touch – a person much like our ordinary selves, in whose company we would not be out of our depth, whose simply expressed opinions might well accord with our own intuitive wisdom. What, then, did John Major have to say about the sentencing of criminals?

'Society needs to condemn a little more and understand a little less'[50]

It was 1993, as John Major prepared to introduce a new tough law-and-order policy. With these words, he was showing the people he was listening to them; he was promising to give them what they wanted; and he was demonstrating he understood why they wanted what they did. In respect of the last of these, what did he actually have in mind? In this context, 'understanding' carries two related strands of meaning. First, in regard to sentencing, the purpose of understanding the causes of crime will be to develop effective rehabilitative programmes. Second, 'understanding' here may connote sympathy for the offender in their plight. Thus, for example, when the underlying cause of a young person's violent behaviour is drug addiction, then we might want to support them through a treatment programme. Moreover, the antecedent circumstances underlying their behaviour with which they did not have the strength of character to cope (e.g. abusive childhood), and their present circumstances which may have been beyond their control (e.g. homelessness), might be seen as favouring a less punitive sanction than would have been otherwise considered appropriate. This line of thinking must be taken as what John Major was decrying.

In its stead, John Major was urging the people to focus on condemning the criminal. What he meant here was punishment by way of the greater use of imprisonment; punishment which would be imposed on criminal offenders at the expense of their rehabilitation. The context of John Major's statement appears to suggest he believed this would be a better crime control strategy, seemingly with no patent awareness that for many types of offender this might not be so. Now, pause and ponder what John Major is really doing here. John Major is, in effect, counselling his country men and women – all common-sensed people like himself – against seeking an understanding, and against exercising this understanding, in respect of the problem of crime and criminals. Moreover, John Major is counselling his country men and women – all decent people like himself – to become a nation of condemners. His is a vision of a less thoughtful, a harsher society. Yet perhaps not so sensible or decent an approach for our drug addict, ugh? More than this, the expression of sentiments such as these risks enlivening the baser instincts in the human heart and emboldening the expression of them.

Contrast this with Churchill's observations about the treatment of crime and criminals, the triteness against the majesty of the language aside. Thus: 'understand less'; how unenlightened! Thus: 'condemn more'; how uncivilized! Moreover, Churchill was in effect challenging the public's common-sense view – one widely held and deeply entrenched – about the treatment of crime and criminals, a matter affecting their personal security. An action surely hazarding political popularity. John Major in confirming what the people thought and wanted to here, thereby courting popularity. Churchill was playing the statesman; John Major was demonstrating political ordinariness.

The point is surely clear. If society is to move to an enlightened approach to the treatment of crime and criminals, as that is understood here, the public will need political leadership from statesmen and stateswomen. These men and women will face a monumental task compared with that of the political ordinaries. These enlighteners necessarily will need to be people abreast of the empirical facts, people able to impart their higher understanding to those with less understanding. Moreover, these men and women will need to be of strong character and resolute convictions. They will be ridiculed and howled down. For the instinctively punitive speak with greater certainty, more loudly and more stridently, than do the thoughtfully moderate.

From this discussion of political ordinariness, we can see its having played a critical role in the undoing of the Macquaries' work. When it came to crime and justice, Bathurst was politically ordinary. And in this chapter, we have seen it undo a modern judicial move toward enlightenment. As a barrier, it remains active today. Yet it is underpinned by five other barriers to a more enlightened system of criminal justice system. These barriers were active too in the Macquaries' time. They, unlike political ordinariness, are to be found within us. Indeed, that the Macquaries' thinking about criminal justice was not tripped up by these mental obstacles is another testament to their greatness. To these barriers we now turn.

Chapter 11

Barriers to the Enlightened Treatment of the Criminal

W HEN MAINSTREAM PUNITIVENESS is challenged, how myopic and ruthless the defence – no questions asked, no quarter given – this, we saw, was the response to the Victorian Court of Appeal's most enlightened judgment in *Boulton*. Thus are we prompted to explore the thinking underpinning this certainty in the punitive status quo. In fact, the nature of and reasons for this thinking are to be found in unacknowledged mental barriers to our accepting a more enlightened treatment of crime and criminals. Here, five barriers are identified: (1) uninformed theory; (2) the common-sense understanding of criminal behaviour; (3) mental and physical remoteness from the phenomenon; (4) respectability (5) criminals as bogey men and women. These barriers are to be discerned in the ideas of the intelligentsia and learned, the great and the good, whose thinking influenced the minds of men and women around the time of the Macquarie era. These very barriers still cause us all to stumble in one way or another along the path to a more enlightened approach to crime today. This is their significance at this point in the present story; herein lies the importance of our understanding them and their potential effects on our thinking.

UNINFORMED THEORY

For the British government, the main aim of transportation was deterrence by way of punishment. Transportation was the punishment, its target being the suppression of crime in Britain. The conditions of penal servitude were not formulated with reform in mind; thus, convict reform when it did occur was an incidental outcome of the system. The Macquaries, as we know, sought to change this within the limits available to them. For them, the conditions of penal servitude should be tailored to maximize the convicts' prospects of reform. In their minds, the effects of this on the deterrence of crime at home counted for naught. Of the reformative potential of transportation, the Macquaries were certain.

Yet in Britain, men properly regarded as social reformers – Bennet was one, William Wilberforce another – were convinced transportation in practice was not, and as a matter of principle could not be, rehabilitative. Some of them vociferously campaigned against it. You see, these men had a better idea – actually, an enlightened idea – so they sincerely believed. The idea these men had in mind was the penitentiary. For them, this alternative was, contrary to transportation, a means of fair punishment and effective reform for the criminal.

Penitentiaries were places where criminals would be confined in isolation or, when not alone, would be forced to remain silent. The inmates' activities there would involve hard work, the reading of morally uplifting literature, and reflective thought. All this would take place in spartan physical conditions and under a regime of strict discipline. Confinement and hard work were the prisoners' punishment for the wrong they had done, and as a deterrent to their future offending. As to rehabilitation, hard work under discipline would instil into the prisoners the work ethic they all lacked. And by means of reading and reflective thought, both under a chaplain's spiritual and moral guidance, the prisoners would come to understand the wrongfulness of their past lives and to appreciate their need for personal renewal.

The man who put the idea of the penitentiary before the British public and made the case for it as an alternative to transportation, was Jeremy Bentham. He prosecuted his case, from late in the eighteenth century until after the Macquarie era, with unremitting vigour and unquestioned certainty. Penitentiaries, like prisons, might assume various physical forms. Bentham himself designed a penitentiary, which he called the panopticon. Its cells were in tiered layers, arranged around a central observation tower, so the prisoners felt themselves under constant surveillance. He even composed a few lines suited to the entrance of a penitentiary: 'Had they been industrious when free, they need not have drudged here like slaves'.[51] Now that tells us something about how he saw the problem of crime! But perhaps it tells us something about him, also. Are these not lines appealing to people whose sentiments towards criminals and their treatment bespeak a degree of contempt and

'The Tread-mill at Brixton'. After a similar image published in the *Gentleman's Magazine*, London, 1822.

vengeance, people who are blind to the social and personal underpinnings of much crime?

To Bentham, the penitentiary had the potential to provide both principled and rational punishment. Punishments would be fair, being meted out in finely graded proportions according to the seriousness of a particular prisoner's crime and need for deterrence. Thus, the more serious the crime, and the consequent greater the need for deterrence, so a longer period of confinement and a more intense regime during that period. Moreover, the punishments addressed what he assumed were the causes of crime, namely, physical laziness and moral wantonness, along with a general lack of personal discipline. In contrast, so argued Bentham, transportation did not achieve these fundamental goals of punishment, either as a matter of principle or in practice. In respect of punishment, Bentham's arguments had much validity. The terms of penal servitude were but most crudely fixed by courts according to offence

'Interior of the Copper & Brass Works'. [Draw]n and published by Pyne and Nattes, [London, c1806].

seriousness. With the first step-up in the term of penal servitude being at seven years and the second at fourteen, it could not be otherwise. Along with this, especially in the Macquaries' time, what a convict had to offer, together with what they might become, were more important than what crime they had committed back in Britain. Moreover, the conditions of servitude experienced by most of the well-behaved convicts did not involve harsh punishment; indeed, they were often more congenial than the circumstances of their lives back in Britain. As we know, it was the Macquaries' policy of rehabilitation and renewal driving these practices. With this policy, the term a convict actually served might bear little relationship to the seriousness of their original crime.

In this light, Bentham's ideas about punishment in respect of transportation had, as matter of legal principle, some merit. What he had to say about rehabilitation, however, represented utter nonsense. For the main body of convicts who were sent to the Colony, the principal causes of their offending were not personal indolence or intrinsic badness. Rather, the cause was the social malaise in which the lower classes found themselves and from which they did not have the means to extricate themselves. They did not work, because there was not work; they stole, were sometimes violent, because they were desperate and embittered; they caroused and lived in wretchedness because they became afflicted with a personal malaise. Their criminal behaviour was morally wrong, but it did not spring from a deep-seated moral wantonness. The majority of these people would work if there was work; most of these people would live at least reasonably decent lives – indeed, often very good lives – if the opportunity was open to them. But it would not come through Bentham's punishment. For under his proposal, once the inmates had completed their term of imprisonment in the panopticon, they would return to their former social circumstances and with the same mentality – the very factors responsible for their offending.

A second innovative British proposal for the punishment and reform of criminals around the time of the Macquaries was the treadmill. Its significance here is that it might incorporate Benthamite ideas, and indeed as a punishment had Bentham's support. Contemplate, then, this image of a treadmill (see p.218).

This particular treadmill was built at Brixton prison in 1821, and was one of several fanned out around the grounds of the prison. These devices, in fact, were favoured as a means of punishment by many of the reformers of the day. The treadmill consisted of a cylinder, laid horizontally, with steps forming its sides and running between each end; a central shaft was connected to two giant millstones, which on turning ground grain. The wheel was turned by having prisoners walk up the steps; one description of this mechanism was the 'never-ending staircase'. The central observation tower reflects the Benthamite idea of the inmates needing to be under constant observation – an essential element of the panopticon – and the treadmill itself meets his requirement of prisoners experiencing constant hard work. (The prisoners being ground honest is how Bentham himself picturesquely – and coldly – explained the principle.) Now, compare this image with the accompanying image of a factory scene (see p.219). It is British, but it might be from Macquarie's Sydney – one of Simeon Lord's factories, in fact – and the men, assignees (see also the farmyard scene, p.113 – and the associated text). Perhaps the futility – indeed, consequent cruelty – of Bentham's thinking now strikes us harder? The work itself was unskilled, and left the prisoners with nothing of which to be proud; the circumstances of the work were degrading, and of no relevance to

'**Bentham**'. G. Watts, artist. J. Posselwhite, engraver. Published by C. Knight & Co., London, [c1833].

the prisoners' future lives. By way of contrast, perhaps we now see more clearly how transportation – specifically, the circumstances under which convicts might serve their term of penal servitude – did provide the very opportunities and general conditions so facilitative of reform and renewal? So how did the undoubtedly brilliant Bentham get it so wrong? To answer this question, we must try and understand Bentham. Let us meet him in this portrait (above) and consider his biography.

Jeremy Bentham was born in 1748. A precocious intellect, he went up to Oxford University in his early teens, then subsequently studied law, but never practised as a barrister. Rather, he chose to be a legal philosopher. His professional predilection was to understand the world by way of legal theory, moral precepts, and ideology. What he needed to know was in his head, his reading, and his immediate world, there to be discerned, thence to be distilled in terms of principles suited to practical application. To Bentham, the problems of this world he chose to address, though practical, were properly treated as intellectual. Hence, was the head sufficient for his needs. On this basis he proceeded to deal with the punishment of criminals. His chain of reasoning must have run something like this. Crime was wrong, so a person's lack of personal morality and moral discipline must underlie their criminal behaviour. Man is rational, so there must be a decision to offend, consciously made, of the pleasing gain (e.g. the avoidance of work) outweighing any possible painful loss (i.e. the punishment). As a consequence, the solution to re-offending will require moral instruction, in a disciplined regime, along with punishment. Moreover, punishment as a response to crime invokes the notion of fairness. In this context, fairness is linked to harshness; thus, in the particular case, the severity of the punishment must satisfy the needs of deterrence and, in association with this, the seriousness of the offence, but no more. Such appears to be the basis, and indeed limits, of his understanding of criminals and their punishment. In this light, we can readily appreciate how he settled on the idea of the panopticon. In this light, it appears clever. Turn a factual light on, and it appears silly.

The fact is, Bentham's apparently exclusive reliance on philosophy and contemplation was a barrier to his coming to a realistic understanding of criminal rehabilitation. In point is, it led him badly astray. But what is the point of all this here, you may ask. The point is, the general public relies on a lay philosophy and personal speculation to form its views on how we should punish the criminals of today. Now, almost certainly you will recoil at this statement, even dismissing it as absurd. You, the practical man and woman being likened to the dreamer Bentham! After all, you probably smiled mockingly at Bentham's other-worldly, somewhat ridiculous visage, as it appears in this portrait of him. And, as a consequence, you may not have been offended by my trivializing presentation of Bentham's arguments, perhaps even chuckling derisively as you read. Yet, those observations were not intended as cheap shots at Bentham; that would be a travesty, for Bentham was one of criminal law's great minds. Rather, they are intended to set up for a fall those who are amused by the academic Bentham's portrait and thinking! That fact is, when the general public – well, the majority of them – pontificate on the punishment of offenders, they and their reasoning will bemuse the informed mind. It is they who appear as though of another world;

it is their solutions to the problem of crime which appear simplistic and ill-founded, part of the script from a tragic comedy. This point is now developed as we consider the second barrier to a more enlightened treatment of the criminal, namely, the common-sense understanding of criminal behaviour.

THE COMMON-SENSE UNDERSTANDING OF CRIMINAL BEHAVIOUR

Meet Henry, Lord Brougham, born in 1778, deemed a product of the Scottish Enlightenment. He like Bentham was a precocious intellect. After completing his schooling at the age of thirteen, he proceeded to read law at Edinburgh University, and thence to practise as a barrister. By the time he entered Parliament in 1810, this polymath had been elected a Fellow of the Royal Society for his contributions to the physics of light. His vanity and aristocratic bearing were in proportion to his intellect; nonetheless, there was a soft side to his character, which allowed him to look upon many of life's losers with the eye of pity. All characteristics – well, certainly the former – consistent with the 1821 portrait of him (see p.224).

Now, although Brougham's intellect shone brightly at atmospheric heights, it was fully functional and at home on the ground. In respect of the latter, he designed and had built a light, four-wheeled, horse-drawn carriage for his convenience and as an affectation. Others liked the idea, and the style caught on; the Brougham carriage was born. This turn of mind was what made him a practical social pioneer. Brougham was able to distinguish philosophical problems from social problems. For the former he appreciated the need for theory, with which his conceptual mind was in its element. However, when it came to social problems, his powerful intellect was grassroots-practical, its method keen observation. Apparently, he thought of pure theory as a means to solutions for social problems unhelpful, even misleading: it could render a man, an idea, foolish, even dangerous, when not born of or tested in reality. In this respect, he was critical of his great intellectual companion, Jeremy Bentham, in fact.

Brougham was not only very, very, clever, he was a humanitarian to boot, not merely in his thoughts, but importantly in his interests and actions. So was he led to the problem of crime prevention. This was important to Brougham because he too believed that transportation as a system of punishment was unfair. Thus he reasoned: if the incidence of criminal behaviour could be reduced in Britain, then the need for transportation would be averted. This was something he first raised in

'Henry Brougham, Esq'e. M.P.& F.R.S.'. J. Lonsdale, artist. R. Fenner, engraver. Published by Knight & Lacey, London, 1825.

the early 1800s, and which he continued to hammer away at in articles and speeches for decades. So, how did Brougham's practical mind attack this social problem?

The convicts, as we know, came predominantly from the under-and working-classes of Britain, their crimes being of the street variety, namely, those of dishonesty and violence, generally of a less-serious order, but frequently not, and in the majority of cases almost certainly represented repeat offending. Brougham was convinced that the immediate causes of their offending were desperate need and alienation in the wretched circumstances of their lives. Moreover, his reasoning ran on, many of these unfortunate people were so placed, not through any fault of their own, but by virtue of social forces beyond their control. All this became so apparent to him as he moved about London, witnessed the courts in action, and thought about what was before him. For preventative measures to be successful, he reasoned, they must address the social causes of crime. They must address the problematic circumstances of their lives. In this idea he found two policy consequences: something which was not being done but would work; something which was being done but would not work.

Brougham's 'something which was not being done but would work' was education. Thus did he champion the building of parish schools for the benefit of the young children of the lower orders, first in the cities, then the countryside. They would be built where 'crime is rife, where people are closely crowded and ignorant'.[52] With this would come the opportunity for them to make something of their lives. Yet, in his treating crime as of social origins, he faced a problem.

The problem Brougham faced was the widespread opposition to his idea. This was founded on the widely held belief that crime was a human, not a social, failing. It was an entrenched belief, among both the general population and the politicians of the day. They would make their case along the following lines: people committed crime because they were bad, but they would only offend when they thought it would benefit them. This represented a reasoned, conscious decision, one having a calculative character. No room here for desperate need; or moments of madness; or minds blind to risk. The solution, then, was a matter of common sense. Criminals must be punished harshly so the punishment on being caught would out-weigh any contemplated benefit. Accordingly, punishment as deterrence was the key to crime control. This, has elements of Bentham's academic understanding of the problem. Indeed, Brougham publicly criticized this idea of Bentham's as being seriously misplaced and providing no sensible basis for crime prevention. This was his 'something which was being done but would not work'. As the grounded Brougham had so clearly discerned, Bentham's theory could not account for garden-variety crime being a largely social phenomenon. Intelligent observation of the circumstances of actual lives, rather than academic theorizing, served Brougham, as it had served Macquarie before, very well. Indeed, Brougham seemed to be proud of his lay approach, one of his articles being entitled, 'Practical Observations upon the Education of the People', first published in 1824 in the *Edinburgh Review*.

Bathurst, driven by Sidmouth, was the leading politician of the Macquaries' day who blindly put his faith in the deterring power of punishment; this, on the basis of criminal behaviour being the product of human failings. When crime continued to flourish, transportation notwithstanding, the solution was clear to him. The conditions of penal servitude were just not harsh enough to outweigh the benefits of a life of crime. Render them more severe, and the scales would tip. So obvious, so simple! It was too obvious, too simple, as the Macquaries well knew; it did not deal with the complexities of the antecedents of the crimes of dishonesty and violence committed by Britain's lower social orders.

This view of Bathurst's, the very view under attack from Brougham, is our common-sense view today. Herein lies the relevance of the preceding discussion. Whether in a gentleperson's club, at the pub, on the golf-course, at the football, a charity working-bee, or just over the back fence – wherever two or more are gathered together – the topic of crime will find its way into the conversation. The interlocutors will lament how life would be so much better if only they felt safe in their homes and when they go out at night. The problem? Soft sentences: too few 'crims' being put behind bars; too few 'crims' not locked up for long enough. The reason behind their conclusions – the current levels of punishment are not harsh enough to deter the criminal – will remain unstated because it is assumed to be so obvious as to be agreed. Views uncritically accepted as sound; well, what else is to be said, they represent the wisdom of the people, those with the common sense. Not the views of aristocratic dreamers like Brougham!

They fact is, for most of us, a belief based on our common sense has the character of certain knowledge. Yet, it is anything but this; better being characterized as a blind and unquestioned faith. When we think about something based on experience, where that experience is lacking we blithely project our current understanding into the unknown. We confidently extrapolate and interpolate from what is often limited experience. How long, despite scientific research to the contrary, did it take Middle-Ages man and woman to accept the world was not flat? And specific to our own time and to crime and deterrence: people like ourselves used to drink to excess and drive; no longer – the now draconian penalties make it not worth the risk. Thus, we make our case for deterrence. No thought that our prison populations may be made up of people who, in the circumstances of their lives, are not so rational nor so self-controlled. How unlike Brougham, a man whose intellectual foundation for his ideas on crime prevention was based on the thoughtful, active and systematic observation of his subject. From this barrier follows the related barrier of mental and physical remoteness from the phenomenon.

MENTAL AND PHYSICAL REMOTENESS FROM THE PHENOMENON

Personal remoteness as a barrier to a more enlightened approach to criminal justice is to be seen when (1) a person speculates about the causes and means of dealing with criminal behaviour, though knowing little about offenders or the circumstances of their offending, and (2) they are oblivious to the importance of this knowledge to their understanding of the problem. This third barrier is not directly responsible for tripping thinking up; instead, it bolsters uninformed theory and common sense as barriers. In fact, personal remoteness has two aspects generally acting in concert. One appears as a predisposition to think in the abstract; the other is actual physical remoteness. It was there to be seen at work in Bentham's legal theory and our reliance on our common sense.

The effect of this barrier can be seen in the lives of some of the leading British parliamentarians of the early 1800s. There can be no better exemplar of this than Sir James Mackintosh. He was born in Scotland in 1765, studied medicine, and subsequently practised as a barrister. Before entering Parliament in 1810, he held a judicial post as the Recorder of Bombay. This is where we first met him in this story and, as we know, where he first met Macquarie and enlarged his younger interlocutor's mind over many a mutually pleasant hour. Mackintosh is held to be one of the finest products of the Scottish Enlightenment, and one of the great figures of the British parliament. This conversationalist par excellence liked to rabbit on, but none so inclined could surpass him in eloquence, or hold the learned of the day so captivated. He opined most intelligently on everything – crime included – in the absence of expertise about anything. Without his cultivation, his eloquence, his intelligence, and his loftiness, he was Everyman – the man and woman in the street, us. We should meet him and learn from his foible. Meet him in the following image (see p.228), around the time of his days in India.

Mackintosh's reforming and humanitarian instincts led him to address the penal system. He spoke against the severity of punishments and the physical wretchedness of prisons as a response to crime. He questioned the deterrent value of the former, and thought both demeaning and soul-destroying, and generally militating against the rehabilitation of criminals. Punishment must be made reformative, he would declaim. Pure Macquarie – the declaiming aside! Yet figure of enlightenment though

Mackintosh was, the depth of his understanding of the general convict's mentality, and the consequential brightness of the light he cast upon their punishment, paled beside those of the Macquaries. For he accepted Bentham's critique of transportation and was convinced of the merits of Bentham's panopticon. The latter was consistent with his championing of prisons – that is, reforming prisons – as properly the principal means of punishment.

Why then, did Mackintosh not go further, and embrace Macquarie's approach to the treatment of crime and criminals? Certainly not because he thought of the man himself as a ratbag or fool. To the contrary, he liked and admired Macquarie; indeed, he would speak well of him when Macquarie came under attack in the British parliament. And he would never have entertained the idea of Macquarie's motives as other than humanitarian, his policies formulated in what he considered to be the best interests of the convicts. Rather, it was Mackintosh's personal remoteness both from the convict at home and from the convicts' lives in the Colony. The former can be attributed in no small measure to Mackintosh's mentality; the latter an almost inevitable consequence of geographical distance. As to mentality, look at his portrait and ponder questions like the following. Does this look like a man who would have enjoyed a beer with the hoi polloi in a London tavern? Or, if he had been stopped by the destitute in a laneway, would he, though pitying them, have been capable of understanding – really understanding – their human weakness? The problem is, these were the places where great numbers of future convicts were to be found. No, Mackintosh was a man who, though waxing confidently about the problems of the real world, had not actually spent any time in it – not because he looked down upon it with disdain, but rather because it presented an uncomfortable personal challenge to him. How different from Macquarie! Macquarie actually enjoyed the company of people like the convict William Redfern and like William Wentworth, the son of an unconvicted highwayman, both of whom had a rough, knock-about side to their characters and social behaviour (recall their portraits – pp.102 and 149, respectively). Moreover, Mackintosh had not seen, as Macquarie had, worthy tenant farmers who once wanted to work hard, nonetheless turn to dishonesty, even violence, in the face of poverty and the general wretchedness of their lives. Nor had he been on the battlefield and seen criminals acquit themselves with honour. Simply, Mackintosh had not seen, nor could he envisage, how so much crime was rooted in the malign circumstances of the many convicts' lives, nor – this is of particular salience – could he appreciate the relevance of this for their treatment as convicts. The personal disadvantage under which Mackintosh laboured will be truly understood when the preceding formal portrait of Mackintosh (opposite) is compared with the caricature of Macquarie (see p.230), one well portraying the rough-and-tumble element in the latter's character.

The other aspect inhibiting Mackintosh's appreciation of the rehabilitative outcomes of Macquarie's treatment of the convicts was physical distance. Mackintosh was in Britain and Macquarie was in the distant Colony. This brought into play three factors individually and together responsible for Mackintosh's misperception of the transforming effects of Macquarie's policies. First, Mackintosh was not able to witness at first-hand the relationship between the convicts' treatment and their reform. Very different from Dr. Bland, who not only observed what was transpiring, but who talked to serving and reformed convicts as patients and fellow citizens. Second, another consequence of this was Mackintosh's necessary reliance on secondary sources of information. These came from free settlers and emancipists, and others. We know about three among them – Marsden and Macarthur, and Jeffery Bent – who spoke of Macquarie and his work most grievously, most unreliably and most mischievously, and whose high-placed contacts made them most influential. As to what weight Mackintosh gave to the less-heard emancipists' favourable words about Macquarie's work, if he even heard them at all, we can only guess. Finally, Mackintosh, being Mackintosh, not being grounded, not having dealt personally with that other side of life, could not conjure up in his mind an image of convicts being transformed in Macquarie's colony by way of a relationship between social milieu and behaviour.

'Lachlan Macquarie'. Mick Paul, artist. 1920s. Digital image from the National Library of Australia, Canberra (PIC Drawer 7711 #S8306).

Perhaps you, the reader, are wondering how this meeting with Mackintosh could serve your understanding of personal remoteness as a barrier to an enlightened approach to the treatment of crime. For Mackintosh is, after all, such an odd-looking fellow, while you are the regular, practical man and woman. In any case, he confined himself to a rarefied intellectual world. Not at all like you! You, who are out and about, battling to get on in life, striving to give your children the best, facing the pressures of everyday modern life. These are the circumstances of life with which Mackintosh was not in touch. Yet, these too are far removed the circumstances in which the genesis of general crime is to be found. Recall, much of this sort of crime is to be found among those facing multiple social and personal deficits, such as family violence, disrupted schooling, unemployment, cultural alienation, low intelligence, troubled personalities. The stark fact is, when it comes to crime and criminals, most of us, like Mackintosh, live in a rarefied world. For we, like Mackintosh, though waxing confidently about the problem of crime, have not actually spent any time subject to such criminogenic circumstances and experienced its effects. Moreover, we, like Mackintosh, have not seen, as Macquarie had, worthy tenant farmers who once had wanted to work hard, nonetheless turn to dishonesty, even violence, unable to cope with, even alienated by, the general wretchedness of their lives. We are not able, as the brilliant Mackintosh was unable, to intuit the link between personal and social malaise and crime, and in turn its relevance to the treatment of the criminal. It is all beyond our ken. Thus, as a preventative measure, we turn to what we do understand in our respectable everyday lives. It is the deterrent power of punishment. Perhaps, mystified and with some frustration you expostulate with more than a hint of ire: 'What else?'

'Respectable' was used just above to qualify the reference to everyday lives, because the element of respectability itself may constitute a barrier to an enlightened understanding of crime. Its influence is not as these first three barriers – theory, common sense and remoteness – acting to prevent a true understanding of the problem, rather it acts to prevent us from wanting to understand the problem. To this fourth barrier we now turn.

RESPECTABILITY

What is here understood by respectability is more than respectability simpliciter, but respectability with that quality with which it is so often infected, namely self-righteousness. There is much to learn today about the effect of respectability on a person's attitude to criminals and criminal behaviour from a good man who once shared a close friendship with a bad man. One of these men – Samuel Johnson – a most noble man, and a hero of Mrs. Macquarie's – appeared earlier in this story. The other we meet for the first time, the reprobate Richard Savage.

Samuel Johnson was born in 1709 in a rural English town where his precocious intellect became patently clear from childhood. Though in straitened circumstances, he went up to Oxford, yet without success – a victim of his social immaturity, contempt for authority, idleness, and episodic anxiety attacks. Apart from being somewhat of a psychological mess, he was odd in manner and appearance. After a short and unsuccessful stint as a schoolmaster, he took himself to London to seek his fortune as one of the literati. His first experience of life there was the world of Grub Street, where he lived. It was a bohemian, impoverished, rough-living world of struggling hacks, along with aspiring authors and poets. In the early part of his life as a poet and writer he enjoyed but mixed success, poverty being his most constant companion. Around this time, another constant companion entered his life, the notorious and enigmatic Richard Savage, whom he found most engaging, and with whom he took to wandering through the streets of London at night.

The circumstances of Richard Savage's birth are somewhat uncertain. What is known, he was born in the last few years of the seventeenth-century and claimed to be the illegitimate son of the 4th Earl Rivers, a claim for which there is some support. Whatever the truth of this, we do know he was a debauched, egocentric, arrogant, prickly sybarite. This poet and playwright, though esteemed in his own mind was, to his chagrin and seething resentment, talked about not so much for the brightness of his writing, as for the darkness of his living. His was a life at once enthralling and appalling to those within its orbit. His was a character both fascinating and repelling to those with whom he dealt. Savage mixed, by virtue of who he was and who he might be, in the best literary circles and with the highest social set. In fact, sometimes with means, though often without means, he was able to live the good life along with them, one which he felt was his rightful due. This way of life, when without means, he maintained by relying on their largesse and by (what today is known as) couch-surfing. And so, he would live the high-life until committing some outrage upon his long-suffering host. Whereupon, dressed as a dandy, and without a scintilla of gratitude or remorse, he would return to the wretchedness and poverty of life on the streets, until … Such was the cycle of his life. There was, however, one major disruption to this pattern. One night, in a London coffee house, Savage became embroiled in a fight, in which a man was killed. Savage himself was charged with murder, and in subsequent proceedings spent some time in prison. Fortunately for him, his powerful aristocratic friends once again came to his rescue. He received a royal pardon. The pattern of his life resumed.

This was the strange man Johnson, in his late twenties, and somewhat of a misfit, met and found most companionable. At this time, Savage was a shadow of his former self, his life one of distress and humiliation. Together they roamed through the city's darker reaches; each lofty, creative mind stimulated by the other, each troubled psyche comforted by the other. And perhaps, just perhaps, the older and worldly-wise Savage, exercising a powerful charm, occasionally led his protégé to indulge in the fleshly pleasures on offer all about them, to the latter's subsequent lasting mortification. This was a friendship of only two years, ending when Savage left London for Wales, his stake in life raised. Some years later he died in gaol, a debtor. Not long after, in 1744, Johnson wrote one of his most admired works, *An Account of the Life of Mr. Richard Savage*.

Johnson, who grew in confidence as he negotiated life ever more successfully, went on to great things, becoming a literary giant not only

'**Johnson**'. J. Reynolds, artist. W. Holl, engraver. Published by C. Knight & Co., London, [1814].

of his age but of the ages. His greatest achievement was his general dictionary of the English language – the first of its kind – in which single-handedly he defined and illustrated by way of quotations over 40,000 words. Now Johnson, no longer a social misfit, no longer mixing with the denizens of Grub Street, was an Establishment figure, his companions being the great and the good, and the very clever. Now too more than merely a paragon of respectability, he was lauded as a most devout man of great piety. Accordingly, his writings were treated as a source of moral principles and wisdom. Indeed, decades later he would influence a young Elizabeth Campbell, as we know. And when he spoke in conversation, his elegance of speech and physical presence – he was over six-foot tall, with the bulk to match – added authority to his words. This is the Johnson of this portrait (see p.233).

With this background, we turn to Samuel Johnson's biography of Richard Savage. We focus on a subtle, easily overlooked amendment in his concluding appraisal of his friend. In this biography Johnson uses Savage's life as a means of exploring what he saw as a man's career blighted and its great promise extinguished by social injustice. It was written at the time when Johnson himself felt overwhelmed by life's harshness and unfairness. This biography is by a man who identifies with his friend in the circumstances of his life, and whose real sympathy is born of personal experience. The relevance of all this to respectability as a potential barrier to enlightened thinking about crime and criminals is to be discerned in Richard Holmes' book, *Dr. Johnson and Mr Savage*.

In this book, Holmes explores the relationship between Johnson and Savage. In the concluding passages we can see the power of respectability to distort our judgements of others, to blind us to what we know to be their true worth, even to embarrass us into letting down a friend in public. The excerpted passage says it all.

> Johnson concludes his *Life* … 'For his Life, or for his Writings, none who candidly consider his Fortune, will think an Apology either necessary or difficult.'
>
> … One might say that against his better judgement – against his judgement as a biographer – young Johnson stood with his friend in defiance of the whole eighteenth-century world.
>
> Yet in his closing lines there lies a curious irony. Johnson does appear to revert to the traditional eighteenth-century idea of biographer as a moral exemplum. From this perspective, Savage's whole career must be condemned, for it shows that 'nothing will supply the Want of Prudence, and that Negligence and Irregularity, long continued, will make Knowledge useless, Wit ridiculous, and Genius contemptible'.
>
> Those are the words on which the biography, as we now have it, actually ends. Is it at the very last, a damnation?
>
> It would be easy to think so, and to find the great Boswellian moralist finally in the ascendant …
>
> When Johnson was correcting his *Life* for the second edition, he wrote against that final, sad dismissive passage the one word: 'Added'. This was not how he had originally intended to conclude his biography. It was a solemn, placatory afterthought; a conciliatory

gesture to the forces of social opinion, which became so powerful in his own life.

His original ending, which stands now as the penultimate paragraph, had been altogether different. It defiantly evokes the world of Grub Street, his own world, and romantically challenges the reader to accept the conditions of Savage's existence. It urges empathy before judgement. 'Those are no proper Judges of his Conduct who have slumber'd away their time on the Down of Plenty, nor will a wise Man easily presume to say, "Had I been in Savage's Condition, I should have lived or written better than Savage".'

Through the force of Johnson's art, it is these words that are always remembered and quoted as his real conclusion about Richard Savage.[53]

Richard Holmes. Digital copy of photograph kindly provided by Helen Ellis of Harper Collins Publishers.

Here we see, through Holmes' nuanced and sensitive mind, a noble and strong-willed man falling victim to the pernicious effects of self-righteous respectability. Johnson's understanding of his late friend's weakness in the face of personal challenges now quelled, even something of shame, he was left with no alternative but the moral condemnation of Savage. It is a most perceptive, surely confronting insight.

Holmes' insight is telling, one of critical relevance to this discussion. As for Johnson, so for us today in our thinking about crime and criminals. From the heights of self-righteous respectability, it is no great step, especially when judging others so apparently different from ourselves, to think of these transgressors, especially the serious transgressor, as evil; it is no great step to not even want to look for any goodness perhaps deep within them.

It is an insight too throwing a light on an aspect of the Macquaries' greatness. Though as Governor and Governor's wife at the pinnacle of respectability themselves, they could still get their heads around the convict mind; the mind of those there through the wretchedness of their circumstances, and the mind of those there through their dishonesty born of greed. In the latter cases, perhaps Macquarie himself saw a younger self, remembered an earlier action of his, and did not forget the part played by the Prince Regent, one who had the power to control his destiny.

This leads to the fifth barrier to a more enlightened treatment of crime, namely, the criminal as bogeyman; indeed, it is one of respectability's sinister products.

CRIMINALS AS BOGEYMEN AND WOMEN

When I was putting together this collection of images, many prints came my way. 'A Fleet of Transports under Convoy' was one of them. Indeed, this print was put before me with enthusiasm. Here it is (opposite). It is a rare, fine print, one most relevant to this story – a group of convicts on their way to the docks for eventual transportation. Yet, at first, I rejected it as relevant. For quite some time, actually!

The faces of the men did not appear to be those of real people. In any case, the image had a disturbing quality about it, one which I found particularly unattractive. Not until I wrote the third-last paragraph in the immediately preceding section did the scales fall from my eyes.

The print is perhaps revealing how these convict men haunted the less conscious reaches of the artist's mind. These convicts – bizarre characters all – are looking at him with an evil eye. To the artist, they stand out as different, peculiar, 'spooky'. Then, when he peers through their eyes and into their souls, the malign, sinister natures of these men become apparent. Surely this is a scene, tinctured as it is with the demonic, to make one squirm, to recoil as though these men are untouchable, to want them out of one's midst. These are not men one would want to come across again. Indeed, they are men one might want not merely punished, but punished and banished, because they appear as though beyond redemption. They are surely evil, without any treasure in their hearts. How can one have sympathy for them? Rather, malign as they appear, do they not invite vengeance? How easy it would be to exaggerate the seriousness of the threat they represent to personal safety and more generally to a nation's moral well-being!

Yet if this interpretation is correct, questions must be asked: why did the artist think these convict men were worth representing; why did he think this unattractive image was worth portraying? Why indeed! Perhaps the image is not revealing to us how the artist himself felt about the convicts. Rather, perhaps he was attempting to open the eyes of the British people to what he understood to be the real reason for their treatment of the convicts as socially worthless and morally irredeemable, as fit only for banishment. Perhaps, the artist was challenging the public to think differently about the convicts. Perhaps the artist's message here

is, 'To regard the convicts as you do, to treat them as you do, this is the image you must have of them in your mind's eye; yet no men in this world have been cast in the image of the Devil'. An artist, better than anyone, will appreciate instinctively that any challenge based on reasoned words must fail in the circumstances of irrational thinking. What is required then is art with its capacity to speak to the unconscious.

By means of this image, we now know what the Rev. Samuel Marsden saw when he cast his eyes upon the convicts, and we are thereby closer to understanding his disdain for them. Now Marsden, as we saw earlier, had much to commend him. He did much to try and make his world a better place. His life was one of righteousness and respectability. Alas, these traits left him with a vulnerability, to which he succumbed. His righteousness morphed into a harsh self-righteousness which expressed itself as punitive condemnation. Thus was he disposed to regard the convicts as he did. As it was for Marsden, so it is for the public at large today. Respectability is a cultural force at work in our society. Indeed, it underpins human decency, a characteristic we properly impute to ourselves with pride. Yet unchecked it has the potential to become self-righteous respectability, and thence a barrier to the enlightened treatment of crime and criminals.

This, and the preceding four barriers, powerful individually, let alone in unison, and operating below the level of awareness, have retarded our progress to an enlightened system of criminal justice system, one according with Lachlan and Elizabeth Macquaries' understanding. Our punishment of criminals is today patently less harsh, yet our mentality is equally punitive. The latter is what is critical when it comes to measuring our state of enlightenment. Yet punitiveness is not a characteristic of everyone. We saw – the previous chapter – evidence of the Macquarie spirit being alive in two judgments of the Victorian Court of Appeal.

* * *

Back in the Colony, the perceptive and well-read Macquaries would have well understood these barriers and their pernicious effects on Britain's thinking about their Colony. How, O how, they would have anguished over their blinding effects on the British public's perception of their policies as transformative, and of the implications of this for the treatment of criminals!

Then, as Lachlan and Elizabeth voyaged back to Britain, these matters no doubt played on their enlightened minds, and must in large measure have cruelled the pleasure attending their return to Scotland, the land of their birth. For Lachlan, despairing that his work was not finished; that once back in Britain he would have to summon up his fast-ebbing reserves of energy to make his case. For Elizabeth, profound bouts of sadness that her beloved, despite everything he had done, felt unfulfilled; that her beloved was not up to fighting for his cause, now being a shadow of the warrior who had first captured her love. The Macquaries' life as a couple was fast drawing to an unhappy close.

Chapter 12

Remembering the Macquaries

EVEN BEFORE BIGGE left the Colony's shores, Macquarie bemoaned the darkness he was sure would soon befall his beloved people. The convicts, those now resident and those who would soon come, faced the visitation of a blight. The illiberal and uncharitable among the pretentious elite had won, of this he was sure. It was to be their colony. It was not to become the land he had promised the convicts, and for which he had fought so tirelessly, indeed working himself to exhaustion. The thought of this drew a veil of darkness across his mind – Himself. 'That it should end this way', was his constant mental refrain. In saying this, there was one particular person in his mind. Himself! As there would be no salvation for the convicts, so there would be no glory for him. Thus did Macquarie despair. Elizabeth – she who was capable of greater detachment than he, and perhaps the possessor of greater wisdom too – had been right: what Bigge was would govern what he would see.

Soon after Bigge's departure, Macquarie learned Bathurst had at last accepted his 1817 resignation. The end of his governorship had mercifully come. Now he must return to Britain forthwith. Bigge's report would be calculated to do him great harm, of this he was certain. Then there were Bennet's calumnies and those of his cheer squad, which still rankled with him. In his own mind he had no alternative but to devote himself to vindicating his name and his mission. Upon setting the date for his departure, that pleasurable sensation accompanying the relief of great pain was his to enjoy, albeit temporarily. Desperate resolution risks myopic preoccupation, risks mental destruction.

'The Arrival of the
Convict Ship *Surry* in
Sydney Harbour'.
G. Ingleton, artist. Copied
from G. Ingleton (Ed.),
True Patriots All (Special
edition, no.39). Angus and
Robertson, Sydney, 1952.

On 12th February, 1822, Lachlan, Elizabeth and their son, together
with the family's old cow – a family favourite – embarked on the *Surry*, a
squared-rigged transport ship, some 120 feet in length, around 460 tons,
and comprising three decks, one having been added recently.

The sight of the *Surry* progressing towards the Heads and framed by
the majestic Harbour would have been a vista to delight the senses of
onlookers. Though as this little ship hit the mighty Pacific, and started to
roll and tumble in the waves, how vulnerable its precious cargo would
have seemed. Indeed, most vulnerable they were, though not from the

elements, for *Surry* was modern and well-built. Rather, the source of Lachlan and Elizabeth's vulnerability lay within themselves: his fragile mental state, and the physical enfeeblement of both. These were to have their impacts in the future. Nonetheless, these also told during their actual departure. As Lachlan and Elizabeth processed from Government House to the pier, they both struggled to savour the moment. They knew smiling faces and grateful waves were due, and these they affected as practised vice-regals. And indeed, they did experience genuine flashes of joy, though their cups were not overflowing. The latter, though there was everything to delight them. The cheering crowds, expressing their heartfelt appreciation to him as their 'Patriot Chief', and to her as their most dutiful First Lady; the melancholy expressions on many of these faces, manifesting the peoples' sadness over their departure; the large flotilla of small craft on the harbour, festooned with flying colours, bidding them both bon voyage; the most fitting grandeur of the setting. What should have been the brilliance of the hour was rendered overcast by dark thoughts. For Macquarie it represented the passing of his beloved Colony, a place he would perhaps not see again. The passing too of his beloved convicts. Though he might be fortunate enough to enjoy the company of the likes of William Wentworth in London, he would never again see most of the little people whose lives he had turned around, and who were to him a great source of joy and personal satisfaction. These things too for Mrs Macquarie, yet more. As she looked at her beloved Lachlan, the emotional turmoil she knew was his, also became hers. As she looked at him, a gaunt face atop a frail body loomed large; and the question 'How much longer will I have him?' would have tormented her. Thus does this black skeletal sketch of *Surry*, without any backdrop, well-match the Macquaries' states of mind and body.

VALE LACHLAN

Lachlan Macquarie, with Elizabeth Campbell, bequeathed to the world a principled approach to the treatment of crime and criminals whose character fully satisfied Churchill's test of civilization. Embraced by a nation, this vision would demonstrate its 'stored-up strength' and 'living virtue'. Indeed, as the antithesis of the conventional wisdom of the day, even the ideals of the dreamers of the time, Macquarie had offered the world an enlightenment. Back in London, he as a great reforming governor should have been celebrated. As a thinker, one who would leave

ART. IV. 1. *Letter to Earl Bathurst, by the Honourable* H. GREY BENNET, M. P.

2. *Report of the Commissioner of Inquiry into the State of the Colony of New South Wales. Ordered by the House of Commons to be printed, 19th June,* 1822.

M R BIGGE's Report is somewhat long, and a little clumsy; but it is altogether the production of an honest, sensible, and respectable man, who has done his duty to the public, and justified the expense of his mission to the fifth, or pickpocket quarter of the globe.

What manner of man is Governor Macquarrie?—Is all that Mr Bennet says of him in the House of Commons true? These are the questions which Lord Bathurst sent Mr Bigge, and very properly sent him, 28,000 miles to answer. The answer is, that Governor Macquarrie is not a dishonest man, nor a jobber; but arbitrary, in many things scandalously negligent, very often wrong-headed, and, upon the whole, very deficient in that good sense, and vigorous understanding, which his new and arduous situation so manifestly requires.

Ornamental architecture in Botany Bay! How it could enter into the head of any human being to adorn public buildings at the Bay, or to aim at any other architectural purpose but the exclusion of wind and rain, we are utterly at a loss to conceive. Such an expense is no only lamentable for the waste of property it makes in the particular instance, but because it destroys that guarantee of sound sense which the Government at home must require in those who preside over distant colonies. A man who thinks of pillars and pilasters, when half the colony are wet through for want of any covering at all, cannot be a wise or prudent person. He seems to be ignorant, that the prevention of rheumatism in all young colonies, is a much more important object than the gratification of taste, or the display of skill.

' I suggested to Governor Macquarrie the expediency of stopping all work then in progress that was merely of an ornamental nature, and of postponing its execution till other more important buildings were finished. With this view it was, that I recommended to the Governor to stop the progress of a large church, the foundation of which had been laid previous to my arrival, and which, by the estimate of Mr Greenway the architect, would have required six years to complete. By a change that I recommended, and which the Governor adopted, in the destination of the new court-house at Sydney, the accommodation of a new church is probably by this time secured. As

The Edinburgh Review on Macquarie. Copied from 'Botany Bay', in *The Edinburgh Review*, 1823, Vol. 38, No. 75, February, p. 85-104 (p. 85).

the imaginative Bentham wondering; as a man of practical ideas, one who would leave the grounded polymath, Brougham, stumped; as a man of erudition in his chosen topic, one who would leave the garrulous guru of the chattering classes, Mackintosh, speechless. But such adulation – this was something Macquarie so craved – he did not get to enjoy. Rather, he had to suffer patent humouring from the kind, and the ridicule of the cruel. And the cruel there were.

None more prominent and cutting was the article by Sydney Smith in the *Edinburgh Review*. This journal, of which Henry Brougham was a co-founder, was intended to provide an outlet for liberal views, and soon established itself as prestigious and authoritative. One day, early in 1823, Macquarie's mental and physical vitality now fast ebbing, an article was brought to his attention. Its argument was neither subtle or gentle. There, on the first page, he was to read:

> What manner of man is Governor Macquarrie [sic] ... [he is] arbitrary, in many things scandalously negligent, very often wrong-headed, and, upon the whole, very deficient in that good sense, and vigorous understanding ...[54]

The image opposite shows the opening paragraphs of the article as Macquarie would have read them. In the concluding paragraphs of the article, added to this catalogue of abuse were 'ignorant' and 'The colony itself, disincumbered [sic] of Colonel [sic] Lachlan Macquarrie, will probably become a very fine empire ...'.[55] In between, the criticism of Macquarie and his work is developed. As part of this, grossly intensifying the hurt, the article confers admiration and gratitude on the two men Macquarie regarded as his vilest bête noires, respectively Samuel Marsden and Henry Bennet.

Macquarie might have expected something better – more insightful – from the *Edinburgh Review*, this scholarly journal, of and for liberal intellectuals. Yet the height of the barriers to enlightenment – in this case patently a common-sense understanding of criminal behaviour, and mental and physical remoteness from the phenomenon – had on this matter proved too great for their kind. This lack of insight would have been infuriatingly all too apparent to Macquarie from the beginning of the article. Thus, in just the third paragraph he would read:

> Ornamental architecture in Botany Bay! How it could enter into the head of any human being to adorn public buildings at the Bay, or to

aim at any other architectural purpose but the exclusion of wind and
rain, we are utterly at a loss to conceive.

You know the answer, which Macquarie must have wanted to scream
out to Sydney Smith and his large audience of sophisticates: 'Do you
not understand? The common man is, as you are, both body and spirit'.
Perhaps in the author's criticism we detect the barrier of 'criminals as
bogey men and women' subtlety exerting its pernicious influence.

Poor Lachlan! The article, considered in its totality, reads as though
the first blow was to serve as the hanging, the body of the article was the
drawing, there being a quick interlude on the rack, and the final blow the

'Loch-na-gael, near Knock on Mull'. W. Daniell, artist and engraver. Published by Longman and Co., London, 1817.

quartering. Macquarie was shattered; he was down. There was worst to come; this was to put him away.

There is in this, sad ironies. Remember, a few years earlier Macquarie, ever sensitive to the weak and downtrodden, had urged Bigge to '[a] vert the Blow you appear too much inclined to inflict on these unhappy Beings'. Now, he was the unhappy being, indelicately suffering blow after blow with a force beyond what was required for fair criticism. Moreover, during his governorship, he had done his best to raise up those whom the British government had trampled underfoot, and to treat as accepted those who had been rejected by them. Macquarie felt these assaults all the more because he was not being treated as he had treated others. Every blow caused his now tenderized mind agony, as he faced what to him was this most unpalatable fact: the great and the good of this land, the people whose admiration had been, and still was, so important to him, had found him wanting. Only one government minister – the fine, sensitive aristocrat who had appointed him (see p.33) – would do anything to try and raise his spirits.

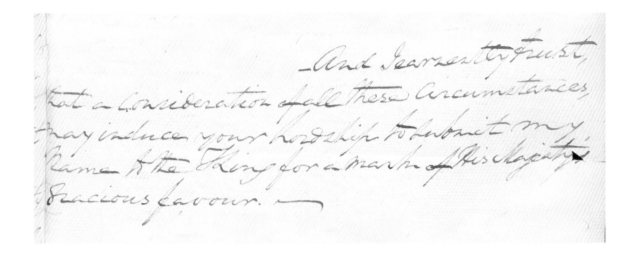

Two images allow us to get inside Macquarie's head and enter his world at this time, and so understand his mood. The first is Richard Read's 1822 portrait of Macquarie (see p.244); the second is William Daniell's 1817 Isle of Mull landscape, portraying the sweeping view across Loch-na-gael to Gruline and Knock, with Ben More in the background (see p. 245).

Contrast this portrait of Macquarie with Opie's, less than twenty years earlier (see p.23). There he projects youth, vibrancy, and optimism – a man who expects the best is yet to come. How different now! Wizen, haggard, lifeless, broken, finished – a man who has lost all and expects nothing in his remaining days. Indeed, the stare of Macquarie's eyes suggests a man who has been left shell-shocked, and now beholds an abyss. When Sir William Orpen painted Winston Churchill in 1916 after the disaster of Gallipoli, which left many tens of thousands of men dead and the reputation of this most ambitious man in tatters, the artist described him as a 'man of misery'. For his part, Churchill found the image confronting, expostulating, 'It is not a picture of a man, it is a picture of a man's soul'.[56] As for Churchill, so for Macquarie.

Loch-na-gael was at the heart of Macquarie's physical world throughout his last years. The little house at Gruline was Lachlan and Elizabeth's retirement cottage; and they spent time at Knock House whilst this humble, dilapidated abode was being made habitable. The landscape about – the water, the mountains, and the land – were the grand vistas his eyes would survey each day. Yet the tonal quality of this image, one almost embracing in scope, portrays better than words Macquarie's mental view of the circumstances of his life. They appeared to him as

Lachlan Macquarie to Earl Bathurst. 12th November, 1822. Digital image from the National Archives, Kew, London.

'His Most Gracious Majesty, George-Augustus-Frederick, the Fourth'. T. Lawrence, artist. E. Scriven, engraver. Published by the London Printing and Publishing Company, [c1840].

a brooding darkness, something smothering his spirits blanket-like.

Nonetheless, among the clouds darkening the night that now was his mental world, there were occasional breaks through which he beheld the flickering light of distant stars. There was the happy family tour in Europe soon after their return to Britain. Then, when in London, there were the royal levees, the ducal parties, and pleasant evenings with friends at the best clubs. Yet was his trauma always at hand. While in Europe, he wrote his reply to the Bigge Report. And at social functions he would collar party-goers and bore them, explaining at length how his governorship was misunderstood and he unappreciated. Then, to his chagrin, after hearing him out politely, they would want to talk about the ideas of the great thinkers of the day, Bentham and Brougham.

Macquarie's preoccupation with his quest for earthly glory manifested itself both in the highest social circles and in official circles at the highest echelons of government. In this, his desperation was unremitting, though his life-force ever weakening. He wrote not one, but several reports to Bathurst, defending is governorship and attesting to his achievements. Aside from these works, he entreated Bathurst to recommend him to the Sovereign. As for the kindly Colonial Secretary, he met formally with Macquarie on several occasions. He thanked him for his assiduous services and conveyed the King's appreciation. As to the merits of his work, Bathurst said nothing. How could he give Macquarie the praise he was so desperate to hear? For the ink on the parchment charting a very different course for the Colony was long dry. As to the knighthood, one can imagine Bathurst saying to his officials after his last meeting with the old governor: 'It just cannot be. To honour Macquarie would be to honour his work'.

A second pair of images portray Macquarie's pre-eminent earthly yearning in his final years. The first is an extract from one of his letters (see opposite), in his own hand, to the Colonial Office. It was written to Bathurst on 12th November, 1822, several months after his return from the Colony. Here, after summarizing his achievements, he concludes:

And I earnestly trust, that a Consideration of all these Circumstances, may induce your Lordship to submit my Name to the King for a mark of His Majesty's Gracious favour.[57]

A plea for a Knighthood!

The second image is a portrait of the King, George IV (see p.247), whose regal splendour symbolized earthly glory to Macquarie. In fact, this particular entreaty for a knighthood was the first of several. Macquarie's persistence on this matter demonstrates how it was obsessing his mind. Indeed, he was most frail and only weeks away from death before he finally accepted this greatest of joys was not to be his. At this time, is it not easy to envisage his devout Elizabeth assuring her most beloved of a greater glory from a greater King? Nonetheless, Macquarie did enjoy at least several gracious audiences with a Monarch scripted to express his appreciation to this well-liked servant of the Crown. We can be sure of this, at least in respect of the first audience, because it was Castlereagh who used his good offices to secure his being received by George IV. Indeed, Castlereagh, who was always solicitous of his gubernatorial appointees, had promised to do more for Macquarie. Nothing came of this. Most tragically, Castlereagh died by his own hand shortly afterwards, and with this act took Macquarie's chance of a knighthood to the grave. Macquarie himself died on 1st July, 1824. Mrs Macquarie, who had rushed down to London from Gruline on hearing of the sudden deterioration in his health, was at his bedside.

Tributes to Macquarie

No doubt in Britain there was a genuine belief, widespread among the people who mattered, even friends and admirers, that Macquarie's case for a knighthood was not overwhelming. Surely, just too many uncomfortable questions had been raised about his administration. Not so in the Colony; there Macquarie had his champions. Principal among this group was the inimitable William Wentworth, now one of the Colony's pre-eminent political movers-and-shakers (see p.149). Macquarie was the man whom he adored and regarded as a father-figure, both to his family and to the greater convict family. To Wentworth, this man had no need for an especial act or monument signifying earthly glory. In his tribute to Macquarie, Wentworth conveyed his esteem for the Governor to the world through a line from Pope, 'Ennobled by himself'.[58] At the time, great comfort to Elizabeth in her grief. Today, a challenge to the punishers in their preoccupation with harshness.

Macquarie would have been touched by this tribute, but he was earthly enough to have preferred the real thing. Nonetheless, he was aware of Wentworth's poem, 'Australasia', which he had written for The Chancellor's Medal at the Cambridge Commencement in 1823. This Wentworth dedicated to Macquarie, saying:

.... I predict, that his Majesty's ministers will soon form a more correct estimate of the zeal, ability, and integrity, with which you have discharged the trust which your Sovereign reposed in you. Calumny is but the foul vapour of a day. As the envious mists that hide the sun quickly disappear, and the glorious luminary breaks forth with renewed force and splendour: thus is it with the benefactors of mankind. Their intentions and acts may be obscured for a season; but the light of their deeds remains behind and warms and cheers through generations.

I feel that the poem ... would have been more complete, if it had contained some allusion ... to that high tone of feeling, that great moral reformation, of which, both by your precept, your example, and your institutions you sowed the seeds among all classes of the colonists — seeds, the fruits of which will descend to their remotest posterity.[59]

Manning Clark. From a 1962 family portrait; photograph kindly provided by Sebastian Clark.

Now, Wentworth was no puritan, 'moral' did not mean to him what it meant to Marsden. Rather, what he meant here was a transformation within the convict spirit, one subscribing to the merits of civil decency, one in which optimism replaces hopelessness, so imparting to the holder the capacity to enjoy a productive life and have fun. This is what justified Macquarie's ennoblement.

Alas, no glory here for Mrs Macquarie!

Manning Clark, in writing his great history of Australia almost 150 years later, wrote at length on what he termed 'The Age of Macquarie', and there was fulsome in his praise of the man. Thus, he wrote by way of conclusion:

To his friends and supporters the whole colony was a monument to his work and he the father of Australia ...

he was the man with the benevolent heart and the sagacious head, who counteracted distress and misery, who gave employment to the convicts, improved the streets, erected buildings of the highest utility and ornament, built the roads, befriended popular freedom, sowed the seeds for the reformation of the convicts …

a man subjected to obloquy, misrepresentation, and incessant vituperation, who passed through that fiery ordeal unscorched … who united the greatest kindness of heart to the most captivating urbanity of manner …

So those who viewed his passing with grief … detected neither what came up from inside the man to lead him on to his destruction …

[t]hose who eulogized his work or execrated his memory … were all unaware that his errors were those of the understanding rather than of the heart …

Though he did not lack the strength to endure such suffering with dignity, in fighting what he believed to be his true deserts, he almost brought himself to derision.[60]

In Manning Clark's panegyric to Macquarie, we see, do we not, Clark understanding history as born in the human soul, its making driven by the human heart, its fruition crafted by the human mind? This is how the present story has sought to appreciate the Macquaries' enlightenment.

ELIZABETH MACQUARIE AS A HEROIC FIGURE

Presumably Manning Clark did not perceive Mrs. Macquarie's pivotal role in the Macquarie governorship because his antennae were not tuned to receive these signals. It might have been otherwise if the writings of the great English novelist, Jane Austen, born in 1775, had been to the fore of his mind at the time. This keen and witty observer of the upper levels of British society, their attitudes, manners and customs, was mentally assembling her material around the very time Macquarie met Elizabeth and sought her hand in marriage.

Perhaps Clark's reading had not included Jane Austen, or perhaps though he read her *Emma* it did not speak to him. For there, Austen gave one of her central characters, a certain Mr Knightley, the line: 'Men of sense, whatever you may chuse [sic] to say, do not want silly wives'.[61] Macquarie was much, much more than just a man of sense. There was a message there for this historian as he sought to understand the Macquarie era.

Mrs. Macquarie was at once both a very old fashioned and a very modern – 'strong' seems to be the going adjective – woman. As her

'Jane Austen' (c1810).
[C. Austen, artist.
Published by R. Bentley,
London, c1870.]

preoccupation in the Colony had been her beloved Lachlan's governorship and its success, then once back and on Mull it was his comfort and happiness during what she accepted in her darker moments were his last few years. To this end, she first set about making their most modest abode habitable. She cleaned out the detritus accumulated as the cottage had lain abandoned, she had it weatherproofed, and she had constructed a small extension. Macquarie himself, in these his last years, spent extended periods absent in London. Elizabeth would have understood this and her Lachlan's desperate need for vindication and recognition. Though herself frail, the pain she felt would have been his, not hers. Though socially isolated, she would not have begrudged her husband the pleasures of London's high society. This is the Mrs Macquarie discerned and captured by the artist in her 1810 portrait (see p.26).

Yet, this Mrs. Macquarie, qua Macquarie's 'dear Elizabeth', was a very different woman from Mrs. Macquarie, qua Marsden, Macarthur and Bent's 'wife of the Governor'. Ellis Bent found it hard to relax in her company. Marsden unwittingly revealed how harshly he had suffered at her hands in his letter to Bigge around the end of his Inquiry. There he wrote (see p.252):

> Both profane and sacred History hath taught us, that it is very dangerous to offend a Lady in Power – John the Baptist lost his Head for this.[62]

The fact is, this was the price powerful men had to pay for attempting to erect barriers between Macquarie and his grand vision for the Colony. Mrs. Macquarie's primary animus towards these men arose from the frustration they caused her beloved Lachlan. And since his cause was hers, they had to expect three shots across their bows, two on her husband's account, and one on her own account. Always, first Lachlan, then herself.

For the leading women in the Colony it was different, and accordingly they wrote differently about her: Thus did Mrs. Macarthur – the Perturbator's wife – opine in a letter to a friend: 'Mrs. Macquarie is very

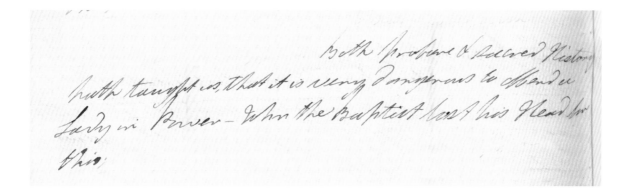

Samuel Marsden to
Commissioner Bigge.
15th March, 1821. Digital
image from the National
Archives, Kew, London.

amiable, very benevolent, in short a very good woman'.[63] But then she was not, as her husband was, aggressively pursuing self-interest at the convicts' expense.

One of Mrs. Macquarie's colonial male critics, the doctor James Mitchell, snidely spoke of her as behaving as though she was the governor. How mistaken, how shallow, this observation! Certainly, his governorship as an office of state was their governorship as a domestic reality. Nonetheless, it was not because she crassly butted in and assumed for herself gubernatorial prerogatives and airs. Rather, it was that Macquarie had instinctively found a great woman and placed her in circumstances where a great cause found her.

How magnificently Richard Read captures the very modern Mrs. Macquarie in his 1819 portrait of her (opposite). Not here demure, sweet, passive, as in her 1810 portrait. Rather, head erect, though with a slight forward thrust; a determined expression framing piercing eyes; energized and purposeful; a woman on the move, on a mission, one who will speak out, who will take no prisoners. The force of this most talented woman's personality is patent. Though this strength is not raw, but cloaked in a mantle of femininity. Nonetheless, perhaps not someone to whom the people could come too close.

This is the Mrs. Macquarie Lachlan came to admire greatly and to love dearly, and – something without which his governorship would have been much less – to rely on as a source of reforming ideas and for sustaining strength. This is a wife who patently was her husband's powerhouse. Yet does justice demand we reappraise her, and deem her a heroic figure?

There is surely more to heroic figures than strength of character and appearance. Heroes see themselves at the forefront of a noble cause; they found their actions on higher, principled ideals; they fight opposition; they

sustain their driving spirit in the face of adversity and despite physical weakness; they achieve against the odds; they leave a legacy. Now, are all these things not true of Elizabeth Macquarie? You will recall her Bible exhorting her to do good, and Johnson telling her that punishment can be justified only to the extent it does good. There was her proactive entertaining of convicts at Government House; her close friendships with convicts of which she was unabashed; her Female Orphan School, one of most grand proportions so as to proclaim the personal worth these lowly girls to the Colony. More generally, she was behind the beautification of the Colony, something to give the convicts a reason to hold their heads high: the botanic gardens were hers; the elegant new hospital bore her architectural mark; and so on. To the end, despite failing health, she sustained her zeal and combatively faced down opposition. In fact, in all the features characterizing the Macquarie governorship, she was there as an equal, one of two prime movers, one of two enforcers. Thus is his legacy of enlightenment her legacy. A heroic figure who, nonetheless, has passed without fanfare into history.

Elizabeth Macquarie's final years were marked by sadness and increasingly failing health. She died peacefully in her cottage at Gruline. It was 1835; she was aged 56 years.

THE MACQUARIES' TREATMENT OF THE CONVICTS AS AN AUSTRALIAN ENLIGHTENMENT

In Scotland – the land of Lachlan and Elizabeth Macquarie's birth and their formative years, and their final resting place – do they not deserve be added as a couple to the pantheon of the great figures of the Scottish Enlightenment? This notwithstanding, the Macquaries' contribution to criminal justice, to history, represents an Australian enlightenment.

By 1817 thoughts of retirement had been increasingly occupying Macquarie's tired mind. With this came the need to prepare the case for his place in British history – so we may easily suppose. When the Macquaries arrived in 1810, there was a certain spark about the daily

Lachlan Macquarie to Henry Goulburn. 21st December, 1817. Digital image from the National Archives, Kew, London.

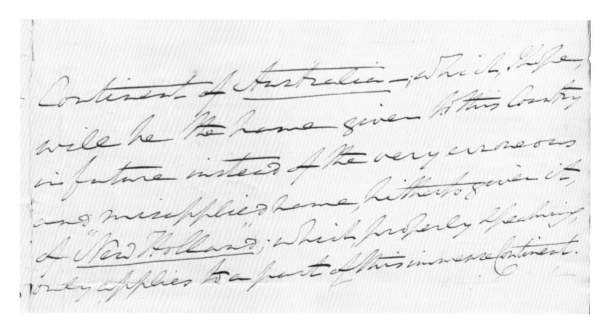

lives of no more than a few of the convicts. Yet, scratch this surface, share an intimate moment with one of them, and one would sense the ache within their hearts. So too for the great majority, though they also bore the constant burden of a heavy heart. No vivid imagination was required on the convicts' part to think of themselves as British garbage, marooned on a moribund, far-flung expanse of land, poor 'sods' living lives for others and without meaning, they being without a worthwhile future. Now, less than a decade later, how different the mentality of the very same convicts and emancipists! A developing sanguine spirit was apparent among them and their children, who as they matured were discernibly stronger and fitter. A far greater number of heads now looked up than looked down. They were the heirs to a new country, a better, fairer country, one in which they could prosper and achieve. They were ready for a new official identity. William Wentworth captured this sentiment in his 1823 poem, 'Australasia':

> Dear Australasia … Shall I … prescient of thy fame
> Foretell the glories that shall grace thy name?
>
> Land of my hope! soon may this early blot,
> Amid thy growing honors [sic], be forgot … [64]

Wentworth, in dedicating this poem to Macquarie, claimed the transformation for his Governor. To Macquarie, though, this was merely a public, independent confirmation of what he had been privately certain for some years. The British settlement was fast losing its character as a colony for the convicts' doom as it was fast becoming a nation for the convicts' future. This, Macquarie determined, required something greater than symbolic recognition. This something must be chipped in stone.

And so, it was on the 21st December, 1817, government business having wound down, Christmas celebrations now being to the fore, Macquarie put pen to paper in a private letter to Bathurst's deputy at the Colonial Office:

> … [the] Continent of Australia - ; which, I hope, will be the name given to this Country in future instead of the very erroneous and misapplied name hitherto given it, of "New Holland"; which, properly speaking, only applies to a part of this immense Continent.[65]

Here it is (opposite) in his own hand.

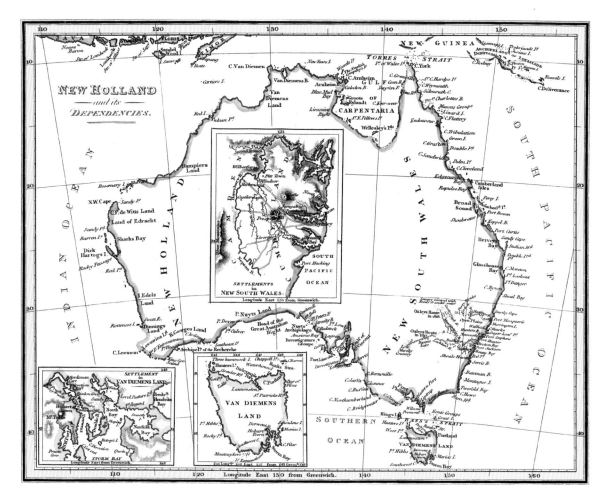

Now, in Macquarie's mind, the convicts and their descendants were Australians, properly thinking of themselves as citizens of a new country, Sydney being its effective capital. His governorship had given them the makings of a land in which they could take pride. On his arrival, the Colony largely unexplored, its infrastructure rude, its buildings for the most part run-down. Now, a Colony whose people – principally comprising convicts, emancipists and their children – were enjoying increasingly convenient, prosperous and engaging lives. To Macquarie in his sanguine moments, it was a wonder to behold. Scenes from this new Australia – a wilderness being opened up (see p.96), a town being transformed into a city (see p.94) – would have been his mental pictures as he drafted this letter. Thoughts too of his convicts cheerily going about their business: the milkmaid on assignment, looking contented, working productively (see p.113); Simeon Lord pleased with himself, having cut

'New Holland and its Dependencies'. Neele & Son, engraver. Published by Sherwood, Neely & Jones, London, 1921.

a good deal (see p.100). Australia was now a new nation; the continent required this new name.[66] A satisfied smile would have taken the weariness and sadness off his face for a moment or two. This Australia was his legacy; his beloved Elizabeth's legacy, too.

This legacy of the Macquaries raises the matter of what is most suited by way of a memorial to them and their work. First, consider how they are currently memorialized and remembered; then we consider something different.

THE MACQUARIE STATUES

Proud generations erect statues, often imposing representational edifices, of their present and past heroes. These are the people we laud and are proud of because in some way they have made the nation greater than it otherwise would be today. By way of statues, we proclaim their deeds and remember their greatness. They serve to tell us about our past and ourselves. They have the capacity to inspire future heroes. We come across them in the most prominent of public spaces. Alas, they not always do these things, or are all of these things. This is the case for the Macquarie statues.

First to Mrs. Macquarie's statue (see p.258). O dear! Better there were none, if only this one. It is located in Campbelltown, a suburb and major centre of greater Sydney, about 30 miles from the heart of the city. Does not prominence connote importance? Do not rulers lead from the seat of power? From this statue, placed as it is on the fringes of the metropolis, what else are we to conclude other than she was peripheral to power. Elizabeth Macquarie, peripheral! Ask Marsden; ask Lachlan, himself. Then there are the most unsatisfactory aspects of the statue itself.

Here Mrs. Macquarie is tending her flower garden – not even a vegetable in sight to accompany this most practical of women. How sweet, feminine, domesticated and dainty a representation it is! And then there is its size. She is of petite proportions, and not even elevated so admirers may behold her. No boldness here, her head bowed and shaded. Elizabeth as Miss Campbell, perhaps, but – what a 'but' it is – not Elizabeth as Mrs. Macquarie. Nothing here to speak of deeds glorious, personal greatness; nothing here to awe-inspire the next generation. A travesty of justice; an opportunity lost! In light of her husband's statue, it gets worse.

Macquarie's principal statue stands in the heart of Sydney (see p.259). It is monumental, projecting power and importance, and glory. Mounted on a plinth approaching human height, the figure itself appears almost twice human height. The statue dwarfs the mere mortals passing by.

Elizabeth Macquarie's Statue. Mawson Park, Campbelltown, Sydney. (Eric Sierins, photographer, 2018.)

Onlookers in the late Governor's presence must strain their necks to admire the man. Macquarie himself is dressed as the military governor he was. He holds his head proudly high; and projects his chest authoritatively. His bulky bronze body glitters in the sunlight. He holds out his hand in a boastful gesture: 'Behold the grandeur of this city; celebrate what I set in

train'. 'Admire me!' It is about architecture, town planning, verdant and colourful landscapes. This invites two questions: are we satisfied with this memorial to Macquarie; how might we image Mrs. Macquarie in a statue, at once majestic and didactic? To these questions we will return, after a necessary digression.

When Macquarie's memory is celebrated in the Australia of today, what is in most people's minds is the physical foundation he – yes, it is 'he' – laid down, one transforming Sydney from a town, characterized by ramshackle buildings scattered about what amounted to little more than an open prison, to a nascent city, where beauty in a flourishing metropolis would matter. This is the message conveyed by Macquarie's statue. As for the convicts; what convicts? Yet the convict is what the celebration of the Macquarie governorship should be about: Lachlan and Elizabeth Macquarie's treatment of the convicts as an enlightenment, as a history tale for today. In this take on the Macquarie governorship, the physical foundation they bequeathed the Colony – significant of itself though it be – is more properly thought of primarily as one of a number of means to this greater end.

What should be pre-eminent in people's minds is Lachlan and Elizabeth Macquarie's true greatness. Greatness, in their discerning goodness where others saw little but badness. Greatness, in perceiving the social roots of much of the convicts' criminality, and the implications of this for their redemption. Greatness, in holding these to be verities, though they were contrary to conventional wisdom, more especially to the thinking of the wise men of the day. Greatness too, in pursuing this enlightenment in the face of official sanctioning and ridicule at Home, and vituperative opposition in the Colony. Greatness, because what they held to be right and proper in the treatment of crime and criminals still represents an enlightenment two hundred years later.

Rare greatness – surely – though a greatness not acknowledged, let alone revered, in the land where they proclaimed and practised this enlightenment. The much-vaunted Duke of Wellington would have dismissed this understanding about crime and criminals as yet another instance of Macquarie's want of judgement! And for this sentiment there would have been widespread agreement at the time. In Australia today, the man and woman in the street on hearing about the Macquaries' work with the convicts would most assuredly agree with the good Duke. For criminal justice is assertively prosecuted as properly and sensibly punitive, and those who commit crimes of any significant seriousness are doubled-damned; first the drawn-out pain of punishment, then the indelible mark of Cain.

In light of this – the Macquaries' treatment of the convicts as an unrecognized and unappreciated enlightenment – how do we treat his statue, and how do we re-imagine hers? Let us leave him alone; let it stand where and how it stands today, at the northern end of Hyde Park, just

Crinum Flaccidum, Macquarie Lily. N. 2123. J. Curtis, artist. Weddell, engraver. Published by S. Curtis, London, 1820.

across from his Barracks for the convicts. Leave his hand pointing down Macquarie Street, past the towering hothouses of finance, all the way to the Opera House, so reminding us how it all began. That it was he who founded the infant Colony's first bank; that it was he who constructed elegant buildings upon the amphitheatre that is Sydney Cove, edifices befitting one of the most beautifully situated cities of the world. Let him in death have the pleasure denied him in life.

As for Mrs. Macquarie, there must be a statue of her, similarly prominent, similarly elevated, equally bold and grand. Next to him, would be most fitting; one arm might be making an affectionate, open-handed gesture towards him. These features together reflecting their work as being the product of their oneness and her devotion to hm. Yet, she would not be looking adoringly at him, but out with him, over their Sydney. Her other arm would be, as his is, raised, but somewhat higher. It would not be in the manner of inviting us to behold her work. Rather, she would be confronting us with a stern, disapproving, censuring finger, her piercing eyes on their highest setting. Mrs. Macquarie would be expressing her displeasure – no, her ire – at the way we treat our criminals. 'Was our work with the convicts for naught?', she would be asking in exasperation and disgust. 'Why are you not interested in what we did, and why we did these things?', she would be demanding. What would Lachlan make of his wife's sharpness of tone here? 'Now Elizabeth', we hear him say most gently, and with a wry smile.

Let the Macquaries' statues represent a history tale for Australia, for the world, today.

* * *

This telling of Lachlan and Elizabeth's story has relied heavily on images. They have been used here as a means of conveying something which could not be said, or said as well, with words alone. In this vein, we conclude with an emblem symbolizing the Macquaries' work. Let it be the Macquarie Crinum (see p.261), discovered during their governorship, and introduced to London's Chelsea Garden in 1819.

The lily itself representing the beauty of Lachlan and Elizabeth's vision of a different path to criminal justice, and the subsequent flowering of their beloved convicts; the lily being a native of the Australian land – land, the price paid by the Aboriginal peoples for this enlightenment.

Kaapay and Kuyan.

Notes

1. Clark, *Occasional Writings and Speeches*. p. 19. (Books: Specific Topics)

2. Williscroft. pp. 303-4. (Legal Materials: Cases)

3. See Widener and Weiner, *Law's Picture Books*. Chapter 1 and Chapter 2. (Books: Specific Topics)

4. Moiety is a form of social organisation in which people and most natural phenomenon are divided into two categories. See Aboriginal Art Online. Aboriginal Society. (Online Materials: General)

5. Aboriginal Art Online. Biographies. (Online Materials: General)

6. Jennie Holtsbaum. Design and Art Australia Online. (Online Materials: General). How this latter aspect relates to the present story is covered in Chapter 10.

7. See State Library of New South Wales' discussion of the painting, 'Sydney from Bell Mount'. (www.sl.nsw.gov.au/collection-items/sydney-bell-mount) (Accessed 4/1/2019)

8. Often conveniently styled, Judge-Advocate.

9. Skilled manual workers.

10. Dickens, *Great Expectations*. pp. 6-7. (Books: Specific Topics)

11. When convicts were on task-work they were set an amount of work for the day, and when completed early, the rest of the time might be theirs.

12. Extract from the letter dated January 31st, 1797. (State Library)

13. As recorded in HRA, 30-4-1810, p.276.

14. Extract from the dispatch. (National Archives)

15. Extract from the letter dated August 18th, 1823. (State Library)

16. Extract from the letter dated March 15th, 1821. (National Archives)

17. '… Henry exploded and is said to have uttered the words: "Will no one rid me of this troublesome priest?"' (The 'troublesome priest' was Becket, Archbishop of Canterbury.) 'Becket, the Church and Henry II', By Dr Mike Ibeji. BBC. (www.bbc.co.uk/history/british/middle_ages/becket_01.shtml) (Accessed 4/1/2019)

18. Extract from the letter dated February 7th, 1821. (National Archives)

19. Undated. As recorded in Ritchie, *The Evidence to the Bigge Reports*. p. 89. (Books: Specific Topics)

20. 'Suggestions'. Addendum to his letter to Bigge – see note 18. In Macarthur Onslow, *Some Early Records of the Macarthurs of Camden*. pp. 349-350. (Books: Specific Topics)

21. As recorded in HRA, 1-7-1815, p. 133

22. Extract from the dispatch dated July 1st, 1815. (National Archives)

23. As recorded in HRA, 28-6-1813, pp. 775-6.

24. Extract from the dispatch dated 28th June, 1813. (National Archives)

25. As recorded in HRA, 7-10-1814, pp. 315-6.

26. Extract from the dispatch dated October 7th, 1814. (National Archives)

27. Scroll of satirical verse.

28. See the cover image of Lynn, J. and Jay, A. (Eds.) *Yes Minister: The Diaries of a Cabinet Minister by the Rt. Hon. James Hacker MP*. Vol.1. BBC, London, 1981 (paperback).

29. As recorded in HRA, 6-11-1819, p. 224.

30. Extract from the letter dated November 6th, 1819. (National Archives)

31. James, *Winston S. Churchill: His Complete Speeches*. p. 1598. (Books: Specific Topics)

32. See HRA, 6-11-1819, pp. 223-4.

33. See note 27.

34. In J. Hirst, *Freedom on the Fatal Shore*. p. 196. (Books: Macquarie Era History)

35. See note 34.

36. See note 34.

37. See for example, Maur, 'Incarceration Rates in an International Perspective'. (Online Materials: General)

38. Waugh, 'Starke'. (ADB)

39. See note 2.

40. [AH] v The Queen [2012] VSCA 302, pp. 7-8. (www.austlii.edu.au) These observations played no part in the actual decision – the reason is apparent in the extract itself. In fact, earlier in the judgment, the Court had declared the inadequacy of the current levels of sentence as

punishments for this category of offence.

41. The other judges were Neave JA and Coghlan AJA.

42. Boulton v The Queen (2014) 46 Victorian Reports 308.

43. The other judges were Nettle, Neave, Redlich and Osborn JJA.

44. In regard to the nature of the CCO, see Boulton, note 42.

45. Bennett and Broe, 'Brains, Biology and Socio-economic Disadvantage in Sentencing'. (Legal Materials: Other)

46. See for example, Vinson and Rawsthorne, Dropping Off the Edge; and New South Wales Law Reform Commission, Sentencing: Aboriginal Offenders. (Books: Specific Topics)

47. This is to be distinguished from the court condemning the offender's behaviour, which is proper and appropriate.

48. This difference is captured in the second aspect of the Kaapay and Kuyan motif. See the text associated with note 6.

49. See for example, Maxwell, 'Non-custodial Dispositions'. (Legal Materials: Other)

50. Macintyre, 'Major on Crime'. (Online Materials: General)

51. J. Hirst, Freedom on the Fatal Shore, p. 16. (Books: Macquarie Era History)

52. Brougham, Speeches of Henry Lord Brougham. p.238. (Books: Specific Topics)

53. Holmes, Dr Johnson and Mr Savage. pp. 226-227. (Books: Specific Topics)

54. 'Botany Bay', Edinburgh Review. p. 85. (Journals)

55. See note 54, p.103.

56. National Portrait Gallery, London. Portrait NPG L 250; see notes accompanying portrait. (www.npg.org.uk)

57. Extract from letter. (National Archives)

58. Ritchie, Lachlan Macquarie. p. 224. (Macquarie Era History)

59. Wentworth. 'Dedication', 'Australasia'. (Online Materials: Macquarie Era History)

60. Clark, History of Australia. p. 379. (Macquarie Era History)

61. Austin, Emma. Vol. 1, p. 62. (Books: Specific Topics)

62. Extract from letter dated March 15th, 1821. (National Archives)

63. Macarthur Onslow, Some Early Records of the Macarthurs of Camden. p. 305. (Books: Specific Topics)

64. Wentworth, 'Australasia'. (Online Materials: Macquarie Era History)

65. Extract from letter. (National Archives)

66. The British explorer, Matthew Flinders, argued for the Continent to be named Australia; this he did around the first decade of the nineteenth century, though on the grounds of geography.

* The material in brackets at the end of each note indicates where the full reference will be found in the Select Bibliography.

Select bibliography

BOOKS: Macquarie Era History

Clark, C.M.H. *A History of Australia I: From the Earliest Times to the Age of Macquarie.* Melbourne University Press, Melbourne, 1962 (Reprinted with alterations 1963).

Clark C.M.H. *A History of Australia II: New South Wales and Van Diemen's Land 1822-1838.* Melbourne University Press, Melbourne. 1968.

Hirst, J. *Freedom on the Fatal Shore: Australia's First Colony.* Black Inc., Melbourne, 2008.

Hughes, R. *The Fatal Shore: A History of the Transportation of Convicts to Australia 1787-1868.* Pan Books, London, 1988.

Hirst, W. *The Governor: Lachlan Macquarie 1810 to 1821.* State Library of New South Wales, Sydney, 2010.

Karskens, G. *The Colony: A History of Early Sydney.* Allen and Unwin, Crows Nest NSW, 2010.

Ritchie, J. *Lachlan Macquarie: A Biography.* Melbourne University Press, Melbourne, 1986.

Walsh, R. *In Her Own Words: The Writings of Elizabeth Macquarie.* Exisle Publishing (with Macquarie University), Wollombi NSW, 2011.

BOOKS: Specific Topics

Austen, J. *Emma.* Vintage Books, London, 2007.

Brougham, Henry. 'Speech on the education of the people'. In *Speeches of Henry Lord Brougham.* Vol. 3. Adam and Charles Black, Edinburgh, 1838.

Clark, M. 'Rewriting Australian history'. In M. Clark, *Occasional Writings and Speeches.* Fontana Books, 1980.

Clark, M. 'The origins of the convicts transported to eastern Australia, 1787-1852'. In M. Clark, *Occasional Writings and Speeches.* Fontana Books, 1980.

Dickens, C. *Great Expectations.* (Eight original illustrations by A.A. Dixon.) Collins' Clear-Type Press, London [early C20th].

Holmes, R. *Dr Johnson and Mr Savage.* Flamingo, London, 1994.

James, R.R. (Ed.) *Winston S. Churchill: His Complete Speeches 1897-1963.* Vol.2: 1908-1913. Chelsea House Publishers, New York, 1974.

Macarthur Onslow, S. (Ed.) *Some Early Records of the Macarthurs of Camden.* Angus and Robertson, Sydney, 1914.

New South Wales Law Reform Commission. *Sentencing: Aboriginal Offenders.* Report 96. NSWLRC, Sydney, 2000.

Ritchie. J. *The Evidence to the Bigge Reports: Selected and Edited by John Ritchie.* Vol. 2: The Written Evidence. Heinemann, Melbourne, 1971.

Robson, L.L. *The Convict Settlers of Australia.* Melbourne University Press, Melbourne, 1965.

Vinson, T. and Rawsthorne, M. *Dropping Off the Edge: Persistent Community Disadvantage in Australia.* Jesuit Social Services, Richmond, Victoria and Catholic Social Services, Curtin ACT, 2015.

Widener, M. and Weiner, M.S. (Eds.), *Law's Picture Books: The Yale Law Library Collection.* Talbot Publishing, Clark NJ, 2017.

JOURNALS: General

'Botany Bay'. In *The Edinburgh Review*, 1823, Vol. 38, No. 75, February, pp. 85-104.

AUSTRALIAN DICTIONARY OF BIOGRAPHY (ADB)

Shaw, A.G.L. and Clark, C. M. H. (Eds.) *Australian Dictionary of Biography.* Vol. 1: 1788-1850 A-H. Melbourne University Press, Melbourne, 1966.

Bathurst, Henry.

Bent, Ellis. By C.H. Currey

Bent, Jeffery Hart. By C.H. Currey

Bigge, John Thomas. By J.M. Bennett.

Bland, William. By J. Cobley.

Cox, William. By E. Hickson.

Greenway, Francis. By M. Herman.

Shaw, A.G.L. and Clark, C. M. H. (Eds.) *Australian Dictionary of Biography*. Vol. 2: 1788-1850 I-Z. Melbourne University Press, Melbourne, 1967.

Lord, Simeon. By D. R. Hainsworth.

Macarthur, John. By M. Steven.

Macquarie, Elizabeth Henrietta. By M. Barnard

Macquarie, Lachlan. By N.D. McLachlan.

Marsden, Samuel. By A.T. Yarwood.

Redfern, William. By E. Ford.

Reibey, Mary. By G.P. Walsh.

Thompson, Andrew. By J.V. Byrnes.

Wentworth, William Charles. By M. Persse.

Online.

Starke, Sir John Erskine. By John Waugh. Australian Dictionary of Biography, National Centre of Biography, Australian National University. (adb.anu.edu.au/biography/starke-sir-john-erskine-18401/text3005) (Accessed 11/12/2018)

OXFORD DICTIONARY OF NATIONAL BIOGRAPHY (ODNB)

Matthew, H. C. G. and Harrison, B. (Eds.) *Oxford Dictionary of National Biography*. Oxford University Press, 2004.

Addington, Henry, 1st Viscount Sidmouth By J.E. Cookson

Austin, Jane By M. Butler

Bathurst, Henry, 3rd Earl Bathurst By N. Thompson

Bennet, Henry Grey By R. Thorne

Bentham, Jeremy By F. Rosen

Bigge, John Thomas By J.M. Bennett

Brougham, Henry Peter, 1st Baron Brougham and Vaux By M. Lobban

Churchill, Sir Winston Spencer By P. Addison

Frederick, Prince, duke of York and Albany By H. M. Stephens (Revised by J. Van der Kiste)

George IV By C. Hibbert

Johnson, Samuel By P. Rogers

Mackintosh, Sir James, of Kyllachy By C.J. Finlay

Savage, Richard By F. Johnston

Stewart, Robert, Viscount Castlereagh By R. Thorne

Wellesley, Arthur, 1st duke of Wellington By N. Gash

Wilberforce, William By J. Wolffe

THE HISTORY OF PARLIAMENT: THE HOUSE OF COMMONS

The History of Parliament: the House of Commons 1790-1820. (Ed.) R. Thorne, 1986. (www.historyofparliamentonline.org/) (Accessed 28/9/2017)

Addington, Henry By R.G. Thorne

Bennet, Hon. Henry Grey By R.G. Thorne

Brougham, Henry Peter By R.G. Thorne

Mackintosh, Sir James By W. Stokes/R.G. Thorne

Wilberforce, William By R.G. Thorne

The History of Parliament: the House of Commons 1820-1832. (Ed.) D.R. Fisher, 2009. (www.historyofparliamentonline.org/) (Accessed 28/9/2017)

Bennet, Hon. Henry Grey By M. Escott

Brougham, Henry Peter By M. Escott

Mackintosh, Sir James By D.R. Fisher

Stewart, Robert, Viscount Castlereagh By D.R. Fisher

Wilberforce, William By D.R. Fisher

LEGAL MATERIALS: Cases

[AH] v The Queen [2012] VSCA 302. (www.austlii.edu.au)

Boulton v The Queen (2014) 46 Victorian Reports 308. (www.austlii.edu.au)

R v Williscroft [1975] Victorian Reports 292.

LEGAL MATERIALS: Other

Bennett, H. and Broe, G. A. 'Brains, Biology and Socio-economic Disadvantage in Sentencing: Implications for the politics of moral culpability'. *Criminal Law Journal*, 2008, 32, 167.

Maxwell, C. 'Non-custodial Dispositions and the Politics of Sentencing'. *Criminal Law Forum*, 2017, 28, 541.

HISTORICAL RECORDS OF AUSTRALIA (HRA)

Deputy Judge-Advocate Bent to Earl Bathurst, 1st July 1815. *Historical Records of Australia*, Series 4, Section A, Vol. 1. Library Committee of the Commonwealth Parliament, 1922.

Governor Macquarie to Viscount Castlereagh, 30th April 1810. *Historical Records of Australia*, Series 1, Vol. 7. Library Committee of the Commonwealth Parliament, 1916.

Governor Macquarie to Earl Bathurst, 28th June 1813. *Historical Records of Australia*, Series 1, Vol. 7. Library Committee of the Commonwealth Parliament, 1916.

Governor Macquarie to Earl Bathurst, 7th October 1814. *Historical Records of Australia*, Series 1, Vol. 8. Library Committee of the Commonwealth Parliament, 1916.

Governor Macquarie to Mr. Commissioner Bigge, 6th November 1819. *Historical Records of Australia*, Series 1, Vol. 10. Library Committee of the Commonwealth Parliament, 1917.

ARCHIVAL MATERIAL: National Archives – Kew, London

E. Bent to Earl Bathurst, July 1st 1815. (dispatch)

J. Macarthur to Commissioner Bigge, February 7th 1821. (letter)

L. Macquarie to Viscount Castlereagh, April 30th 1810. (dispatch)

L. Macquarie to Earl Bathurst, June 28th 1813. (dispatch)

L. Macquarie to Earl Bathurst, October 7th 1814. dispatch)

L. Macquarie to Henry Goulburn, December 21st 1817. (letter)

L. Macquarie to Earl Bathurst, November 12th 1822. (letter)

L. Macquarie to Commissioner Bigge, November 6th 1819. (letter)

S. Marsden to Commissioner Bigge, March 15th 1821. (letter)

ARCHIVAL MATERIAL: Mitchell Library (State Library of New South Wales) – Sydney

E. Macquarie to C. Whalan, August, 18th 1823 (letter)

L. Macquarie to M. Maclaine, January 31st 1797 (letter)

L. Macquarie to C. Macquarie, January 31st 1797 (letter)

ONLINE MATERIALS: General

Aboriginal Art Online. Biographies of Lockhart River Artists. Rosella Namok. (www.aboriginalartonline.com/art/lockhart. php) (Accessed 2/11/2015)

Aboriginal Art Online. Aboriginal Society - Moieties. (www. aboriginalartonline.com/culture/moieties.php) (Accessed 2/11/2015)

Design and Art Australia Online. Rosella Namok: Biography. (www.daao.org.au/bio/rosella-namok/biography/) (Accessed 18/1/2016)

Crimmins, J. 'Jeremy Bentham', Stanford Encyclopedia of Philosophy, Spring 2017. (stanford.library.sydney.edu.au/ archives/spr2017/entries/bentham/) (Accessed 8/1/2019)

Macintyre, D. 'Major on Crime', Independent, Sunday February 21st 1993. (www.independent.co.uk/news/major-on-crime-condemn-more-understand-less-1474470.html) (Accessed 3/1/2019)

Maur, M. 'Incarceration Rates in an International Perspective', April 2017. The Sentencing Project. (www. sentencingproject.org/publications/incarceration-rates-international-perspective/) (Accessed 28/2/2019)

ONLINE MATERIALS: MACQUARIE ERA HISTORY

Macquarie, Elizabeth Henrietta. Lachlan and Elizabeth Macquarie Archive, Macquarie University. (www.mq.edu.au/ macquarie-archive/lema/biographies/embiog.html) (Accessed 4/4/2013)

Macquarie, Lachlan. Lachlan and Elizabeth Macquarie Archive, Macquarie University. (www.mq.edu.au/macquarie-archive/lema/biographies/lmbiog.html) (Accessed 8/3/2018)

Macquarie, Lachlan. Scots and Australia. Education Scotland. (www.sath.org.uk/edscot/www.educationscotland.gov.uk/ scotsandaustralia/lachlanmacquarie/index.html) (Accessed 17/11/2015)

Wentworth, William Charles. 'Australasia'. Lachlan and Elizabeth Macquarie Archive, Macquarie University. (www. mq.edu.au/macquarie-archive/lema/1823/australasia2.html) (Accessed 20/8/2017)

Wentworth, William Charles. 'Dedication' for Australasia'. Lachlan and Elizabeth Macquarie Archive, Macquarie University. (www.mq.edu.au/macquarie-archive/lema/1823/ australasia2.html) (Accessed 20/8/2017)

Index

Note: The following abbreviations have been used – LM = Lachlan Macquarie; EM = Elizabeth Macquarie.

Page references in *italic* refer to illustrations. The abbreviation *n* refers to notes.